JOURNEY
TO
FULFILLMENT

JOURNEY
TO
FULFILLMENT

CONSTANCE BRADFORD SCHUYLER

To order additional copies of this book, contact:
Xlibris Corporation
1-888-795-4274
www.Xlibris.com
Orders@Xlibris.com
26166

CONTENTS

Family Trees 6

Introduction 7

1. Background 9
2. Courtship and Marriage 39
3. Early Family Life 53
4. Across the Continent 73
5. Life in the Philippines 87
6. Home Leave and Back to the Philippines 106
7. Deipnosophistical Society 121
8. Back to School 141
9. Doctoral Dissertation 157
10. New Ventures 175
11. Career Shifts 201
12. Family Celebrations 220
13. Back to the Deipnos 248
14. From Academia to Administration 272
15. Nuptials 303
16. The Next Generation 329
17. More Grandchildren 356
18. And More Grandchildren 374
19. Retirement 394
20. Rough Sledding 412
21. Golden Anniversary 434

Photographs *447*

Schuyler Family Tree

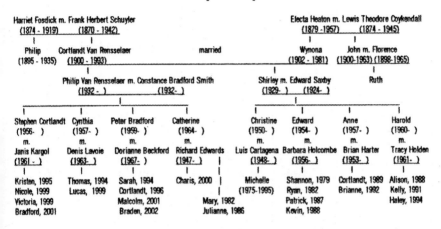

Harriet Fosdick m. Frank Herbert Schuyler
(1874 - 1919)   (1870 - 1942)

Electa Heaton m. Lewis Theodore Coykendall
(1879 -1957)   (1874 - 1945)

Philip   Cortlandt Van Rensselaer   married   Wynona   John m. Florence
(1895 - 1935)   (1900 - 1993)   (1902 - 1981) (1900-1953) (1898-1965)

Philip Van Rensselaer m. Constance Bradford Smith   Shirley m. Edward Saxby   Ruth
(1932-)   (1932-)   (1929-)   (1924-)

Stephen Cortlandt	Cynthia	Peter Bradford	Catherine		Christine	Edward	Anne	Harold
(1956-)	(1957-)	(1959-)	(1964-)		(1950-)	(1954-)	(1957-)	(1960-)
m.	m.	m.	m.		m.	m.	m.	m.
Janis Kargol	Denis Lavoie	Dorianne Beckford	Richard Edwards		Luis Cartagena	Barbara Holcombe	Brian Harter	Tracy Holden
(1961 -)	(1963-)	(1967-)	(1947-)		(1948-)	(1956-)	(1953-)	(1961-)
Kristen, 1995	Thomas, 1994	Sarah, 1994	Charis, 2000		Michelle	Shannon, 1979	Cortlandt, 1989	Alison, 1988
Nicole, 1999	Lucas, 1999	Cortlandt, 1996			(1975-1995)	Ryan, 1982	Brianne, 1992	Kelly, 1991
Victoria, 1999		Malcolm, 2001				Patrick, 1987		Haley, 1994
Bradford, 2001		Braden, 2002	Mary, 1982			Kevin, 1988		
			Julianne, 1986					

Smith Family Tree

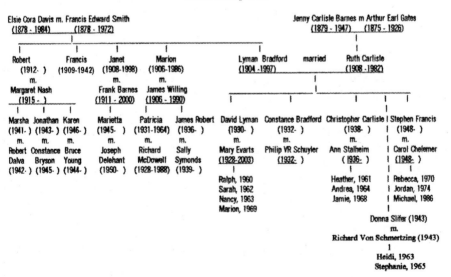

Elsie Cora Davis m. Francis Edward Smith
(1878 - 1984)   (1878 - 1972)

Jenny Carlisle Barnes m Arthur Earl Gates
(1879 - 1947)   (1875 - 1926)

Robert	Francis	Janet	Marion		Lyman Bradford	married	Ruth Carlisle
(1912-)	(1909-1942)	(1908-1998)	(1906-1986)		(1904 -1997)		(1908 -1982)
m.		m.	m.				
Margaret Nash		Frank Barnes	James Willing				
(1915 -)		(1911 - 2000)	(1906 - 1990)				

Marsha	Jonathan	Karen	Marietta	Patricia	James Robert	David Lyman	Constance Bradford	Christopher Carlisle	Stephen Francis
(1941-)	(1943-)	(1946-)	(1945-)	(1931-1964)	(1936-)	(1930-)	(1932-)	(1938-)	(1948-)
m.	m.	m.	m.	m.	m.	m.	m.	m.	m.
Robert	Constance	Bruce	Joseph	Richard	Sally	Mary Evarts	Philip VR Schuyler	Ann Stalheim	Carol Chelemer
Dalva	Bryson	Young	Delehant	McDowell	Symonds	(1928-2003)	(1932-)	(1936-)	(1948-)
(1942-)	(1945-)	(1944-)	(1950-)	(1928-1988)	(1939-)				

David Lyman branch: Ralph, 1960 / Sarah, 1962 / Nancy, 1963 / Marion, 1969

Christopher Carlisle branch: Heather, 1961 / Andrea, 1964 / Jamie, 1968

Stephen Francis branch: Rebecca, 1970 / Jordan, 1974 / Michael, 1986

Donna Slifer (1943)
m.
Richard Von Schmertzing (1943)

Heidi, 1963
Stephanie, 1965

INTRODUCTION

When I was young I often asked my mother, "Do you think I'll ever get married"? My mother's reply was always "yes", to which she would immediately add, "the Blaisdell girls were shy like you in high school, but they both found husbands when they went to college". I would sigh and walk away thinking, "I wish I could find a boyfriend now." I lived in a small town in New England where I had a reputation as a wallflower. I was young for my grade and usually had only one close girl friend in each grade in school. As a student in junior high school I went with most of my classmates to ballroom dancing classes. When the dance teacher told the boys to take a partner, most of them rushed to ask the more popular girls. I was in the group of girls that were asked, reluctantly, to dance after all the "good" partners had been chosen.

During the first two years of high school I was extremely shy. I enjoyed my academic studies, but being a good student did not bring me popularity with other students. About the time that I feared I was stuck in a rut in that small town forever, my parents announced that my father had taken a new job in Washington DC. My life was about to change.

The family moved to a suburb of Washington DC and I began my junior year in high school. Washington was a cosmopolitan city with a transient population because of frequent job turnover in government jobs. Newcomers were welcomed and it was easy to make friends. Fortunately I was asked to join a cluster of students and, for the first time in my life, I felt accepted by a warm group of friends. One Sunday, a girl who lived down the street invited me to attend a church youth group that was meeting at her house. I was somewhat timid about going as I was still very shy with strangers, but I accepted the invitation.

The meeting began with refreshments in the dining room. Then the group moved into the living room for the program and discussion. I held back and stood behind a large chair at the entrance to the living room. A young man from the group came over to me and said, "Why don't your come in and join the others?" I replied, "I'm too shy," but he insisted that I join them. His name was Mike and this was the beginning of a lifelong love.

1

Background

Both Mike and I were born in 1932, but there the similarity of our lives stopped. Mike grew up in a very different atmosphere than I did. His father was an army officer and his family had moved around the country and the world every few years before they moved to Washington DC. Mike was an extrovert and felt very much at ease in the social world of his family.

Mike's family descended from the early Dutch settlers in this country. On his father's side, the first descendent to come to Albany, New York was Philip Schuyler, sometime before 1650. His oldest son, Peter, married Maria Van Rensselaer from another of the first families to settle in that area. Another of the first leading families in that area was the Van Cortlandts. Mike's father, Cortlandt Van Rensselaer Schuyler, was named after all of these families. He was born in Arlington, New Jersey on December 22, 1900. He attended Columbia High School in South Orange, New Jersey where he met his future wife, Wynona Coykendall, a descendent of Samuel Coykendall who fought in the battle of Springfield in the Revolutionary War. In the fall of 1918, after two months of his senior year, Mike's father was accepted for the United States Military Academy and graduated in June of 1922, eleventh in his class of 102, having served as cadet captain in his final year. On graduation he was commissioned a second lieutenant in the Coast Artillery Corps. He married his high school sweetheart the next year, after she graduated from Wellesley College. As a young man Mike's father was thin and tall, 6'3" in height. He served in a succession of appointments as an artillery officer early in his career and was assigned as an instructor of mathematics at West Point from 1928 to 1930. During that time their first child was born and they named her Shirley. Three years later Mike was born on August 4, 1932 in the U.S. army hospital in Panama while his parents were stationed there. Before he was born, his mother and grandmother discussed at length whether his name should be Cortlandt or Philip Van Rensselaer Schuyler, if he turned out to be a son. They finally agreed on the latter, but after the baby was born, his father declared, "I don't care what you name him, I am going to call him Mike," and the nickname stuck.

When Mike was two, his parents moved to Fort Monroe, Virginia. They lived in a small house next to the chapel on the army post. From there his parents were assigned to Fort Leavenworth, Kansas during 1936 and 1937. Mike would long remember the hot summers and freezing cold winters in Kansas. Something happened in Kansas that would plague Mike for the rest of his life. When he was four, he had mastoiditis that ruptured his eardrums. It happened before the discovery of antibiotics and the doctors were unable to cure the infection. The infection became chronic and even years later, after the discovery of antibiotic drugs, it could not be cleared up. The infection destroyed Mike's eardrums and he lost much of his hearing.

From 1937 to 1939 his father was reassigned to Fort Monroe. The family was given a larger house this time and Mike was old enough to remember the layout of the house and racing his sister downstairs to breakfast each morning. He attended a small school on the post and recalled playing army games with his friends on the ramparts of the fort. There was a large swimming pool on the post that the family enjoyed during the long hot Virginia summers. During the second stay at Fort Monroe, Mike's grandfather, Frank Herbert Schuyler, came to live with the family for several years following the death of his beloved wife, Harriet. Mike greatly admired and loved his Grandpa Schuyler. He remembered him as dignified and gentle, a person of integrity who was fascinated by history. When his elder son, Philip, died in 1935, he left substantial debts of his business. Frank Schuyler left his successful career as a stockbroker and spent the next five years operating his son's business and paying off his son's debts. He always took Mike's side unobtrusively in family matters. The family had a rule that in order to have dessert, the children had to finish everything on their plates before the adults finished their dinner. Each evening Grandpa Schuyler would play with the last bite on his plate until he saw that Mike had finally finished his dinner so that he wound not miss out on dessert.

In 1939 Mike's family moved to Washington, DC and in 1942 they moved to Richmond, Virginia, the headquarters of the Army Anti-Aircraft Command. Shirley began high school in Richmond and Mike became a real cut-up in school. His father was so concerned about his son's behavior that he took time off in the midst of his wartime responsibilities to take him on a week's camping trip. This made a deep impression on Mike. Years later he would recall:

> In 1943, when I was eleven years old, I was giving my parents quite a few gray hairs, to such an extent that they were sincerely worried about the direction where I was headed. As is the case so often in parenting, Dad did not know what to do, so he decided that some special attention was required. He took a week off from his work to take me camping, just the two of us. I had a wonderful time with him. This was during the most

critical days of World War II, a time when senior officers did *not* take time off from their assignments. But Dad felt that a member of his family needed his time more than the U.S. Army did for that week. I don't know if that effort on his part turned me around—as parents we never know the long-term effects on our children of specific actions we take. But within a short time after our camping trip, I did reform and did not cause my parents an abnormal amount of grief from then on.

Mike's father was a man of integrity and honor and he taught Mike those principles. Mike has always remembered one lesson that his father taught him about honesty. At his father's funeral Mike told this story:

> When I was a teenager, Dad had left me with instructions concerning a specific task, and told me to leave him a note as to whether his instructions had been fulfilled. So I left a note that was intentionally misleading without actually making a false statement. I was quite proud of my clever wording. But when Dad learned the truth, he scolded me severely and gave me a definition I would never forget. "A lie," he said, "is the intent to deceive." I have recalled that definition many times and have tried hard to abide by it.

While Mike lived in Richmond he took on his first job—delivering *The Saturday Evening Post.* One day when he and his friends were riding their bikes, a car stopped next to them and a man asked the group if any of them would like to sing in a boy's choir. They all said "no" except for Mike who said "maybe." The man told Mike to meet him at the Episcopal Church that evening to join the All Saints Episcopal Church Boy's Choir. Mike joined the choir and enjoyed singing even though he wasn't a particularly good singer.

In January 1943, Mike's father was named Chief of Staff of the United States Anti-Aircraft Training Command with training camps throughout the country, where thousands of troops were trained and dispatched to combat theaters. In the fall of 1943, Mike's father was commissioned a Brigadier General and assigned the command of the largest anti-aircraft training center at Camp Davis, North Carolina. He left the family in Richmond to take command of his new post. At the end of the school year the family moved to Wrightsville Beach to be near Mike's father at Camp Davis. Mike obtained a job setting up pins in a bowling alley and enjoyed living near the beach with his family that summer. Occasionally Mike would ride his bike up to Camp Davis and spend the night with his father.

In the fall of 1944, Mike's father was appointed by President Roosevelt as the United States Representative to the Allied Control Commission for Romania. This commission was established under the Yalta Agreement for the government of Romania for the period of the Allies' occupation. The three nation commission consisted of senior Russian, British and American military members, with the Russian in the position of chairman. The Russians were occupying Romania and pushing the country under communist rule. Mike's father sent messages of excellent analysis and insight back to the United States and demonstrated skill in furthering United States interests and policies. One experience was revealing in what he confronted and how he handled a crisis. There had been a severe drought in Romania and he was appalled at the signs of starvation throughout the population. When he appealed to the chairman of the commission, the Russian's response was, "let them work things out for themselves." Mike's father made a direct appeal to President Truman, who, in one week, sent a supply ship with three million K-rations to the stricken area. The Romanian Red Cross distributed the food and thousands of lives were saved. After visiting many small villages and seeing their gratitude to the Americans, Mike's father commented, "Never have I felt prouder to be an American."

When Mike's father first went to Romania, World War II had not yet ended and no army dependents were allowed overseas. Thus, Mike's mother took him and his sister to live with her parents, Louis Theodore and Electa Heaton Coykendall, in their home in Maplewood, New Jersey. Mike adored and admired his grandfather Coykendall, whom he called Papa. Mike was deeply influenced by his grandfather's values and personality. Shirley attended Columbia High School in South Orange and Mike went to Maplewood Junior High School. In March 1946, when Mike's father was allowed to have his family join him, Mike and his mother moved to Bucharest. Shirley chose to remain with her grandmother so that she could finish her last year of high school in New Jersey. In Bucharest Mike's father let up on his usual strict discipline of Mike because he felt that Mike was in an unusual situation among mostly grown-ups and military officers. He allowed Mike to attend cocktail parties and mingle with the junior officers. For his first year of high school while he was in Romania, Mike was tutored by the wife of a Romanian Field Marshall imprisoned in a Russian prison camp.

In January 1947 the Department of the Army awarded the Distinguished Service Medal to Mike's father for his work as the United States Representative on the Allied Control Commission from November 1944 to September 1946. The citation read:

> General Schuyler performed outstanding service for the department and the nation in a position of responsibility. He ordered and directed the American representation on the commission that was established to supervise the respective governments with the terms of the Armistice agreement. The successful performance

of this integrated Allied task is in a large part due to
Brigadier General Schuyler's consummate tact and his
intelligent and thorough appreciation of the many
complex international problems involved. His
accomplishments have been of great importance to the
Armed Forces and have served to raise the prestige of
our Nation abroad.

The Bucharest news commented, "It was the first time any
United States Army General was presented with a United States
Award while United States troops stood at attention in the center
of a Russian stronghold behind the Iron Curtain."

In 1947 Mike's father returned to Washington DC for duty as
Chief of Plans and Policy of the Army's Operations and Plans
Division. Here he became deeply involved in the fast
developing concept for a North Atlantic alliance. He assisted
in the preparation of basic policy papers and participated in the
discussions and committee work that culminated in 1949 in the
birth of the North Atlantic Treaty Organization (NATO). In 1950
General Eisenhower was nominated as Supreme Commander
of all NATO forces in Europe. In early 1951, when General
Eisenhower, with his Chief of Staff, General Gruenther, arrived
in Paris and began the organization of the Supreme
Headquarters, Allied Powers, Europe (SHAPE), Mike's father
was promoted to Major General and accompanied the group as
General Gruenther's Special Assistant. In 1953 General
Gruenther became Supreme Commander and he made Mike's
father his Chief of Staff. At that time Mike's father was promoted
to Lieutenant General and later to full General. He retired at his
own request in November, 1959, having spent eight years at
SHAPE, six of them as Chief of Staff. He considered his
association with SHAPE as the most rewarding, challenging
and inspiring period of his career. On his farewell visit to the
Netherlands, Queen Juliana personally decorated him with the
Order of Orange-Nassau in the degree of Grand Officer. He

was also decorated by the governments of France, Belgium, Germany, Italy and Luxembourg. At his retirement ceremony he received his second United States Distinguished Service Medal with oak leaf cluster.

After he retired from the Army, Mike's father accepted the position of Executive Assistant to the Governor of New York State, Nelson Rockefeller. He was made Commissioner of General Services and Chairman of the Civil Defense Commission of New York State. He stayed for ten years, then resigned to care for his wife who had become ill with Alzheimer's disease. She died in January 1981. In his 80's Mike's father married the widow of an old acquaintance, General Honnen. He spent the last years of his life with his second wife, Helen, in a retirement home in San Antonio, Texas. Many retired officers lived there and he enjoyed an active social life until he died at 93 years of age. Mike's father respected the ideals of West Point—duty, honor, country—but, most of all, he respected the ideal of family.

Mike's mother, Wynona Coykendall Schuyler, was born in Maplewood, New Jersey on August 18, 1902. She attended Columbia High School in South Orange, New Jersey where she met Mike's father in 1916. She was a charming outgoing young woman with a sensitive nature. She loved music and chose it as her major in Wellesley College. She became an excellent pianist and organist and enjoyed these skills all through her life. She played the organ at the local church wherever she lived and was often the choir director as well. She was a good athlete in tennis, golf and bowling and won trophies for her skill as a horsewoman. She worked for the Red Cross periodically in her life. She was a devoted army wife, moving to a new location almost every two years. She adored her husband and was very proud of him and his accomplishments.

Mike remembers her as a loving mother who used to sing to him as a small child. His favorite song was *The Owl and the Pussycat*. His mother took him to Sunday school every week and often discussed religion with him. She especially liked to read Marcus Aurelius and she discussed his writing with Mike. She tried to accommodate Mike when he felt that he needed something special. When he wanted to join the cub scouts he asked her if she would be his den mother and she agreed to do so. During World War II, Mike was invited to go on a cookout with the Scouts and he told his mother that he needed to take a steak to cook. She told him that ration points were scarce and steak required a lot of points. She managed to scrape together some extra ration points and gave him his steak. Mike remembered his mother as a good cook. He especially liked her casseroles and after we were married he always wanted me to make casseroles for him.

When Mike's father was away on special assignments, his mother took on the responsibility of both mother and father to him. She educated Mike about sex and taught him manners and how to dance. She encouraged her children to become independent and to think for themselves. She invited me to spend three months with the family in Paris when Mike's father was Chief of Staff of NATO and she made me feel like part of the family. When Mike married me and we had children, she welcomed us all into her heart. She was always willing to care for a baby if the family had to travel to a special event. She gave classy and original gifts to her children and grandchildren. I could distinguish which of Mike's clothes had been gifts from his mother as they were always of the best quality. When the grandchildren grew older, she gave them the "in" things for gifts. The biggest and most wonderful gift that she gave to the members of the family was a set of suitcases, one for each member of the family, when we were assigned to the Philippines for two years. Each suitcase had something special about it that identified it as appropriate for a specific member of the family. For example she gave Cathy, who was four years old, a very small green suitcase. It was a quality Samsonite case and Cathy could fit all her little shorts and dresses in it as well as carry it herself. She used it through college and then gave it her own daughter to use, still in excellent shape. A gift that she gave to Mike when he was in college, which was unusual for a mother to give her son, was an original painting of a nude woman to hang in his room at college. She was living in Paris at the time and told Mike that she figured all college men had nude pictures in their rooms so she would rather he have an original from Paris instead of a clipping from a magazine.

In June 1947, when Mike's father was reassigned to the Pentagon, the family moved into army quarters in Fort Myer, Virginia just outside of Washington, DC. For his last two years in high school, Mike attended Woodrow Wilson High School in the District of Columbia. In the middle of his junior year he joined a youth group called Pilgrim Fellowship (PF) sponsored by the Congregational Church of Washington. He was soon elected Vice President of the group and was charged with program planning. At a PF picnic in August before the start of his senior year, Mike noticed "a cute little curly headed girl." He saw me again at the first PF meeting of the new school year. A friend down the street invited me to the meeting. I was shy and Mike had to entice me to join the group discussion in the living room after refreshments had been served at the dining room table. After the PF meeting, he offered to drive me home. I lived four houses up the street, but he managed to take every one else home first and drop me off an hour later. This was the beginning of our long courtship.

My family came from New England stock. Both of my father's parents were descendents of William Bradford who arrived on the Mayflower and was the governor of Plymouth Colony and author of *History of Plymouth Plantation*. My mother's father was also descended from Bradford and her mother was descended from John Alden and Priscilla Mullins, also members of the original Pilgrim group who came to America in 1620.

My grandfather on my father's side, Francis Edward Smith, left school at age fourteen to support his mother after the death of her husband. He went to work as a clerk and rose to become a senior partner in the investment firm of Moors and Cabot in Boston. He was self-educated and enjoyed reading, especially the works of Rudyard Kipling and Mark Twain. He fell in love with Elsie Cora Dyke when he was a young man. He had to pursue her for some time before she agreed to marry him. After they were married they bought a big house in Winchester, Massachusetts. They filled the house with five children, three boys and two girls. The first child, Lyman, was born in September 1904, the next one, Marion, in 1906, then Janet in 1908, Francis, Jr. (Buddy) in 1909 and Robert in 1912.

In 1908 my grandfather purchased a small house on a six-acre piece of land on the rocky shore of Rockport, Massachusetts. He bought the property from an eccentric man, Mr. Reynolds, who owned a mansion and a substantial tract of land that he called Paradise Cliffs. The road that ran by the Smith and Reynolds houses was appropriately called Eden Road. The Smith home was the only house on the road besides the Reynolds estate. It had been the home of the caretaker of the Reynolds mansion. When my Grandma Elsie's children were young she felt isolated in the Rockport house and she hid the children when peddlers came to the door for fear they might kidnap them. As their family grew, my grandparents put a large addition onto the house that almost doubled its size. The addition made the house very spacious. There were six bedrooms, one of which could sleep five people easily. They called that room the dormitory room. The size of the dining room was almost tripled, allowing the family and their guests lots of room to savor the home cooked meals. The living room was also large and the kitchen was a big sunny room with an ample pantry on one side and a shed on the other. The whole house was dark green, both inside and out. There were porches on three sides of the house with beautiful views of the ocean. They built a big garage and a playhouse for the children. They even added a tennis court when the children reached their teenage years. The children learned to swim off the rocks and enjoyed exploring caves in the rocks and fishing on Seaweed Island.

My grandfather adored his five children and ten grandchildren. He also was a scoutmaster for a troop of fourteen boys of whom he was very fond. He was a devoted father and scout leader. The scouts used to take the train to Rockport and camp out in tents in the yard. He taught his children, grandchildren and scouts to play ball, skip stones across the water, swim and fish. He liked to catch fish and put them alive into a saltwater pool under the seaweed at low tide on a reef. Then he would take children down to the fishing place and tell them that he could catch a fish with his bare hand. The children were amazed to see him pull a fish out of the pool with his hand.

In Winchester he liked to take his children and their friends into the woods and tell them to look under rocks for gifts that the elves hid there. He had previously hidden shells under the rocks before he took the children there. A neighborhood child told his mother that he found a shell under a rock. She didn't believe him but when he took her to the place where he had found the shell she turned over a rock and found a pretty shell there. My grandfather usually collected the shells to use again after the children left, but he had overlooked that one. The mother called the Smiths and my grandmother explained to her what her husband had done. My grandparents lived two houses behind my family and, at Christmas, all the grandchildren went to their house for a big celebration. Grampy liked to have the grandchildren perform plays and sing after opening the gifts at

Christmas and he was always offering them a dollar to draw a picture, create a story or read a classic book.

My Grandma Elsie was a brilliant woman with amazing energy. She earned her way through Boston University by playing the violin in a musical quartet in the Boston area. She was a prodigious reader. In her journal, she listed all the books that she read each year from the time she was ten years old. She read an average of 38 books a year over the next twelve years and then, in 1901 when she was in college, she hit an all time high by reading 87 books in one year. The list that year included 18 books in languages other than English. She read classics in Latin, Italian, German, French and Spanish. In the next three years she continued to read large numbers of books averaging 64 per year. After college, Elsie got a job in a one-room schoolhouse in western Massachusetts. She taught children in five different grades. The next year she taught a single class in eastern Massachusetts, after which she married my grandfather and bore their five children. With her vast knowledge from her reading and her teaching experience, she decided to teach her five children at home. She continued to read great numbers of books and no challenge daunted her. One day her husband brought her the complete works of Anthony Trollope, over forty books, and she read them all. She taught all of her children at home and they all went to college.

My father, Lyman Bradford Smith, was the oldest child. He was an avid reader like his mother and she claimed that his love of reading made teaching him at home an easy task. My father finished his home education three years ahead of his age group, so upon finishing his high school level schooling, he spent a year at Browne and Nichols School to learn German. He would later become conversant also in French, Spanish, and Portuguese, and able to read Latin, Greek and Italian. He entered Harvard at the age of sixteen and majored in botany. He went on to earn a Ph.D. in botany and become the world expert on the Bromeliaceae family. Near the end of his life he wrote a three-volume encyclopedia of all the bromeliads in the world. His siblings also attended college. Marion went to Mount Holyoke, Janet to Wellesley, Buddy to Harvard and Bobby to Dartmouth. Bobby, the youngest went on to Harvard Medical School and became a world famous pediatric anesthesiologist. His seminal text in this subject was published in eight editions.

After the children finished college and had families of their own, my grandmother continued to have a positive effect on them. She made clothes for the grandchildren and cooked big cinnamon buns for each family every Sunday. She used to make me my own special jar of grape jam from the concord grapes that grew in her yard. When I was nine years old a terrible tragedy occurred in the family. My Uncle Buddy died from an operation on his lung. Grandma was devastated. She went into a long deep mourning. A neighbor snapped her out of it one day when she asked, "Elsie, would you rather that he had never been born?" My grandmother's solution to her grief was to do for others. She began to do volunteer work in Winchester Hospital. She also made clothing for charitable groups.

Grandma Elsie had an enormous amount of energy and drive. Not only was she a extraordinary reader and great teacher, but she was a very skilled seamstress. She had always knitted and sewed clothes for her children and grandchildren, and with the onset of World War II, she started to make clothes for the Red Cross, as well as her family. Over half the items she made were for charity. In 1940 she made 117 pieces of clothing for the Red Cross including 15 sweaters, 25 children's dresses and 25 surgeons' gowns. In 1941 she made 242 items for the Red Cross including 38 baby gowns and 165 boys' shirts. In 1942 she made 112 pieces of clothing for the Red Cross and the next year 150 pieces. As the war progressed, she began doing volunteer work five days a week in five different hospitals. In 1944 she made 535 pieces of clothing and hospital supplies such as sheets, towels binders, bed pan covers and surgical glove cases. In 1945 as the war came to an end, she continued to work in hospitals and make clothing for refugees as well as hospital supplies. She did volunteer work in Massachusetts General Hospital well into her seventies. Her volunteer hospital work during the war included working in clinics, wards, laundries, kitchens, and cafeterias. She washed beds, folded linens, made surgical dressings, ran the post office and even acted as the elevator operator. In her later years at Massachusetts General she started a cafeteria for visitors and worked hard at stocking it and staffing it. Another volunteer activity that she undertook was reading regularly to a blind student at Harvard University. She was interested in helping the blind in other ways and learned to type Braille. She typed many textbooks for Perkins Institute for the Blind. In addition to all of this volunteer work, she still found the time and interest to be attuned to all that went on in her family.

When my father was a child his great Aunt Cora, a teacher, first interested him in botany and also in stamp collecting. They spent time together identifying local wild flowers. My father had afternoons off from his home studies, during which time he investigated New England natural history, identifying plants and animals in the woods near his home and in the tidal environment at Rockport. He collected plants and kept lists of his findings. From the age of twelve, he dated his identification of local plants in the *Field Book of American Wildflowers*. The book is still on the bookshelf at Rockport almost 100 years later. He also joined the Boy Scouts of America and rose to Eagle Scout. Any other free time that he had as a child was devoted to reading.

When my father graduated from Harvard, his father wanted him to follow his career as an investment broker, but his father agreed that, if after a year's trial in the business, his son still wanted to pursue graduate study in botany, he would support him. There was never any doubt in my father's mind that he wanted a career in botany, so his father sent him to Harvard graduate school after his one year in the investment business. In his Ph.D. program at Harvard, my father specialized in the Bromeliaceae family and went on to become the world expert in that family of plants.

While pursuing his doctorate, my father met a neighborhood girl, Ruth Gates, whom his mother often drove to Radcliffe College in Cambridge, when she took her son, Lyman, to graduate school at the same location. A romance blossomed and they were married in June 1929 right after my mother graduated from Radcliffe. My grandparents treated them to a honeymoon in Europe.

Upon receiving his Ph.D., Father began his first job at Harvard's Gray Herbarium. Botany became the overwhelming passion of his life. He traveled widely to discover new species of the bromeliad genus. He even did botany research in England and Switzerland while on his honeymoon. During his career he was the author of more than 500 publications on botany, the largest of which was a 2142-page monograph on the Bromeliaceae family. His research on this family of plants spanned more than sixty years and during his career he amassed the single largest collection of herbarium specimens of the Bromeliaceae in the world. He continued to work on his research into his nineties, receiving numerous awards and having 42 bromeliad plants named after him.

My father worked at Harvard University in Cambridge, Massachusetts for the first 18 years of his career and then at the Smithsonian Institute in Washington D.C. for the last 43 years of his life. Father enjoyed wrestling and bicycling as hobbies and he bicycled eleven miles to work and back every day until he was in his seventies. He was a member of the Harvard wrestling team in college and continued as an amateur wrestler at the YMCA into his sixties. Father was small in stature and wrestling gave him an outlet for his aggression. He had a bit of a mean streak in him and he delighted in telling stories of how he got the better of bullies when he was a boy.

My mother, Ruth Carlisle Gates, was an only child. Her father, Arthur Gates, did not attend college, but successfully worked his way up to senior management in Traveler's Insurance Company. He was a loving and tender father who died at the age of fifty from rheumatic heart disease. My mother was 18 at the time of his death. Her mother's name was Jenny Barnes Gates, but she disliked the name Jenny and wanted to be called Jane, even by the grandchildren. She met her husband-to-be in a church youth group. She worshipped him and was heartbroken at his death so early in life. She was in her forties when she became a widow and never wanted to marry again. Jane earned her way through Radcliffe College by writing documents in script. She was very short, 4'10", while her husband was 6'2". After his death, she found comfort in eating and became almost as round as she was tall. She loved to eat maple sugar on thick slices of white bread and bought maple sugar in gallon tins. She and my brother David enjoyed reading Latin together. She was very religious with strict principles—no smoking, no alcohol and no dancing and playing cards on Sundays. Her one outlet was listening to the Lone Ranger program on the radio three times a week. She was a deacon and the treasurer of her church and would tolerate no noise or wiggling from me during the church service on Sunday. Most of her life she did not own a car, but when she became sixty, she took driving lessons and bought a car. Extensions had to be put on the pedals so that she could reach them to drive. Jane was a frugal wife and a very strict mother.

My mother was a lonely little girl. She had make-believe friends as a child. Her only real friend, Connie Williams, lived across the street and she named me after her. My mother adored her loving father and maternal grandfather. When her father died she was forced to give up living at college and came home to live with her mother and her grandmother, Carrie Barnes, both strict and humorless women. While living at home my mother was offered a ride to Radcliffe each day by a neighbor, my future Grandma Elsie, who drove my father to Harvard graduate school each day. My father fell in love with my mother and began to court her. Coming from a puritanical family, his courtship was very proper. When he first proposed marriage, my mother refused him, as he had never even tried to kiss her. My father was devastated by her rejection and asked his mother what he should do. She told him to try again, and the second time my mother said yes. Mother was fascinated with Father's large family. She became very close to his sisters, Marion and Janet, and enjoyed telling me all about the lives of his parents and siblings.

My parents' first three children were born while they were living in Winchester, Massachusetts. David was born in 1930, I followed in 1932 and Bunkie came in 1938. Their last child, Stephen, was born in Kensington, Maryland in 1948. While Father was engrossed with his botanical research, Mother spent her time raising their children and participating in community activities. During World War II, she was Director of Home Hospitality for servicemen in Winchester Massachusetts. She called people in the community requesting them to offer their homes for hospitality to soldiers and sailors who were stationed in Boston, far away from their families. On weekends and holidays busloads of servicemen would pull up in front of the Smith house and unload. In a few minutes all of these men in small groups would be on their way to warm homes throughout the community. My parents always took a few men into their own home. They entertained over 200 servicemen during the war years and some of the men became life-long friends of the family. Mother felt a deep obligation to help servicemen away from home during the war. She also canvassed for blood donors during and after the war and donated over 100 pints of blood herself. After the war Mother was elected to the Winchester School Board and became an active member until she moved away in 1947.

When her family moved to Kensington, Maryland in the fall of 1947, Mother's community service was directed to other areas. She became president of the county YMCA, a trustee of the local junior college, and an active member of her church and four women's clubs. Although she worked for several organizations, the lion's share of her effort was personal service for individuals in the community and her family. She taxied disabled people, called on friends in nursing homes and made countless loaves of oatmeal bread for everyone she knew. She donated untold hours of time to reading to blind people. When she received her first assignment from the organization for the blind, the recipient turned out to be the same man that both Grandma Elsie and I had read to while he was a student at Harvard. My mother brought joy and enthusiasm into the lives of everyone she encountered. Her home was a haven to travelers from all over the world, complete with free room, board and transportation to wherever her guests needed to go.

Mother's family, however, was the most important aspect of her life. She was a tremendous help to my father in his botanical work—accompanying him on collecting trips, proof-reading page after page of many of his publications and co-authoring one tract covering 37 species of plants. After the children were grown, she proofread all 2,142 pages of his last publication, a three-volume encyclopedia of bromeliads of the world. She was devoted to her children and their spouses and was wonderfully attuned to the subtleties of their lives. She was a superb mother to her children. She read to them when they were small and was compassionate and giving to them all.

Mother not only brought up four children of her own, but she took in a 16 year-old foster child whose own family had rejected her. Her name was Donna and the whole family accepted her with love. When she married and had children, they became Mother's grandchildren. Mother cared about every aspect of her children's lives, and when they married, she loved their wives and husbands as her own children. When the grandchildren arrived, she welcomed them all and gave them the same love and understanding that she had given her children. Mother knew how to be available without intruding or smothering. When there was good news to share—a new baby, a child's report card with all A's, she was proud and happy. When there were concerns and problems, no matter how large or small, she sought solutions and was willing to give sacrificially of her time and energy. She was the communication center of the family.

Though it was her nature to be doing for them always, Mother believed that her children should grow through education to be independent, self-sufficient, useful citizens, and she furthered their education with loving interest and care from reading nursery rhymes to encouraging doctoral work. She also taught her children the strong moral principles that she and Father shared—honesty, integrity, duty and determination—but to these she also added compassion.

Their only daughter, Constance Bradford Smith, was born on May 5, 1932 in Boston Massachusetts, the second child of four. I had a brother David who was two years older and, later, two younger brothers, Christopher and Stephen. Christopher was nicknamed Bunkie because he was born on the date of the battle of Bunker Hill. I lived in Winchester, Massachusetts until I was 15 years old. I was always very attached to my mother. I loved to have her read to me and tell me stories about other people.

Mother, however, was not a good disciplinarian. She let Father take care of that aspect of raising the children. Father was very strict and punished us frequently. When we were naughty, Mother would tell Father when he came home and he would spank us. He also believed in locking me in my room as punishment. My brothers long remembered the threadbare look of the door on my bedroom after I had pounded on it over the years in frustration at being locked in. Father would not tolerate any disrespect from us and he punished us if we challenged his authority. Like many men who were caught up in their professional ambitions, he gave little positive attention to his children. It was Mother who raised the children and tended to their daily needs.

As a small child I was tested for intellectual readiness and approved to begin kindergarten at age four. My parents sent me to school at that early age, but the teacher soon noted that my social skills were not mature enough for the classroom regime. I almost failed kindergarten because of my disruptive behavior. My father dealt with the problem by having me locked in my room all afternoon on days when I brought home a critical note from the teacher. Although Mother was generally loving and kind, she was acquiescent in my father's strictness in this situation. By the end of the year, my behavior had improved sufficiently for me to be promoted to grade one. Mother met with the first grade teacher to warn her about my background in kindergarten, but at the end of the first term in grade one, I received a mark of excellent in conduct.

As I grew older, I chose to spend a great deal of time in my room playing romantic games with my dolls. I involved the dolls in candlelight weddings, banquets, birthday parties, baptisms, church services, illnesses and exotic vacations. I had only two male dolls, Bradford Ruth and John. Bradford Ruth was bigger so he played the part of father, minister, doctor and teacher. John was made of wood with joints that bent. He could stand on his head and move his arms and legs. He played the part of a teenager or young father. My younger brother Bunkie liked to watch the drama that I created for my dolls. I allowed him to sit and watch as long as he didn't touch the dolls.

From the first through the fourth grades, I attended a two-room school across the street from my home. I enjoyed school immensely, learning the basic skills in reading, writing and arithmetic, as well as all the verses of patriotic songs. In the third and fourth grade classroom we built a house together. The boys made furniture for the house and the girls made curtains.

On Sunday mornings I went to Sunday school followed by the church service. In church I sat with my grandmother Jane and watched my mother up in the front of the church singing in the choir. She used to nod off during the sermon. It seemed to me that we sang the same hymns over and over. I learned all the verses by heart; later in life, I enjoyed singing them without the need of a hymnal. My favorite hymn was *The Church's One Foundation.* Jane was very strict about my behavior in church. If I fidgeted or coughed she would squeeze my leg and pop a cough drop into my mouth.

When I was ten, a Catholic friend of mine took me to her church. I was so fascinated by the rituals that were followed in her church that I went home and told my mother I wanted to join the Catholic Church. Mother told me that I should first investigate the meaning of the Baptist Church that our family belonged to. I enrolled in the confirmation class of the Baptist Church. I learned that, in my church, individuals were not baptized as babies, but, rather, each person made the decision to join the church when he or she was old enough to understand the concepts of the Baptist denomination. Before people could be baptized they had to take a class that taught them the meaning of baptism. If they still wanted to join the church they could declare their intention and undergo the immersion used in the Baptist church. After I took the class I decided to be baptized. My mother said that she could only see the curls on top of my head when I was baptized because I was so short.

On Sunday afternoons when I was in elementary school, I sometimes played tag football in the schoolyard with Father, David and other neighborhood boys. Father often threw the ball to me because none of the boys bothered to guard me. Father praised me when I caught the ball and made unexpected touchdowns. In the winter, my grandfather taught me to ice skate on Long Pond in the woods behind his house. I also liked to toboggan and ski down the long banking in his yard. I loved to spend time with Grandma Elsie who made all my clothes. My favorite clothes were the beautiful smocked dresses that she made for me. I wore homemade dresses all through high school, and in my adult life I continued to wear only dresses.

Grandma Elsie invited me to her house in Rockport for two weeks each summer. These were some of the happiest times in my life. The yard abutted the rocky shoreline across from two islands. There were picturesque coves between the granite points along the shore. Grampy taught the grandchildren to swim in natural pools formed by the rocks. He also taught us to fish and clean the fish for cooking. I loved to play double solitaire with Grandma Elsie, even though I could never beat her at the game. She was as fast as lightning. She could always outrun me for a bus or a train even in her old age.

My aunts, uncles and cousins also spent summers at Rockport. Aunt Janet and Uncle Buddy were still single when I was a young child, and they took a great interest in the first three grandchildren, David, Patsy and me. Patsy, who was the same age as I, was the first child of Aunt Marion and Uncle Jay who rented a small house nearby each summer. David spent a lot of time with Uncle Buddy going on bird watching trips and fishing from his boat, while Patsy and I spent special time with Aunt Janet. Patsy and I played together in a large playhouse that Grampy had built. When we were old enough we were allowed to spend the night in the playhouse. Patsy and I were like sisters as we were the only girls in each of our families. Grandma Elsie made us twin dresses and we played all sorts of make-believe games on the rocks near the green house.

As we grew older, Patsy and I liked to watch Aunt Janet get dressed for her dates. She was beautiful and had many boyfriends, but she did not get married until late in her thirties. She brought Frank Barnes to Rockport in the early 1940's and Patsy and I were very taken with him. I used to stare at him at the dining room table until he became embarrassed. Patsy and I urged Janet to marry him and eventually she did. He was always a favorite uncle of mine.

As the years went by, my grandparents built another small house on the Rockport property so that they could get away on their own from the growing number of family members visiting the big green house. Later, in 1954, they built their dream house on another part of the property. Before they died they gave the green house to Lyman and the other two houses to their daughters, Marion and Janet. Their son Buddy had died and their youngest son, Bobby, had a house on Cape Cod and he was not interested in Rockport. They left him their Winchester house so that each child was given a house.

Starting when I was eight years old, my father gave me lessons in typing, Spanish and shorthand. He paid me five cents a page to type his botany papers. On Saturdays David and I bicycled to Cambridge with Father to work at Harvard's Gray Herbarium. I drew pictures of bromiliads for his publications and David typed for him. David and I also went on collecting trips with Father and learned to preserve the plants in big presses.

Sometimes he would pay us a penny a piece for some plant that he was collecting.

When I was young, my family did not own a car, so I used to walk to church or downtown with my mother to shop for groceries. There was a steep hill that led out of town and up to Highland Avenue where we lived. I used to sit on a wall at the bottom of the hill and refuse to walk up it. This dislike of hills lasted throughout my life. My friends and I used to walk downtown to the movie theatre every Saturday to watch the Tarzan serial and whatever war picture was being shown. We had to cross the railroad tracks and often took a short cut that was not at the regular crossing. Then one afternoon I saw a movie in which a man caught his foot in a switch and was run over by a train. After seeing that picture I was terrified of getting my foot caught in a switch, but I still took the short cut.

Growing up during World War II was a unique experience. During the war Americans were united in their view that our country was fighting for the survival of the free world. We felt that God was on our side and our country was devoted to stopping our enemies from conquering the world. We joined together in rationing items needed to fight the war. The feeling of togetherness and cooperation throughout our country engendered pride in our nation. The media created a sense of patriotism in Americans and convinced them of the "rightness" of winning the war against the "evil" powers. I was fascinated by war movies. My favorite was *So Proudly We Hail* with Claudette Colbert and Veronica Lake. I saw the picture with my friends on Saturday and then went to see it two more times after school during the week that it was being shown in our town. It was about heroic nurses in the Philippines and may have been one of the influences that later made me want to become a nurse. Grandma Elsie gave me books that she thought would interest me about the war; my favorite was *The Burma Surgeon,* about heroic nurses and doctors who cared for soldiers and civilians fleeing from the Japanese through Burma.

During the years of World War II my mother was head of home hospitality for soldiers and sailors in Winchester. My family converted our attic to bedrooms and entertained servicemen at our home on weekends during the war. Mother frequently invited young women from the community to dinner with the servicemen. After dinner they would sing popular songs around the piano while my mother played from sheet music. Some British sailors returned to our house a number of times. Several life-long friendships developed and one British sailor by the name of Horace named his first son David after my brother who played football with him on Sunday afternoons.

Many of the servicemen visited Rockport with our family during the summers. Grandma Elsie had lost her son, Buddy, in an unsuccessful operation in 1940, and in her grief she no longer enjoyed being in Rockport. She also did not like to be there during the war years when blackouts were required at night. Therefore, she allowed our family to spend extended summer vacations in the Rockport house during World War II.

Those were wonderful summers for our family in the beautiful setting by the sea. Going down the long driveway to the green house one could see Straitsmouth Island standing in a royal blue sea. The island was about a mile long with a white lighthouse and a red light keeper's house at one end. The island was covered by green vegetation. It was a bird sanctuary where visitors were not allowed. To the right of Straitsmouth was Thatchers Island, with twin lighthouses rising from it. By the rocks where everyone swam, there were small islands, or reefs, that popped out of the ocean at low tide. These reefs had a rich brown colored seaweed on top and as the water receded, golden seaweed emerged under the brown. I loved to swim to those reefs covered with seaweed, starfish, periwinkles, sea urchins and other sea life. I would sit on the seaweed looking at the islands in the royal blue sea and watching the waves break around me as they hit the sides of the reefs.

The servicemen soon adapted to swimming off the rocks in the cold water and then coming up to the house for hot showers and some of Mother's delicious cooking. David and I got to know the three Evarts girls whose parents rented the house across the street. Emily, Mary and Sally Evarts became life-long friends of our family. David eventually married Mary, and Emily and I became close friends years later when we brought our own families to Rockport every summer. The Evarts girls owned a small sailboat in which they raced other boats on Sundays. They always came in last in their group, but they enjoyed sailing anyway and sometimes took David and me out on their boat. The Evarts girls played a special hide-and-seek game with us, called Beckon Beckon, every evening before dinner. We all swam together off the rocks during the day and at night after dinner we would gather in the green house to play games.

The large dining room, with a huge oak table in the middle, was the center of activity in the Rockport house. The walls were stained dark green, as were all the walls in the house. There was a large framed map of the world at one end of the room, and under the windows at the other end of the room was a rowboat that had belonged to Uncle Buddy. During the daytime the sun streamed in through seven large windows making the room very light and warm. The house had no insulation, so studs of the walls stuck out and the braces between the studs were covered with treasures from the sea collected by the children. The dining room table served a variety of uses. Everyone gathered at the table for delicious home cooked meals and after dinner the table was cleared for rousing games of round-robin ping-pong. People would line up at both ends of the table and take turns hitting the ball and running around to the opposite end of the table to hit the ball again. After everyone was exhausted, we played cards and board games, murder in the dark and the all-time favorite game, charades. At the end of the evening we would sit around the table snacking and talking until bedtime. The Evarts family also provided home hospitality to servicemen so, at times, there was a big crowd in the green house. On VJ day, at the end of World War II, David, Emily, Mary, Sally and I walked up to the ice cream stand that was half way to town. We bought red, white and blue ice cream sticks and shouted hurrahs all the way home as we ate them.

After the war was over I started high school in Winchester. I walked to school each day with my best friend, Ruthie Sheehan. I was young for my grade and not at all sophisticated. I still wore the dresses that Grandma Elsie made for me and I was not allowed to wear lipstick. My cousin Patsy was not allowed to wear lipstick either, but as soon as she arrived at school she went to the girls' room and applied lipstick and makeup. She also wore the "in" clothes of that day, plaid skirts and sweaters. Patsy became a cheerleader and was popular with the football players. Grandma Elsie tried to help me feel mature by taking me to Filenes Department Store in Boston and buying me some sweaters and skirts.

Grandma Elsie was my treasured confidant during my early teens. I spent a great deal of time at her house helping her cook, watching her knit and sew and sharing concerns with her. My grandfather was also good to me, taking me ice skating in the winter and encouraging me to read and write stories. Later when I was in college he took me skating at the Cambridge Skating Rink, where we watched stars such as Dick Button and Peggy Fleming perform, and he taught me how to dance on skates. While I was at Radcliffe, Grampy took me to my first and favorite play, *The Student Prince,* and one of my favorite movies, *I'm a Yankee Doodle Dandy.* When he picked me up to take me to the movies, he carried a large pile of newspapers under his arm. When we got to the theatre, he would put them on my chair so that I could see over the person in front of me. He paid for both David's and my college education.

When I was in the ninth grade, my Grandmother Jane developed cancer of the bladder. There was no cure in those days. She kept her illness secret and, because of strong Puritan principles, she refused to take any pain medication. She suffered at home for two years never showing how much pain she endured. My mother took care of her until she died at the age of 68. My parents and I were the only ones who knew of her suffering. I was in her house when she took the call from the doctor and overheard her diagnosis. Sometimes I saw the agony in Jane's face when she thought no one was looking. The experience left me with a dread of cancer that haunted me all through my life. After Jane died our family moved into her house and sold our old house that was across the street. I disliked the year that I lived in Jane's house and often had nightmares about that house later in my life.

A year later a wonderful change came into my life. Father was offered a job at the Smithsonian Institute in Washington, DC and our family moved to Kensington, Maryland, a suburb of Washington. Shortly before we moved Mother discovered that she was pregnant with her fourth child, so a whole new life was about to open up for us. In Kensington we found a lovely house with five bedrooms, a large living room with a fireplace, a big front hall, a traditional dining room and a big kitchen with a breakfast nook. My parents bought the house and we moved into it in the summer of 1947 before my junior year in high school. That fall Bunkie entered the fourth grade in Kensington Elementary School, David entered Harvard College and I went to Bethesda-Chevy Chase High School, three miles away from our house. I often rode the school bus, but sometimes I rode my bicycle to school.

Shortly after I started my junior year in high school, I met a friendly girl named Joyce who invited me to join her group of friends. The members of the group were very friendly and accepted me readily. They did not smoke or drink alcohol, which made life easier for me coming from a non-smoking, teetotaling family. I liked my new teachers and friends and enjoyed my first year at this new school. In March 1948, Mother gave birth to a son, Stephen Francis Smith. He was an adorable baby and I enjoyed helping Mother take care of him.

2

Courtship and Marriage

At the end of the summer of 1948, I was invited to a Congregational Church picnic in Rock Creek Park in Washington, DC. I met a college man who was active in the Moral Rearmament movement. He drove me home and when we were there he asked my mother if he could take me to a movie. Mother did not like the idea of my going out with a college man and did not allow me to go. Later she reconsidered and did let me go on one date with him. He didn't ask me out again as he felt that I was too restricted. At the same picnic another young man, Mike Schuyler, also noticed me. He met me shortly after that at a meeting of the youth group of the church. The group was called the Pilgrim Fellowship (PF). A girl in the group who lived down the street from me had invited me to the meeting that was being held at her house. Mike was smitten and told his best friend to leave me alone as I was going to be his girl. He drove me home after the meeting and we began to date. So began our romance.

Mike lived in Virginia and went to school in Washington. I lived and went to school in Maryland. We met and dated in the PF group of the Congregational Church in Washington. It was all a bit confusing, but also very wonderful. I was very nervous when we began dating because I was afraid that I would not be able to carry on an interesting conversation with Mike. I read up on all the current news and tried my best to be conversational. A month later, Mike told me that I didn't have to fill every minute with conversation—it was all right to be quiet sometimes.

When Mike arrived at my house to pick me up for our first date, Father said to him, "Do you want to wrestle?" Mike had never wrestled, but he felt he should accommodate his date's father's wishes, so he agreed to try it. Father took him out on the front lawn and promptly wrestled him to the ground and pinned him. This was his introduction to the obsession of wrestling in our family.

On our first date Mike drove some of the PF group to Great Falls, Virginia after the PF meeting. We all went out on the rocks to look at the waterfall and when we got back to the car we found it sunk in the mud. We had to call a tow truck and by the time the car was towed out it was nearly dawn. When Mike brought me home Mother was not pleased with the hour that I came home and I wasn't allowed to go out with Mike again for several weeks. However, it wasn't long before Mike had completely won over Mother, who told me that Mike would be a perfect husband for me. Ironically, Mother's strong approval of Mike turned me off for a time, but then I also began to think he was nice.

Our relationship waxed and waned in the beginning, but soon we discovered that, in fact, we were right for each other. After I joined the PF Mike and I volunteered to write and present sermons on Youth Sunday. I was very nervous so I practiced my sermon over and over in front of the mirror. The church service went well and our mothers were both there to hear us. Mike's sermon was practical and mine was idealistic. Our mothers were proud of us and were pleased to meet each other for the first time.

Both of our fathers played tennis and we used to discuss which father was the better player. We decided that we would ask them to have a match to see which one was better. They gamely agreed to the challenge. Mike's father was six feet three inches tall and my father was five feet three inches tall. They were both good players, but Mike's father seemed to just stand still and hit the ball while my father had to run all over the court to return the ball. Diplomatically we did not declare either one the better player and they took us out after the match for ice cream sodas.

Mike and I both had jobs in the Washington area the summer after we finished high school. Mike worked in a stone yard while I was a secretary to a friend of my parents. At the end of the summer, my mother invited Mike to Rockport for a week. During that week, I took Mike to Winchester to meet my grandparents and they both like him. After our visit, we went for a walk in the woods in Winchester and Mike proposed to me. We knew that we would have a long wait until we finished college and could get married, but we planned our life ahead. We decided that we would have four children, two boys and two girls, and even decided on names for them.

When Mike graduated from high school he was sixteen. His father felt that he was too young for college, so he sent him for a year to Philips Academy in Andover, Massachusetts. I had been accepted at Radcliffe College in Cambridge, Massachusetts. We were only an hour apart by train, so we saw each other regularly on weekends. While Mike was at Andover he joined the wrestling team so that he might hold his own in my family. He also joined the track and cross-country teams. He won letters in all three sports.

In my first year at Radcliffe I developed a love of reading that stayed with me throughout life. My favorite courses in my freshman year were Humanities I and II where I first read Dante's

Divine Comedy, which became my favorite book. I volunteered
to read to a blind Harvard graduate student who turned out to
be the same student that Grandma Elsie read to during his
undergraduate years at Harvard. Later my mother would also
read to him when she lived in Kensington and he was employed
at the Library of Congress in Washington. While I was at
Radcliffe, my brother David was on the Harvard wrestling team.
He did not have a girl friend, so I went to the Harvard wrestling
meets to cheer for him and we often went to movies together in
Harvard Square during the week. On weekends I went to
Andover to tea dances or Mike came down to Cambridge to
take me out or study in the library with me. Grandma Elsie let
us stay at her house on the weekends that Mike came down.

Mike went back to the job as a worker in a stone yard in Virginia
the summer before he started college and I worked as a waitress
in Bethesda, Maryland, two of the most physically exhausting
jobs either of us would ever have. At the beginning of the
summer Mike's parents drove to Andover Academy to move
out Mike's belongings. While they were in Massachusetts they
visited my grandparents at their Winchester home. The meeting
between Mike's parents and my grandparents was interesting
to observe. My grandmother sat up straight as a ramrod in her
chair and spoke politely to Mike's parents who were most
gracious in their conversation with her and her husband. I think
that they were all a little relieved when the visit concluded.

After the meeting with my grandparents, Mike's parents drove
Mike and me to my parents' house in Maryland. On the way we
stopped in New York City and his parents treated us to an
evening at the Waldorf Astoria. Vic Damone was the singer
and we danced to his wonderful music and sipped cokes at our
table. The next day we drove to Princeton to see Mike's dormitory
and visit some old friends of his parents, Colonel and Mrs.
Routheau. Colonel Routheau was a professor of military science
and the director of ROTC at Princeton and he and his wife

offered to let me stay at their home when I visited Mike on weekends. Their house was a large colonial mansion right next to the Princeton Stadium. They were always gracious to me whenever I stayed with them.

In the fall, Mike entered Princeton University and his parents moved to Paris. Mike made my family's house his home base during his four years in college. He planned to major in engineering as he considered it a good background for working in industry. However, he also wanted to get some liberal arts education and Princeton encouraged this for engineering majors. He found that he liked his liberal arts courses best and got his best grades in those courses.

My second year at Radcliffe was a traumatic one. There was a five-hour trip between Radcliffe and Princeton and I was often away from Mike for six weeks at a time. We talked every night on the phone and I was often in tears during those calls as I missed him so much. At the end of the fall term, I decided to take a semester off and become a nurse's aide, as I had always been interested in nursing. I took a Red Cross course and then worked in Gallenger Hospital, a federal prison hospital in Washington. This experience was a real eye-opener. There were patients with delirium tremors running around screaming language that I had never heard. I stuck it out, however, until the summer when I took a job as a counselor at Camp Goodwill for underprivileged children. That summer Mike's parents wanted him to join them in Paris. While he was there he worked in the United States Embassy Commissary to earn spending money for the next year at Princeton.

At Camp Goodwill each counselor was responsible for the girls in her cabin. One night a copperhead snake curled up on the floor beside a camper's bed and when the counselor noticed this she placed a wastebasket upside down over the snake with a rock on top. I considered this quick thinking. After we evacuated the cabin, we summoned the male counselors to kill the snake. A number of the campers came from abusive families. One twelve-year old girl, who had been sexually traumatized by her stepfather, wet her bed each night and had to wash out her sheets each morning.

I was asked to be the Nature Counselor and lead groups of children through the woods to help them identify wild flowers and trees. I also became the camp storyteller. I would memorize long fairy tales and then tell them dramatically to all the children around the campfire each evening. I loved doing this and it was a precursor to my teaching as a college professor years later. While I was at the camp I developed a crush on Ned, one of the male counselors. When Mike came home from Paris at the end of the summer I was lukewarm in my relationship to him. Camp Goodwill gave a farewell party for the counselors and Mike insisted on going to the party with me. When I saw Mike next to Ned I realized what a wonderful person I already had and lost all interest in Ned.

I returned to Radcliffe in the fall of 1951. I lived in a co-op house called Peach House where the students took turns cooking the meals. While I was away at Princeton for a weekend with Mike, my classmates signed me up to cook dinner the night that the Dean of the College had been invited to dinner. It didn't faze me. I prepared my mother's recipe for chicken a la king and made strawberry shortcake for dessert. I liked Peach House and Mike came to dinner occasionally. He stayed at my grandparents' house when he came up for weekends, and Grandma Elsie invited me to come to her house also on the weekends that Mike was there.

While I was living at Peach House, my cousin Patsy came to see me. Patsy was very much in love with Dick MacDowell, a young man whom she had met on the beach at Rockport the summer that Mike first came to Rockport. Sadly, her parents were opposed to her dating Dick because he was from a different background and religion than they were. The more serious Patsy became about her relationship with Dick, the more opposition she received from her parents. When she came to see me she had decided that elopement was the only way out of the situation and she wanted to know how I felt. I told her that I supported her decision because there didn't seem to be any other solution. Patsy and Dick eloped soon after that. Her family never accepted Dick, but when the grandchildren started to arrive, they accepted Patsy back into the family and became doting grandparents.

I majored in English literature at Radcliffe. My favorite courses in the major were those covering the 18th and 19th century English novels. I never read as many books in a year as Grandma Elsie, but I did have to read three or four books a week for my English and history courses. I did well in my courses at Radcliffe, but I still pined to be closer to Mike. At the end of the 1951-1952 academic year I decided to transfer to the nursing program at Columbia University, which was only an hour away from Princeton. Before I made the decision I called Grandma Elsie to see if she approved of nursing as a career. To my surprise, Grandma Elsie told me that she had always wanted to be a nurse.

Before I started Columbia in the fall of 1952, I accepted an invitation from Mike's parents to spend the summer with them in Paris where they were living at the time. Grandma Elsie volunteered to pay for my voyage to Paris and Mike traveled for free on a troop ship as an Army dependant. My ship left from Quebec, and because the shipping line lost my ticket, I was put in a first class cabin on the way over. I had a wonderful time and met some nice people. One of them was an art teacher named Alec and another was a nurse named Joyce. Alec offered to give us a tour of the Louvre when we reached Paris. So while Mike was working one day, I met Alec and Joyce at the museum and Alec gave us an instructive tour of the art treasures at the Louvre. Mike and I also went sightseeing at Versailles with them and he liked them a lot.

That summer Mike had a job in the United States Embassy Commissary and I did volunteer work in the American Hospital in Paris. I also tutored an Army dependent in algebra. What a wonderful time we had for three whole months in Paris. We spent every cent that Mike earned going to nightclubs and movies. The previous summer Mike and his mother had explored nightclubs trying to find ones that they thought I would enjoy when I came to Paris the next summer. One of the first spots that Mike and I went to was one that he and his mother had picked out. It was a little hole in the wall in the Montmartre section of Paris called the Lapin Agile (the "Jumping Rabbit"). It was a dark room with paintings all over the walls. People sat on wooden benches and a pianist, singers and storytellers entertained us. The audience joined in the singing and had a wonderful time. Another spot that we visited was the Caveau de la Bolee. It was in the catacombs down a flight of narrow stone steps. There were red checked cloths on the tables and the entertainment was an accordion player, a guitar player, a master of ceremonies and some singers. The entertainers told stories, sang songs and talked to the people in the audience whom they included in the stories they were telling. One story was about an old haunted castle in which, at 11 o'clock, a girl screamed. They were speaking in French so I could not understand them. When the master of ceremonies came to the scream, he went around the room asking the women to scream. When he came to me, I was too shy to scream. The accordion player had noticed that I seemed nervous, so he banged a tin door with a big crash and I jumped and screamed and every one laughed.

Mike and I liked to sit at sidewalk cafes and watch the people go by. One spot we particularly liked was Café de la Paix, next to the opera house. We went to a few of the more famous nightclubs and shows such as the Novelle Eve, the Lido and the Follies Bergere, which had spectacular settings and costumes. The night that we went to Novelle Eve we danced and watched three shows until 3:30 a.m. Then we went to Les Halles in the open market district and had onion soup, a French tradition. The market was full of people at 4:00 a.m. Mike bought me a bouquet of pink rosebuds and we watched the sun come up. We went home and slept all day. We also went to some student nightclubs on the left bank of the Seine that we enjoyed.

On several occasions we joined Mike's parents when they attended cocktail parties. At one party I met General Gruenther, Mike's father's superior, and I really liked him. Mike admired him greatly. Another time we were invited to a party at Field Marshall Montgomery's chateau. There was a big band and about 400 guests there. I met General and Mrs Ridgeway, but did not find him as personable as General Gruenther. When Mike introduced me to Field Marshall Montgomery, General Gruenther teased me saying, "bringing a girlfriend to Paris is like bringing a ham sandwich to a banquet." Mike's father's position in NATO meant that his mother had many elegant dinner parties. I tried to be on my best behavior but sometimes after dinner, when it was time to return to the living room for liqueurs, the guests had to wait for me to find my shoes under the table. Mike's father was very good-natured about my habit of taking off my shoes. I never learned to like wearing shoes.

Mike's parents took us on some special trips. We visited the cathedral at Chartre, which had the most magnificent stained glass window that I have ever seen. We also went on a trip along the Loire River to see some spectacular chateaux. The third trip with them was a visit to Switzerland. We drove to Dijon in France the first night and stayed in a darling little hotel. The next morning we drove to Geneva, had lunch and went on to Montreaux. We stayed in an elegant hotel on the side of the mountain overlooking the Castle of Chillon. Mike and I walked down the mountain and went through the castle. We bought a copy of Byron's *Prisoner of Chillon* and read it after we toured the castle.

That afternoon we took a scenic drive to Interlaken. Swiss chalets were snuggled in the mountainside and pretty wildflowers were everywhere. We enjoyed a picnic lunch that the hotel had given us in a scenic spot with gorgeous views all around. When we reached Interlaken, Mike's parents had reserved rooms in a grand hotel. We had cocktails that evening and breakfast the next morning in Mike's parents' suite. On the first night after dinner Mike and I went out to a small café with violinists playing. Our last stop was at Berne where we saw the famous clock with the little figures striking the gong at noon. We ate lunch in a charming beer garden and then drove back to France. We spent the night in the picturesque town of Bescancon and drove back to Paris the next day.

Back in Paris we went to more movies and nightclubs. One night we ate dinner on the Bateau Mouche, a small boat that travels up and down the Seine serving dinner as it goes. We both had steak and wine and listened to the musicians playing all evening. The trip was over two hours and we thoroughly enjoyed it. For our final date we chose to go to Monseigneurs, a sumptuous restaurant. The walls were covered with blue velvet and there were huge portraits in gold frames under sparkling chandeliers. There were silver candelabras and gorgeous floral arrangements all around the restaurant. We were serenaded all evening by violinists. The only libation available was champagne so we had to order a bottle of champagne. We thought that we could nurse one bottle all evening, but no such luck. The violinists came to our table and showed us how they could put their champagne glasses on their violins and drink with no hands. By the end of the evening they had consumed three bottles of champagne from our table. Mike was so ebullient that he tipped every one generously even the doorman. It was a super celebration.

For a final treat, Mike's parents took us to a grand spectacle at Versailles. We had front row seats right by the reflecting pool. There was a platform rising out of the pool and a ballet performance was held on the platform with gorgeous lighting effects that were reflected in the water. After the ballet performance all the fountains of the palace were lit up in different colors followed by an hour of fireworks. It was the most spectacular display that I had ever seen and there were thousands of people watching it. I didn't want to go home at the end of the summer. We had had such a wonderful time and Mike's parents were so good to us. We decided to announce our engagement after we returned to the United States.

In the fall of 1952, Mike began his junior year at Princeton and I started in the nursing program at Columbia. We took advantage of New York City's amusements during the next two years. Mike's father generously provided Mike with an allowance after he returned from Paris, as Mike had spent all his summer earnings on enjoying Paris nightlife with me. In the beginning of the fall we budgeted Mike's allowance so that we could go out to fancy restaurants with big bands for dancing once in a while. We loved to dance and we continued to go dancing whenever we could throughout our lives. Our other favorite entertainment was going to the movies which we also continued to do regularly all through our lives. We found a charming inexpensive restaurant in Greenwich Village that we frequented most weekends before going to a movie. Princeton and Columbia were so close to each other that we could see each other almost every weekend.

The nursing major at Columbia was a grueling program, but I loved it. My favorite specialty was obstetrics, my least favorite was psychiatry. In the nursing program there was a group of eight students who dated Princeton men, so every weekend we took the train to Princeton together. Party weekends at Princeton were an experience out of F. Scott Fitzgerald. There was a street lined with Princeton clubs, each with its own band so that students and their dates could wander up and down the street visiting each club. Princeton was a male college at the time, so women from many colleges would flood the campus on big party weekends. There was a lot of excitement and gaiety until the wee hours of the morning. The women were put up on the second floor of the clubs, often in rooms holding 30 or 40 women in triple bunk beds. Little sleep was had as women came in at all hours and some got up early to go to Mass.

I was glad to have a room at the Routheaus' and, later, after Col. Routheau retired, I was invited to stay at the home of a botany professor who was a friend of my father. The only problem with that arrangement was that Professor Pittendrigh had four small children who woke up early and played in the living room where I was sleeping. There were strict rules at Princeton that all women must be out of the dorms before 7 p.m. Mike and I had been brought up by principles that dictated waiting for marriage before becoming intimate. College rules in the early fifties helped keep students on a straight and narrow course, but it was frustrating to not even have a suitable place to kiss goodnight at either Columbia or Princeton.

For the summer of 1953, Mike obtained a job at Goodyear Tire and Rubber in Akron, Ohio. I had to work in the hospital all summer as part of my nursing program so he hitchhiked to New York City every Saturday to be with me. He slept at the YMCA on Saturday nights and spent Saturday evening and Sunday seeing New York City with me. He took the midnight bus back to Akron on Sunday nights.

We continued to see each other almost every weekend during Mike's senior year at Princeton. Mike insisted that we not get married until he could support me financially. As he approached graduation Mike had two job prospects that he was considering—Goodyear Tire and Rubber Company in Akron,

Ohio and Union Carbide Corporation in Bound Brook, New Jersey. He agreed to marry me if he got the job in Bound Brook as I could then commute to New York City for the last year of my nursing program. Mike said that if he got the job in Akron, we would have to wait another year to get married. I told him that I would quit school if that happened. Luckily the Union Carbide job came through and we were married on June 16, 1954 the day after Mike graduated from Princeton. Late in the afternoon of his graduation day, the entire wedding party drove to Winchester, Massachusetts for the wedding rehearsal at 10 p.m.

I had wanted my cousin Patsy to be my matron of honor, but she was unable to do so because the birth of her second child was imminent. I chose my closest friend at Columbia as my maid of honor, and Mike chose his roommate of four years at Princeton to be his best man. Fifteen of our friends were in the wedding party and over two hundred guests came. The wedding was held in the same church where my parents were married 25 years before. The reception was held in the church parlor. My relatives were all teetotalers, so the church seemed like the most appropriate place for a non-alcoholic reception. Grandma Elsie invited all of the wedding party to her house for dinner following the reception. By that time we were on our way to the hotel in Boston that we thought we had kept a secret from our friends. However after we had dinner in the hotel and went to our room we received a call from the lobby. It was the best man and several other friends who told Mike that he had forgotten his toilet kit. After Mike returned to the room with his toilet kit, his friends sat in the bar toasting us until the wee hours of the morning.

Mike spent the $250 that his Grandfather Schuyler had left him for a four-day honeymoon at Mirror Lake Inn in Lake Placid, New York. We had a snug little room overlooking Mirror Lake and we were in heaven. Everyday we had breakfast in bed and then went to see the local scenery, taking a picnic lunch. We visited beautiful waterfalls and scenic mountain views and went to children's attractions such as the North Pole and a mock western town. After four days we came back to reality. Mike started his job at Union Carbide and I went back to school. We rented a nice garden apartment with a living room, bedroom and small kitchen in Plainfield, New Jersey right on the bus route to New York City.

Mike had opened a new door at Columbia Nursing School. No one before had ever been allowed to marry while in the program. Those who did marry were expelled. All nursing students were expected to be completely committed to nursing and only nursing. Mike went to the Director of Nursing and told her that we had waited six years to be married and he urged her to allow me to marry and remain in the program. He convinced her to do just that. Many of the nursing faculty were horrified that I became married while still a student. Some were convinced that marriage would keep me from devoting myself completely to nursing. Because of their attitude, I was determined to prove to them that I could succeed at nursing even though I was married. I studied hard and succeeded in becoming the valedictorian of my class.

3

Early Family Life

During the first year of our marriage, when I wasn't studying, we had great times with other young people. Mike had a group of bachelor friends at Union Carbide who wanted to be introduced to beautiful nurses. So Mike and I arranged lots of blind dates and we went on outings at the Jersey shore or to parties at the "Farm", a house that seven of the bachelors shared. We also found a number of young married couples at Union Carbide parties to socialize with. We formed a group to celebrate New Year's Eve together and after 50 years we are still spending New Year's Eve with one of those couples, our best friends, Dick and Beverly Weber. We made fast friends with the Webers at the first Union Carbide Christmas party where Beverly and I became acquainted over a huge bowl of shrimp.

My last year in the nursing program was difficult. I was only permitted to spend the night at home if I was scheduled to work the following day from 10 a.m. to 7 p.m. I tried to get as many of these shifts as I could, but head nurses were not always accommodating. When I couldn't spend the night at home I would take a 5 p.m. bus home and spend two hours with Mike before taking the bus back to Columbia. I frequently told Mike that I wanted to quit school, but he always urged me to try it for one more month. When I finally made it to the end of the program in September 1955, I received a Bachelor of Science degree from Columbia University. Mike, of course, was there for my graduation, looking very proud. Also on hand were my parents, my brother David and his wife Mary and my grandparents, who were then 77 years old. Grandma Elsie offered her dream house in Rockport to us for a second honeymoon after I graduated. We had planned to start a family as soon as I finished college and we did just that.

I spent the fall of 1955 studying for my board exams to become a registered nurse. Mike kindly helped me write the 300 thank you letters for our wedding gifts that fall so that I could study. I passed all the sections on the exam with scores of 97 or better. We enjoyed taking Sunday rides in the car in our first years of marriage. One Sunday when we were out driving we passed a development of new houses in Piscataway. We thought that it would be fun to look at the model house so we turned into the development. We were quite taken with the new little house and, as we left, Mike looked at the brochure for the development. He was amazed to see that the mortgage would not cost any more than the rent that we were then paying for our apartment. He also saw that we could get a four and a half percent Federal Housing Authority mortgage loan. The realization hit us that we could buy a house before the new baby came. We put a down payment on the house and spent the winter choosing wallpaper, paint and furniture for the baby's room. We moved into the new house in the spring, several months before the baby arrived. Mike decided to go to graduate school at Rutgers University in the evenings. He started out taking one course a week, but took a heavier schedule as he went on.

We found a Congregational Church in Bound Brook only ten minutes away from our new house and joined it two days before the baby came. At the orientation meeting before joining the church, the minister urged me to join the women's group. Mike immediately said that we would only do church work together as we had been separated for so many years. We agreed to run the Junior High Fellowship together in the fall.

When I found out that I was pregnant I told Mike that I wanted to go to my doctor at Columbia for my maternity care. Mike was somewhat dubious because it was an hour and a half drive from where we lived in New Jersey to the hospital in New York. The obstetrician at Columbia assured Mike that there would be plenty of time to get to the hospital with a first baby. He was wrong! On the day the baby arrived I awoke at 8:15 a.m. and told Mike that I was going into second stage labor. He called the doctor who said it must be a mistake as no one starts labor in second stage, especially with a first baby. He agreed to meet us at the hospital. Mike drove like crazy up the New Jersey Turnpike while I pushed the baby towards birth in the back seat. When Mike got off the turnpike he drove through ten red lights and screeched to a stop at the emergency room door. He ran in calling for a stretcher. When I got to the delivery room there wasn't time to take off my clothes before the baby was delivered. It was all over six minutes after we arrived at the hospital. The resident had to deliver the baby because the obstetrician did not arrive until an hour and a half later. He lived ten minutes from the hospital, but obviously did not believe Mike's story on the phone.

The baby was born on June 8, 1956. He was a beautiful eight-pound boy and we called him Stephen Cortlandt Schuyler, the name that we had decided on five years earlier. I nursed him for seven months until I became pregnant again. Our second child came one hour after the first labor pain, but we had become wiser and went to a local hospital and doctor. Nevertheless Mike was very nervous at the thought of getting me to the hospital in time for future deliveries. Our second child was born on October 12, 1957, an adorable little girl with black hair and brown eyes. We named her Cynthia, but would call her Cindy.

We were very busy washing, drying and folding diapers. With two babies in diapers, Mike decided that we needed a drier, so that we would not have to defrost frozen diapers hanging on the line that winter. He bought our first television set with an eight-inch screen so that I could watch TV while I folded diapers. It turned out to be a great help in distracting Steve while I nursed Cindy. His favorite program was Captain Kangaroo and he especially liked to watch the big dancing bear on the program. The only break that I got from child-care was my once a week trip to the grocery store on Saturdays while Mike stayed home with the children. I did get to socialize with the other mothers in the neighborhood as we watched our children together in each other's yard.

Mike took on several projects to improve our first house. He built cabinets in the family room and a very attractive breakfast nook with benches in one corner of the kitchen. He also built a beautiful big patio outside the back door. It was his first experience with manipulating wet cement, so it took three truckloads of cement to get the hang of flattening the cement before it dried. He colored the cement squares green and white and built a sturdy railing around the perimeter. We had many summer parties on that patio.

In 1958 I decided to practice my nursing skills in a local hospital. Mike watched the children while I worked one evening a week. Middlesex General Hospital, where I worked, was an overcrowded, understaffed old hospital in New Brunswick, NJ. I was responsible for the care of 24 adult patients, as well as for giving medications to six children in the pediatric ward, where a practical nurse was in charge who was not qualified to do it. Adult patients were sent directly to my floor from the operating room, as there was no recovery room. My only assistant was a nurse's aide, so I enlisted the help of relatives in watching post-operative patients for signs of distress. This job was challenging, but I enjoyed it. However, the next year I discovered that I was pregnant and I resigned my position at the end of the summer.

While I was pregnant with our third child, Mike took the family on our first vacation retreat. He had always used his vacations to do work around the house, so this was a big treat. We rented a cabin for a week at Lake Wallenpaupack in the Pocono Mountains. We had a wonderful time swimming in the lake and going to children's attractions in the area. When we came home, I told Mike that we should take a vacation like that every year. Mike said that we could not afford it, so we began to look for alternative types of vacations.

In December of 1959 when I went into labor, Mike became frantic. He rushed me to the hospital, and when the staff asked us to fill out forms before going up to the labor room, he got very excited and said, "We can't do that now, my wife has babies very rapidly!" He rushed me upstairs in a wheelchair, but it turned out that I was having false labor pains. They sent me home and Mike looked quite sheepish as he passed the front desk. The next day, December 7th, we went back to the hospital and the baby was born. It was a cute little baby boy and we named him Peter Bradford Schuyler. I felt a deep affection for him and couldn't stop looking at him when they brought him to me in my hospital room.

The next day the doctor came into my room and told me that there was something wrong with Peter. The pediatric nurse had reported that he vomited his feeding when he returned to the nursery. They had taken x-rays but could not determine what the problem was. Dr. O'Brien, the family doctor who had delivered Peter, suggested sending him to Columbia Presbyterian Medical Center for diagnosis and care. He told me that it was important to have a specialist treat Peter. I was very upset. I adored Peter from the moment that I first saw him. I had not been discharged from the hospital yet, so my mother held Peter while Mike drove them into New York City.

When they arrived at Babies Hospital at the Columbia Medical Center Mike's parents were waiting for them. A resident doctor met Mike and took over the case. He wanted to operate on the baby immediately. Mike would not let him touch Peter. Mike called Dr. O'Brien in New Jersey and told him about the resident's intention. Dr. O'Brien said, "Let me talk to him." When the resident took the phone, Dr. O'Brien chewed him out and told him that he himself had much more experience than the resident and that he didn't send the baby to Columbia for a resident to operate on. He told the resident to find a top specialist immediately to care for Peter. The resident did as he was told and got the best specialist in the hospital.

The specialist was far more cautious than the resident, doing more tests and waiting for results before going into surgery. Mike took Peter to have x-rays and wouldn't let anyone else touch him. He undressed him and dressed him again until the specialist was ready for him. That specialist saved Peter's life. He saw that Peter had a mid-gut mal-rotation. His small intestines hung straight down from the duodenum rather than twisting around like normal. Part of the small intestine was intertwined with some ligaments that were squeezing it like a rubber band, thus preventing the passage of food. Rather than incise the intestine, the surgeon simply cut ligaments that were squeezing it, so that food could pass through. He left the mal-rotated gut hanging there and said it would function fine even if it were not in the position normally found in human anatomy. By not incising the gut, the specialist avoided the complications that would have accompanied such major invasive surgery in a tiny baby.

A few days later I was able to view Peter through the window of the intensive care unit. When he came out of intensive care into a room, I was able to hold him again in my arms. I sat in his room and cried as I held him to me. The mother of the other child in the room told me that her baby was severely retarded. I thanked God for our good fortune with Peter. Peter was a happy baby. I never put him down after we brought him home. I cooked, vacuumed and did most of my housework with Peter in one arm. Mike's mother sympathized with me having three small children in diapers, so she arranged for us to have diaper service. Mike bought a second car for the family so that I would have one at home while he took the other to work.

In January 1960 when Peter was a month old, I mentioned to Mike that I wished I could have interesting discussions with adults; my conversations with the neighborhood mothers centered on child rearing. Mike gave me his usual answer to my complaints, "Well, why don't you do something about it?" So I did. I invited two couples who were close friends to come to the house. One couple was Dick and Beverly Weber, whom we knew from Union Carbide Corporation, and the other couple was Tom and Simi Long, whom we knew from our church. I proposed that we form a reading and discussion group. Every month one person would chose a book for the whole group to read, and then that person would become the discussion leader for the book. We asked the Webers and the Longs to each invite another couple to join the group, so that it would not be just Schuyler friends.

We decided to start right away in January. Beverly Weber chose the first book and the Longs agreed to hold the meeting at their house. We had not invited any other couples yet, but we decided to proceed with the original three couples until we found the others. The discussion at our first meeting was lively and we knew that we had a good thing going. A few months later the Longs and the Webers each invited their neighbors to join the group. These five couples became the original reading and discussion group that would last for over forty years. We subsequently named the group the Deipnosophistical Society (Deipnos for short).

At the end of the spring semester of 1960, Mike graduated from Rutgers with an MBA in Finance. I took pictures of him in his cap and gown holding baby Peter with Steve and Cindy standing on either side of him. In the summer of 1960, we decided to join a local swim club so that the family would have a place for relaxation during summer. We belonged to the club for the next seven years. The children took swimming lessons there and the family ate suppers at the picnic tables beside the pool most weeknights. Sometimes there were adult swim parties and we played water basketball with our friends. It was a good social environment for the whole family. The next year, when Mike was transferred to New York City as the manager of the financial analysis group at Union Carbide Chemical Company, he would drive directly to the swim club from the train station for supper.

In August 1960, my brother Bunkie married Ann Stalheim in Garretson, South Dakota. Mike suggested that we go out to the wedding for our vacation trip that year. Peter was only eight months old, so Mike's mother volunteered to take care of him while Steve and Cindy went with us. We traveled overnight on a train in our own private roomette with sleeping facilities. We marveled at the great expanse of flat treeless land in the middle of the country. When we reached the Stalheim farm in Garretson, South Dakota we fell in love with Ann's father, Ollie Stalheim, who was the friendliest man that we had ever met. In fact, all the people in South Dakota that we met were very friendly. The clerks in the stores were never hurried or impatient as clerks in the East often were. We had a great time at the farm where Ann's mother served huge meals three times a day. She explained that farmers need substantial meals because of all the hard physical work they do in running a farm. The children loved seeing the animals and enjoyed playing hide and seek and running through the stalks of corn that rose way above their heads. The wedding was delightful in the little country church. We were impressed by the unity of the congregation as everyone pitched in to help at the wedding reception in the church hall.

When we returned from the wedding, Mike returned to investigating an inexpensive way to take family vacations. Early in 1961 he noticed an advertisement for a used collapsible camping trailer for $100.00. We decided to buy it and become a camping family. We figured that we could afford the one-dollar fee for a campsite each night and thus could start taking regular vacations with the children. We took our first camping vacation in the summer of 1961 at Rogers Rock at the northern tip of Lake George in New York. It rained the entire ten days that we were there, yet we still loved it. We made new friends and one-year-old Peter spent the whole time pushing his truck in the dirt under the tent canopy. The children all had yellow ponchos with hoods that they wore to play out in the rain. Every summer for the next eight years the family went camping. For four years in a row we camped at New York State campsites at Rogers Rock, Thousand Islands on the St Lawrence River, the Finger Lakes in the center of the state and at Taconic Lake near Albany. Then we expanded our horizon by camping at Prince Edward Island, West Virginia, The Gaspe in Canada, New Hampshire and Cape Cod. Our longest camping vacation was a four-week trip across the country to Wyoming and back across Canada.

In the fall of 1961, Steve started kindergarten in the school just one block away from our house in Piscataway. We had decided that the little house in Piscataway was not big enough for our growing family. There was little storage space in the house, no attic or cellar and the closets were tiny. We started looking at other houses in the area. We almost made final decisions on a number of houses, but each one was not quite right for us. We did, however, find a floor plan that we liked. I took the plan to a builder in Bound Brook to determine how much he would charge to build it. He told me that he had already built a house just like the plan and he wanted me to come and see it. When he told me the cost of the house, I replied that we could not afford it. Mike had given me a limit of what we could spend and the house was well over that limit.

The builder asked me to follow him to the house in question so that he could get a floor plan for me to take home to show Mike. When I stopped the car in front of the new house, the children all jumped out and ran into the house after the builder. When I chased after them to gather them back into the car, I saw the inside of the house and liked it. When I got home I showed the floor plan to Mike. He was so excited with the plan that he went to see the house that night with a flashlight. The next day Mike called the builder again and he agreed to lop off one quarter of the price. We took it on the spot. I had been a good bargainer without even realizing it. So in February 1962, we became owners of our dream house at a price that we could afford.

On the outside the house had white shingles with red brick facing under the picture window in front of the living room. There was a double garage on the side of the house at the end of a long driveway. Inside, the house was multileveled. There was a long hall leading from the front door to the closet at the other end. On the right side of the hall were five steps leading up to a large living room with a cathedral ceiling. A wrought iron railing separated the room from the hall. The front of the living room looked out on the front lawn through a huge picture window. On the opposite side of the living room were two steps leading down to a formal dining room. A wrought iron railing separated the living room from the dining room. The kitchen was to the left of the dining room on the same level. It was a large room with a big picture window looking out on an expansive back yard with tall oak trees at the far end. I decided that the breakfast table should go right in front of that window. At the front of the kitchen there were two sets of stairs, the one at the end led up to the living room and the one on the right led down to the front hall. Across from those steps on the other side of the hall was a large family room with glass doors leading out to the back yard. There was a small bathroom off the family room. The garage was adjacent to the family room and across the hall from the garage was a door to the cellar.

Up ten steps from the living room were three big bedrooms and two bathrooms. The main bathroom was very elegant with three different levels (one of the selling features of the house). At the top of the stairs from the living room one could turn around to the right and go up two more steps to a large fourth bedroom. The third level of the main bathroom also led into that bedroom. We loved the house so much that a few years later we refused to sell it when we went to the Philippines. We rented it to a nice couple and came back to claim it two years later.

When we moved into our new house in February, Cindy immediately became best friends with Debbie Handen, also four years old, who lived next door. I was worried about Steve changing schools in the middle of the year. I spoke to Miss David, the principal of the new school in Bound Brook, and found her to be very supportive. Steve seemed to like his new teacher and school. That summer the family went camping at Thousand Island State Park on the Saint Lawrence River in upstate New York. We found a site right on the river and set up our little camping trailer. Steve went fishing with Mike and caught a little fish that he proudly held up for a snapshot. The teenage boys in the next campsite found a big black water snake for him that didn't thrill me too much. Peter was the only early riser in the family so Mike and I worked out a system to allow each of us to get enough sleep. I got up at 6 am with Peter and watched him play for three hours. Then at 9 am Mike and the other children got up and I went back to sleep.

In the fall of 1962, Cindy started kindergarten at Smalley School. I felt that with two children in school I would have time to do some volunteer work. I decided to teach a Red Cross Mother and Baby class for the Adult Education Program at Bound Brook High School. I taught the class for the next seven years and thoroughly enjoyed it. At the same time Mike was asked to take the position of Sunday school superintendent at the Bound Brook Congregational Church. The church had a large membership at the time, so there were four classes for each grade, requiring a total of 32 teachers. I helped him line up teachers and took on a class myself. Soon Mike convinced me to become the director of the primary level and later to join him as co-superintendent of the Sunday school. After working with the Sunday school program for a year, we recognized that the quality of the curriculum was unsatisfactory. We decided to do a comprehensive revision of the entire curriculum. We enlisted the help of the teachers and asked Gene Brokaw, a former superintendent of the Sunday school, to coordinate the endeavor. We held regular meetings both at our home and at the church to review a number of church school curricula. After a few months of intensive work, a new curriculum was voted on and purchased for the next school year. This experience would prove an excellent background for me when I undertook curricula revisions in the future as a college professor and administrator.

Mike and I enjoyed involvement in church activities. There was a couples club that we were active in, called the Congregates. We made many friends in the group including Tom and Simi Long who had three children the same age as our children. One of our favorite groups in the church was an adult bible study group, led by our minister, Olin Lewis, in his home on Sunday evenings. Olin had a Ph.D. in philosophy as well as a graduate degree in divinity. We were inspired by his erudite observations and found they helped us sort out and confirm our own religious beliefs. Another religious study group that I joined was made up of church women in their 60's, 70's and 80's. The coordinator of the group was Mrs. Wood, a lovely widow whom I highly respected. The group was a prayer group, but we shared our personal lives also and I learned a great deal about the feelings and thoughts of older people.

That fall I had a miscarriage. To cheer me up Mike bought me an adorable little puppy. She was just a mongrel, probably with more beagle genes than any other type of dog. We named her Ginger and she was the hit of the family. Mike strung a wire across the back yard so that she could run and play on a long leash when we were not home. She loved to bark at the mailman, but once when her chain broke she didn't know what to do and backed away. She was terrified of cats if they turned and hissed at her. She loved to chase rabbits, but never came close to catching one. The family took her camping and Steve always brought water to her on the campsites. The children were very fond of Ginger.

In the summer of 1963 I became pregnant with our fourth child. We spent our summer vacation at the Finger Lakes State Park in central New York. The children loved the beach and the activities around the campsite. They took turns washing the dishes in an old baby bathtub. Peter had to stand on the bench of the picnic table when it was his turn to do the dishes. We went to see the local scenic spots and at Watkins Glen we were caught in a torrential rainstorm that thoroughly soaked all our clothes. I made out well as Mike bought me a new dress and raincoat to replace my wet clothes. There was a trunk full of dry children's clothes in the car that was kept there for emergencies, so the children all had outfits to change into. Mike also had some dry clothes in the car. After everyone was outfitted in dry clothes, we all went out to dinner in a nice restaurant.

Mike and I decided to learn about art history during that vacation. We bought a set of art seminars published by the Metropolitan Museum of Art. The set, written by John Canaday, contained twelve portfolios of paintings with comments on elements of painting and art appreciation in each one. There were twelve full color 10" by 12" reproductions contained in pockets inside the front cover of each of the twelve portfolios. Every night of the vacation we studied the seminars by kerosene lamplight at the campsite picnic table after the children were asleep. We enjoyed the experience and learned a lot about art. Years later I would use the same set of portfolios in an art course that I taught in college.

In August of 1963, Mike and I agreed to house a student from Nigeria for two months prior to beginning his studies at Princeton University as a sophomore in the fall. His name was Biodin Kasim and the whole family was delighted with him. We bought him some warm clothes for the winter weather and welcomed him into our family. He returned to our house for all his vacations for the next six years. After he finished his undergraduate degree he went on for a masters degree. The first year he was here, Steve took him to his class for "show and tell". Biodin wore his native robes and Steve was so proud leading him down the street on their way to his school. The children in Steve's class asked him questions about all the wild animals in Africa. Biodin had never seen a wild animal as he lived in Lagos the capital of Nigeria. He got a big kick out of the visit however. Biodin felt right at home with our family and tried to do whatever he saw us doing. We took him up to Rockport for a visit before college began. We all went down to the rocks and jumped into the ocean, so Biodin did the same thing. However, when he got in the water it was over his head and he started to flounder. Mike rushed over and pulled him up on the seaweed. He couldn't swim but he wanted to follow everything we did. In October Biodun enjoyed helping us put on a big birthday party for Cindy. There were fifteen little guests at the party so we set up a big board on sawhorses in the garage for them to eat on. Mike ran the games in the back yard with Biodun's help.

Early in 1964 a tragic event occurred. My cousin Patsy was stricken with leukemia. She was pregnant with her seventh child and the disease moved very rapidly to stamp out her life and the life of her unborn child. She was 32 years old when it happened and she left six small children between the ages of ten and two. I was in the seventh month of pregnancy but insisted on going to Massachusetts to Patsy's funeral. My doctor told Mike to stop every hour on the trip and have me walk for a half-hour at each stop. The funeral was devastating to everyone there.

On April 6, 1964 I gave birth to our fourth and last child, Catherine Schuyler, to be called Cathy. This time my labor was eight hours long. Our minister's wife, Charlotte Lewis, drove me to the hospital, as Mike was on a business trip in northern New Jersey. She was very nervous during the trip, as she knew my history of very short labors. Mike drove down from his conference and met us at the hospital and for the first time he was able to sit with me during labor. He fell asleep but I was happy to have him there. Cathy was a beautiful baby with curly blonde hair and a happy disposition.

Soon after Cathy was born, Mike had an operation on his ears. He had new eardrums inserted as his original drums had been eaten away by the chronic infection that had followed his ruptured eardrum when he was a toddler. I went into the New York Ear and Eye Hospital to be with him and found him dressed in his street clothes much to the nurses' consternation. Mike never would wear a hospital gown if he could avoid it. The operation was a success and provided a modicum of improvement in Mike's hearing.

Soon after Mike went back to work, I also developed an ear infection. I woke up one morning and thought that I had experienced a stroke. When I called the doctor he told me that I had labyrinthitis. I had to lie flat on the floor to keep from vomiting and fainting. Mike was in New York City and Cathy was upstairs in her crib. I telephoned my friend Simi Long and she came over immediately and took right over. Simi was familiar with the condition, as her mother had had it. She was very helpful and comforting. However I had to remain prostrate on the kitchen floor until Mike came home and carried me upstairs to bed. Mike and I had been planning to attend Mike's tenth Princeton reunion, but when his roommates arrived to pick us up we had to tell them that we could not go with them. I was very lucky as the labyrinthitis cleared up soon and did not affect me permanently as I heard was the case with other people.

I had become depressed about my cousin Patsy's death after the birth of Cathy. My doctor recommended that I talk to a psychiatrist. I was reluctant, but Doctor O'Brien assured me that I was not crazy and that I only had to make one visit. The psychiatrist said that I was too much of a perfectionist and told me to read *Atlas Shrugged* by Ayn Rand. It was a very long book by a feminist author whose main point was that one should be self-centered. This was diametrically opposed to my Christian view of life. However, I read the book—though it took me quite a while. The children long remembered seeing the book in my room for many months. The effort of reading the book seemed to clear up my depression, so maybe the psychiatrist had a good idea after all.

Dick MacDowell was so overwhelmed by Patsy's untimely death, that he married his secretary three months latter. She was a wonderful woman who took over the family and brought up Patsy's six children as her own. Patsy's mother, Marion, was also very instrumental in helping the children adjust. They all loved their "Nana" (my Aunt Marion) and their new mother. As years went by Mike and I continued to see the MacDowell children who were close to the ages of our own children. In the summer, their Nana lived in the house adjacent to my parents' house in Rockport, so we saw them every year. When Cindy was fourteen years old, she took care of three small children who lived next door to Aunt Marion, her favorite aunt. She visited her aunt on her daily break from her baby sitting duties. She became very fond of her MacDowell cousins that summer and invited Susie MacDowell to visit her for a week in Bound Brook in the fall.

Cathy Schuyler was a joy as a child. When she was a baby she sat in a seat in the middle of the kitchen table during meal times and the other children kept her entertained. As she grew she was always laughing. She related to other people in the friendliest manner and everyone seemed to enjoy her company. In the summer of 1964, Mike's mother, who then lived in Albany, New York, took care of baby Cathy while the family was camping nearby at Taconic State Park. I drove to Albany from the campsite several times so that I could be with Cathy and one night we let her sleep in the camping trailer with us. The other children made friends and enjoyed the beach at the park. Later that summer, we took the older three children to the World's Fair while Grandma Wy again took care of Cathy.

In the winter of 1965, Mike thought that it would be good for us to take a short vacation alone without the children. We decided to go skiing at Jug End Resort in the Berkshires for our first winter weekend vacation. We had seen the resort on our way to visit Mike's parents in Albany on our way home from Rockport. The resort was in a beautiful location and had a lovely lobby with a huge granite fireplace. We stayed in our own private cabin and enjoyed the continental breakfasts in the main lodge. We practiced skiing on a gentle slope next to the lodge. We had a wonderful time and decided to make a habit of a winter getaway weekend vacation each year. We had been using a wonderful woman as a baby sitter, Ann Kobazak, who cared for the children like a grandmother. She was willing to stay at our house while we were away for a weekend. She was very responsible and good to them. Thus we felt comfortable about taking winter vacations in the future.

In the summer of 1965 the family visited the World's Fair on Long Island where Mike carried Cathy in a carrier on his back. We also went camping at Prince Edward Island that summer. Cathy was one year old and played in the dirt as Peter had done at Roger's Rock several years before. We camped beside the beach and the children played football in the grass along the beach. The water temperature was bearable for swimming as Prince Edward Island is surrounded by warm water from the Gulf of Saint Lawrence. We enjoyed a lobster feast at a local church one evening and the next morning took a ferry to Nova Scotia. In Hamilton we visited a fish cannery where the children were all given hats with the cannery's name on them. We drove around the outside edge of the island and the scenery was lovely. Our favorite spot on Nova Scotia was Peggy's Cove because it reminded us of Rockport, Massachusetts.

Later that summer, Mike had to go on a business trip to West Virginia. I suggested that we all go along and camp while he was at his conference. His boss was amazed when he put in an expense account for one dollar per night on that business trip. On the way home from West Virginia, the universal joint in the station wagon broke. We were near a tiny town on the Ohio Pennsylvania border. There was one motel, one restaurant and one garage in the town of Claysville, Pennsylvania. It was Friday afternoon and the mechanic could not get a new part until Monday. Mike had to get back to New Jersey for a business meeting, so he suggested that I stay at the motel with the four children until the car was fixed and then drive them all home. I agreed to stay with the girls if Mike took the boys home with him on the plane and got a sitter while he went to work. He agreed.

In the fall of 1965, Peter started kindergarten at Smalley School. Mike took on the job of Cubmaster of Pack 43 that same year.

He thoroughly enjoyed planning the programs and working with Steve on making his Pinewood Derby racing car. Not long after he accepted the job Mike convinced me to become a den mother. He assigned me all the obstreperous boys, "character builders" as he called them. Mike didn't want to lose his other den mothers by giving them the hard-to-handle boys. I worked all week trying to prepare an interesting program for my one-hour den meeting each week. The boys in my den included: Eddie, who could easily be thrown into a screaming tantrum when provoked by the other den members; Martin, who could not resist hitting other boys when they came close to him; Geoffrey, who insisted on talking to me constantly as I tried to direct the group; Steve, who was excitable and often did not listen to my directions; Chris, whose mother often came with him and talked to me while I was trying to control the group and, finally, my one perfect cub scout, Philip, who did everything he was told and was continually cheerful and friendly.

I kept them busy making craft projects such as totem poles out of large boxes. To do their crafts I lined them up around the ping-pong table. I thought that I had put ample space between them, but they managed to push or flick others on the head when they passed them going to the sink to wash their hands. Once a month the different dens presented one of their projects to the whole pack. One of the most challenging projects for my den was rehearsing a play to be presented at the Pack meeting. The presentation was well received, but no one knew the effort that went into the result that was displayed. After I had been a den mother for a couple of years, Mike made me a den mother chief, which had all the same challenges of a den mother and a few more.

As I became more involved in community activities, Mike offered to hire a woman to help me clean house once a week. We found a gem, Sophie Mikolowski, who not only cleaned the house but also became a wonderful friend. Sophie had a large house in South Bound Brook. Her husband was not able to work so she supported him. Her only son was married and lived in Massachusetts when she started working for us. One summer we drove her up to see her son on the way to Rockport. She liked the huge rocks that she saw in New England. Sophie loved to garden and she had all kinds of plants—flowers, vegetables and fruit trees. She kept us supplied with tomatoes from her garden and pears from her tree. She was fond of the children and the feeling was mutual. She loved to show me pictures of her grandchildren when I drove her home. She took care of her husband and when he died she went to live with her son's family. They gave her part of their yard for her own plot to garden. We continued to correspond with her until she died in her nineties.

In the winter of 1966, we decided to take another weekend skiing vacation. We stayed in a lovely cabin in the woods at Split Rock Resort in the Pennsylvania Poconos. We improved our skiing and enjoyed dances at the main lodge in the evenings. Mrs. Kobezak, our wonderful baby sitter, took excellent care of the children while we were away. In May of 1966 Biodin graduated from Princeton University with a Bachelor of Science in Aeronautical Engineering. Mike and I went to his graduation and met his girlfriend, Dupe, from Nigeria. They would later marry when Biodin was in graduate school in Ohio.

4

Across the Continent

By the summer of 1966, Mike's yearly vacation time had been increased to four weeks. We figured that four weeks was enough time to drive to Wyoming to visit my brother David's family and drive home again. We planned to camp out every night all the way there and back. We bought a large station wagon with big front and back seats and two small seats facing each other with a table between them way in the back. It was a perfect setup to separate the children and thus to keep peace on long trips. Steve and Peter sat in the back seat while Cindy and Cathy sat way in the back where they could color and read. It actually worked out well on the long trip across the country. We also bought a new camping trailer for the two girls and us to sleep in and a small pup tent for the boys. The trailer had a table and benches in it and a big attached canopy with screened sides for eating outdoors. Mike put curtains beside the beds in the trailer to give us some privacy. The children's clothes were stored in individual bins that could be stacked on top of each other for traveling. We had acquired an assortment of cooking utensils including a collapsible oven. Ginger rode under Mike's feet as we drove out west.

We spent the first night of the trip west at Mike's sister's house in Carlyle, Pennsylvania. Shirley was married to Ed Saxby, a

United States Army officer who was getting advanced training at the Army Military College in Carlyle. We set up the trailer in their backyard and spent the night and the next day with the Saxby family. Our children enjoyed playing with their Saxby cousins. The next night we spent in Indiana in a field next to railroad tracks. We were awakened periodically by the sound of freight trains passing by. The next day we drove to Devil's Lake in Barabo, Wisconsin. The campground and the lake were beautiful and the family enjoyed swimming and hiking beside the lake. Our next stop was the Stalheim farm in Garretson, South Dakota. We were all delighted to see Ollie Stalheim again and his wife, Odessa. They treated us royally. We visited some local scenic spots near Garretson and then drove on to the Bad Lands.

The colorfully eroded landscape of the Bad Lands is made up of pinnacles, rock tables and fossil beds. As the brochure said, "One of the most unusual drives that you can take in all of the USA is through the Bad Lands of South Dakota." We felt like we were in the middle of a western movie, but we didn't see any cowboys or Indians hiding behind the rocks. We drove on through the Black Hills of South Dakota. In Custer State Park friendly donkeys came up to the car begging for handouts of food. The children were delighted to feed them. On the western edge of South Dakota we stayed at the Whispering Pines Campground. We went to see Mt. Rushmore and then visited the town of Deadwood, where we stopped at Saloon #10, "the best known bar throughout the entire historic west." We were told that Wild Bill Hickok was shot in the back there. The bar was decorated with stuffed animal heads and birds; it looked like a scene from a Hollywood movie and we half expected to see a cowboy with drawn guns walk in the door at any moment. We saw the Boot Hill graveyard where Hickok and Calamity Jane were buried and toured a gold mine where we were given some fools gold. After leaving Deadwood we crossed into Wyoming and found a cow pasture in which to spend the night. We had to be careful where we stepped.

The next day we drove across Wyoming to my brother David's ranch outside of Cody. As we drove on Interstate Highway 90 we saw nothing but black dirt. There were exits that turned off route 90, but for many of them, there were no roads at the end of the exits. During the trip, we decided to have a picnic lunch so we took the next exit off and drove into a field with a few cow skulls and evidence of more recent cattle presence. When we reached David and Mary's ranch we were warmly greeted. Our children enjoyed playing with their cousins who were about the same age. During our stay, David and his family took us to Yellowstone National Park a little north of their ranch. We saw Old Faithful, Mammoth Hot Springs and the beautiful lower falls of the Grand Canyon of Yellowstone. They also took us to the Buffalo Bill Museum and the Whitney Gallery of Western Art. I loved the paintings of Charles Russell, Frederick Remington and Albert Bierstadt. Peter liked Russell's paintings and had several of them in his room at college years later. Mike and I liked the grandeur of Berstadt's paintings and, on a subsequent visit to Cody, we purchased a large reproduction of one of his paintings for our home. We stayed several days at David and Mary's ranch. We all went swimming in the South Fork of the Yellowstone River that runs through their property. The children rode on their horses and we all climbed the mountain behind their house. Mary cooked us delicious meals of fresh venison, home grown vegetables and home made peppermint ice cream with thick chocolate sauce, which we remembered for years to come.

After being spoiled by David and Mary for five days we headed toward Montana. We drove to Glacier National Park through magnificent scenery. We found a site deep in the woods and set up our camping ensemble. There was no running water so we brought big pails of water from the mountain stream and boiled it on our camp stove for drinking and cooking. We decided to go swimming in the stream, but the water was so cold that the children jumped out faster than they jumped in.

We hiked and took lots of scenic pictures of the family surrounded by colorful wildflowers with mountains in the background. Luckily we did not see any grizzly bears. (After we returned to New Jersey we read in the paper of a grizzly bear that killed four campers in Glacier National Park.).

Our next destination was a ranch outside of Calgary, Alberta, Canada. There we visited the Soutzos. Constantin and Ioanna Soutzo were friends of Mike's parents when they were in Romania. They were from Romanian nobility, but were forced to leave when the Communists took over their country. They immigrated to Canada and bought a 3200-acre ranch near Calgary, which they operated as a family endeavor. Two of their three children lived on the ranch with them. Their son Sandy helped his father run the ranch. Their daughter Ioanna lived in her own house on the ranch with her husband, John Tarnowski, and their three daughters, Rosabelle, Danuta and YoYo. Danuta developed a crush on our son Steve and gave him a beautiful picture of an Indian girl that she had made.

While we were there Mike enjoyed riding horseback with Constantin around the ranch and working in the fields with Constantin and Sandy. The women brought them hot tea and sandwiches at mid-day. Mike remarked with surprise how refreshing hot tea was when he was sweating from working in the hot sun. Our children played with Ioanna's children on the swings in the yard, rode on the tractor and went horseback riding on the ranch. Before we left, Ioanna and her children took us to Banff National Park in the Canadian Rockies. We visited Lake Louise and Moraine Lake surrounded by seven mountain peaks. The scenery at Banff was the most spectacular that we saw on our trip.

We left Calgary the next day for our drive home across Canada. On the first day we saw a herd of elks and a moose. We camped at Moosejaw in Saskatchawan that night. On our eastward trip we saw beautiful scenery at first, but then it began to rain and continued to rain for days. One night outside of Winnipeg we punctured a tire. It was after midnight and it was raining hard. Mike changed the tire and then declared that we could break our camping streak and stay in a motel for the night. We drove along until almost 2 a.m. looking for a motel and finally spotted the White Orchid Motel. We pulled into the parking lot ready to fall into real beds when Mike spotted a sign that read, "Camping in the back." He was delighted, but the rest of us were not. Mike drove to the back, set up the trailer and announced that we should take showers while we had the bathhouse to ourselves. The children and I were too tired to resist so we did what we were told.

We drove to Ft. William in Ontario where we embarked on a cruise from Port Arthur. We saw part of Lake Superior on the cruise and later we went fishing in the lake. We visited an amusement park the next day, always a hit with the children. The most memorable event of the rest of the trip back was on another rainy day. We needed to stop and wash clothes and ourselves. There was nothing but mud around the campsite, so Mike and the older children decided to have a football game in the mud. Cathy watched for a while and then decided to join in the fun. She just sat down in a big puddle in her pink snowsuit and wallowed in the mud. After the game was over they all took showers and I tried to wash some of the mud from their clothes in the shower. Then we drove to a laundromat with all the muddy clothes. We received a lot of surprised looks from the other people there.

At the end of the trip we camped at Green Gables campground near Niagara Falls and near another amusement park, much to the children's delight. We went to see the falls, where everyone wore yellow slickers to keep from getting wet from the spray. The falls were truly an awesome sight. On the last day of our vacation we stopped for the night at Albany and had dinner and breakfast with Mike's parents before going home. When we returned to Bound Brook, the local paper interviewed us about the trip. A big picture of all of us, including Ginger, in front of the camping trailer was displayed across the front page of the *Bound Brook Chronicle*. Steve, age nine, kept a detailed journal of the entire trip. Cindy and Peter wanted to be a cowgirl and cowboy, respectively, for quite a while after the trip. Peter asked Mrs. Kobazak if she would be his cook when he grew up to be a cowboy. She agreed and, for years afterwards, they talked about their plans as cowboy and cook.

Early in 1967 we went to Killington, Vermont for our third annual winter weekend vacation. We rented a beautiful cabin with a king-sized bed. The skiing on Killington Mountain was steep and exciting and we really enjoyed flying down the slopes. At the end of our first day a light snow began to fall. We had taken the lift to the top and Mike took off down the mountain thinking that I was right behind him. I was standing still at the top of the hill and somehow my ski caught on something and I lost my balance. As I fell my ski boot did not come off the ski. I heard a snap and as I looked at my left leg it was twisted completely out of line from its normal position. I reached over to set it back in position and heard another snap. I realized then that my leg was broken. I called for help from Mike but he was half way down the slope and could not hear me. There were no skiers nearby, but finally some one saw me from the lift as it neared the top. Soon the ski patrol arrived with a toboggan to take me down the mountain. That was the bumpiest and most painful ride I ever endured. By the time we reached the bottom and they had put me in an ambulance I had lost consciousness. When I came to Mike was with me and we were again enduring a bumpy ride over dirt roads on our way to the emergency room in the local hospital. While I was lying on a stretcher in the emergency room I was hoping that the doctor could set my leg and then Mike and I could go to see the movie, *Georgie Girl,* that was playing at the theater in town. But it wasn't that easy. The x-rays showed that my leg was broken in three places and would have to be set and have a large cast applied. We cancelled our hotel reservation and Mike stayed with me until I was settled for the night in my room.

Mike stayed through Sunday, but he had to leave Monday night to get back to the children and work. He called my mother who came to Bound Brook to take care of the children for the next week. I was in a great deal of pain and the pain medication was not helping. Finally, after three days of agony, the doctor had more x-rays taken and discovered that the bones were not in alignment. Sharp segments of bone were sticking into the muscles causing spasms and pain. The doctor scheduled me for surgery the next day. He set the bones and put steel pins in both bones of the lower left leg. Mike's mother came to Vermont to be with me right after my operation. She said that she could hear me yelling as I came off the elevator. I wasn't making much sense and I had a notion that the doctor had put my leg on backwards so I kept asking Mike's mother to look at my leg to see if this was so. She obligingly went over and looked at my leg over and over again to reassure me that the leg was properly aligned and the cast was on correctly. I deeply appreciated her coming to be with me after that operation. By the end of the week I was able to go home. Mike came up with a mattress in the station wagon and drove me home. When we pulled into the driveway my mother was standing there with her suitcase packed ready to leave. She had endured a very challenging week with our four children.

Mike carried me into the house and put me down in the family room. We pulled out the hide-a-bed in the family room where we would sleep for the next three months. Mike got the older children off to school in the morning and left Cathy in the family room with me. Cathy was two, almost three, and very responsible for that age. She was a helpful good-natured little girl and very obedient. She could go upstairs and get me what I needed from my description of which drawer it was in. I was somewhat depressed at first but our minister's wife, Charlotte Lewis, came over to help me out when I felt desperate. Steve was also a big help to me while I was laid up and took good care of Cathy. The people in the church and the neighborhood were wonderful to us. Louise Raycob, a friend from church, organized people to bring family dinners to us for one whole month, and friends were extremely generous in the delicious meals that they brought. My best friend in the neighborhood was Ella Handen, Debbie's mother. She brought me lots of nourishing food and visited me often. I received numerous get-well cards from friends, relatives, church members, my Sunday school class and my cub scouts.

Mike wanted to get paid help to live in for a while when I first came home, but I was against the idea. He told me that I would have to learn to use crutches if I refused to have paid help. I had a four-inch heel put on my right shoe so that I could swing my cast through when I walked on crutches. After a while I was mobile and could go to church and the movies if I brought a stool along to prop up my foot. I even learned to drive the station wagon with one foot. I went back to teaching my Mother and Baby course with my cast on. I only missed one week of class. The cast stayed on for three months and the doctor cut a window in it so that I could scratch my leg with a bent coat hanger. When the time came to remove the cast I felt that I had lost all support in my leg. The muscles had shrunk and I still had to walk on crutches. My leg had been purposefully bent in the cast, but I could not straighten my leg after the cast was off. The doctor sent me to physical therapy and eventually the muscles strengthened, the leg straightened and I was my old self again ready to go dancing every week with Mike. At the end of May we went to Columbus, Ohio for the wedding of Biodun and Dupe. Biodun asked Mike to be his best man.

During the next two summers the camping trips were scaled down in length. In 1967 we took two smaller trips. First we went to New Hampshire where we drove by picturesque countryside and ate picnic lunches on big rocks in the middle of streams. Mike and the boys climbed Mount Washington while the girls and I sat at the bottom in a local restaurant. The boys came back with stickers that read, "I climbed Mt. Washington." The family especially enjoyed the Shelbourne Museum, which depicted early American life. Later in the summer we drove up to the Gaspe, the Canadian peninsula along the Saint Lawrence River. We camped on a bluff overlooking the river and trudged up and down a gravel road to the beach each day. The scenery was magnificent, but there was little else to see in the area. All we found on the way home was a little zoo with mangy animals.

That fall Steve skipped the sixth grade and entered junior high school. His sixth grade teacher said that he knew everything she was teaching the class and she recommended that he go into seventh grade. Steve had been restless in elementary school and he found the atmosphere in junior high more satisfying as he moved from class to class and studied more interesting and challenging subjects. I agreed to become co-superintendent of the Sunday school that year. My partner was Barbara Anderson, an old friend from Winchester, Massachusetts, who just happened to move to New Jersey and join the Bound Brook Congregational Church. We enjoyed working together and things ran smoothly. Cathy was three and had started nursery school at the church so Barbara and I had mornings free to handle the affairs of the Sunday school.

At Christmas time we had a tradition of making cakes and brownies for families who were shut-in or having problems. In December 1967, one of the families whom we visited was the Crosses. Mr. Cross was the caretaker for the Middlebrook Club, a small building in our town with a large hall that was rented out for social occasions. The Crosses were the only black family living in our town at that time. They had four children about the same ages as ours. Their son, Martin, was one of my cub

scouts and he had sent me a card when I broke my leg. When
we arrived with brownies for the family, their mother, Gloria,
was overwhelmed with gratitude. She told us that she didn't
know anyone in town and had just come back from Trenton
Hospital after being treated for a nervous breakdown. Trenton
Hospital was known for its harsh treatment of mentally ill
patients. She told us of her shock treatments and the hospital's
degrading practice of hosing down patients in the nude. We
talked for quite a while and she told me that she wanted to go
back to school to become a practical nurse and try to turn her
life around. She asked me if I would tutor her if she went to the
community college. I volunteered to tutor her every week for
the next year. She came to my house on Sunday afternoons and
we went over her lessons together.

Early in 1968 Mike started to think about leaving Union Carbide
to gain some different kinds of experience at another company.
But before he left Union Carbide he decided to take advantage
of their international operations so the family could experience
life in another country. He applied to Union Carbide
International to place him in an underdeveloped country for a
couple of years. While he was waiting to hear about a foreign
assignment he took the family on our last camping trip in the
United States for a while. We took a short trip to New Bedford,
Massachusetts. We stayed at a privately owned campsite that
featured nightly hayrides, which the children really enjoyed.
While camping in New Bedford we drove out to the end of
Cape Cod for a day. We swam on the ocean side of the National
Park at the end of the cape where the water was 58 degrees.
The children loved rolling down the sand dunes and racing
Mike down them. At the end of the day everyone in the family
changed into dressy outfits and went out to dinner at the Pirates'
Cove Restaurant in Provincetown at the tip of Cape Cod.

In August 1968 my brother Bunkie and his family were
scheduled to move to Panama for a couple of years. As we also

planned to go abroad and might not see them for some time, I decided to go out to South Dakota to say good-by to them. Mike was tied up with business, so I took Steve, Peter and Cathy with me and drove to the Stalheim farm in South Dakota. Cindy stayed home to cook for Mike and be with her friend Debbie Handen. The big station wagon that we had purchased two years earlier was ideal for taking children with me. Steve sat in the front seat and was my navigator. He read road maps easily and kept me going in the right direction. Peter sat alone in the back seat reading comic books and Cathy sat in the far back coloring and reading books.

The trip went well with easy driving on interstate highways until, near the end, we had to drive on a two-lane highway with big trucks coming the other way. I became so unnerved that I stopped every hour for coffee and more comic books for the children to keep them occupied. Steve long remembered that leg of the trip. When we reached the Stalheim farm we were greeted enthusiastically. Ollie Stalheim put us up in an uninhabited house on the farm. There was no running water in the house, so everyday the men came and flushed the toilets with water stored in giant milk cans. There was a big tree in the yard with a rope swing and a tree house for the children to play in. Cathy was very taken with the new kitten in the family.

On the trip back we drove through Iowa so that we would be on interstate highways all the way home. But even those big roads weren't perfect. One stretch of route 80 was missing the white lines between lanes. A big thunderstorm came up and we couldn't see where we were going. We decided to call it a day and found a motel at 5p.m. After a hearty dinner, a good night's sleep and no more rain, the rest of the trip went well.

Early in the fall of 1968 Union Carbide International informed Mike that he would be working in their battery manufacturing operations, but could not inform him yet as to the specific location. They sent him to Toronto, Canada for six weeks to learn about battery manufacturing. After two weeks in Toronto, the company sent Mike home for a week to be with his family. When he was about to return to Toronto, I told him that I didn't want to be away from him for three more weeks. I suggested that he find an apartment for the six of us in Toronto for the last two weeks he was there. I told the principals of the children's schools that I was planning to take the children out of their classes for two weeks. All of the children were excellent students and the principals did not object to their leaving. Mike found an apartment with a kitchen, living room and bedroom for less money than Union Carbide was paying for him to stay at a fancy hotel.

I drove all the children to Toronto in one day. It was a stressful trip, but we kept up our spirits by playing records on Cathy's little phonograph. We played the same song over and over again. We finally arrived in Toronto about midnight, and settled into our little apartment. Living in Toronto was a great adventure for all of us. The children slept in a hide-a-bed and two cots in the living room and we slept in the bedroom. I cooked all our meals in the apartment kitchen so we lived frugally. We found a baby sitter in the apartment complex and Mike and I went out to some very charming lounges in the evenings. Toronto had many interesting places to see. We took the children to parks and went ice skating near an old castle. Steve was old enough to explore the city on his own and found it fascinating. On Halloween we made costumes for the children and took them to a posh suburb to go trick-or-treating. We had each child write a report for school on their experiences in Toronto. When we returned to Bound Brook, Union Carbide International assigned Mike to the position of Treasurer and Chief Financial Officer of Union Carbide Philippines. He was to begin his new assignment in February 1969.

During the week of Christmas, 1968 Biodun visited us with Dupe and their baby girl, Ayodele. She was an adorable little girl and our children were fond of her. I baby sat with her while her parents visited New York City for a day of sightseeing. We started to prepare for our trip abroad. We lined up appointments for a series of immunizations for the family and entered a whirl of good-by parties starting at the end of December and extending to February 17th the day before we left. On January 4th we invited over a hundred of our friends to a January Jubilee. Ninety-two came and we had a wonderful time. We bought 100 champagne glasses and 140 regular glasses. I baked six loaves of date-nut bread, made 240 turkey sandwiches and several dips and cooked two five-pound hams and nine pounds of Swedish meatballs. Champagne was flowing and we ended with a sheet cake and coffee. The party lasted until 3:30a.m., and a great time was had by everyone.

We were invited to numerous dinners in January and February. The Congregates at our church had a dinner in our honor and our book group held an extra meeting so that we could have two more discussions together. Friends had us to dinner in their homes and many of them invited the children as well. I went to Gloria Cross' graduation and the party afterwards on January 31st. How proud her family was of her and so was I.

To prepare us for living in the Philippines, Union Carbide arranged for the family to receive an orientation to life in that country. The young woman who oriented us had never been to the Philippines and must have obtained the "facts" of her orientation from an outdated book. She told us that we should leave all our good furniture at home as the humidity of the Philippines would ruin it. She also told us we should not take our dog with us, as dog meat was a favorite food in that country. These outdated facts did not represent modern Manila where we would live. We found that most new homes were air-conditioned and that many families had dogs as pets. The misinformation that we received led us to leave our best furniture in storage and our dog with Mike's parents in Albany while we were gone. When we arrived in the Philippines we realized that we needed dining room furniture, so we had to buy a second dining room set.

At the beginning of February we drove the family to Winchester, Massachusetts to say good-by to Grandma and Grampy and the aunts and uncles. The next day we drove to Albany to say good-by to Mike's parents and to leave Ginger with them. The day before we left the movers came to finish taking our thing and that evening we had dinner at the Webers house with our best friends, the Deipnos. Then Dick and Beverly Weber took us to the motel at Newark airport to spend the night so that we could catch an early plane in the morning. Mike's parents came to see us off.

5

Life in the Philippines

Our plane left Newark Airport at ten in the morning of February 18, 1969. Neither Mike nor I had ever visited San Francisco or Hawaii so we decided to spend a couple of days in each place on our way to the Philippines. We arrived in San Francisco at noon pacific time and toured the city that afternoon and the next day. After we arrived we checked into the Sheraton Plaza Hotel and walked through Chinatown. We took the cable car to Fisherman's Wharf and meandered around enjoying the sights. We ate dinner at the Franciscan Restaurant on the wharf and rode the cable car back to the hotel. After the children were asleep, we checked out the Red Garter nightclub in the hotel. In the morning we rented a car, drove over the Golden Gate Bridge and up to Muir Woods to see the giant redwood trees. In the afternoon we came back to the city, drove down the winding street to Cort Town and then over the San Francisco Bay Bridge to Oakland to see Berkeley University. We took a cable car ride across town and back and had dinner in a restaurant overlooking the Bay. That evening we went back to the Red Garter again.

We flew to Hawaii the next morning where we stayed at the Reef Hotel on Waikiki Beach, with a view from our room of Diamond Head. We relaxed, swam at the beach and ate at the hotel that evening and the next day. On the third day we rented a car and drove to the Polynesian Culture Center to see model villages of Samoa, New Zealand, Fiji, Tahiti, Hawaii, Tonga and Polynesia. We had a buffet lunch at the center and drove around the island to view the coast. On Sunday morning, the day we were leaving, we decided to go swimming in the big breakers that we had seen the day before at Koko Head Beach. There was no lifeguard and we should never have gone in the water. Steve was nearly carried away by a rip tide, but Mike reached out to him and pulled him back. That was one of the scariest and dumbest chances that we ever took. We went back to the hotel, showered and packed. We flew out of Hawaii that afternoon. It was a ten-hour trip to Tokyo and we lost a day as we crossed the international dateline.

Our trip to the Philippines took us ten days. In addition to our stopovers in San Francisco and Hawaii, we took a three-day vacation in Japan. In Tokyo, we stayed at the Okura Hotel and had breakfast in the room every morning. Tokyo is a fascinating city. The people there appear to be very conscious of germs as many of them wore surgical masks on their faces. While in Tokyo, we visited a big department store. We gave each of our children 1000 yen to spend as a reward for their good behavior on the plane. Cindy decided to start a miniature china collection and spent her money on blue and white Japanese china. Cathy wanted to collect dolls from different countries and bought a small doll in a Japanese costume. The boys bought toys. For dinner we went to the Zakura restaurant where five kimono-clad waitresses doted on the children. They brought them green tea ice cream as a treat for dessert. It tasted ghastly, but Steve tried to be polite and ate all of his serving. Then the delighted waitress brought him another big serving. We told him he did not have to eat it.

On one of the days in Japan, we took the Bullet Train to Hakone to see Mt. Fuji. Unlike the usual temperate weather of Japan, it was snowing. We had not brought winter coats as we thought the weather would be warm on the trip as well as in the Philippines. We huddled around a wood stove in one of the shops in Hakone while the children bought souvenirs. We admired Mt. Fuji, then took the train back to Tokyo, where we ate dinner at the Imperial Theatre Restaurant while we watched Kabuki dancers. The following morning we took a train to Kamakura to see the Great Buddha statue. It was still snowing, so we kept stopping at coffee shops to huddle near their stoves. After seeing the Buddha we returned by train to Tokyo. The train was also cold. We took hot showers at the hotel and went out to a Japanese restaurant for dinner. We couldn't read the Japanese words on the menu, but fortunately the menu items had pictures of the dishes with numbers next to them. All we had to do was hold up the appropriate number of fingers for the menu item we wanted.

On February 28th we flew to Manila where we were met by the president, vice president and treasurer of Union Carbide Philippines. For the first three nights, Union Carbide put us up at the Sheraton Hotel. Then we moved into a three-room furnished apartment in the Gilarmi Apartment Complex. We lived there for a month while we looked for a house to rent. While we were living in the apartment the children enjoyed swimming in the Gilarmi pool every day. Mike arranged for one of his employees, Gloria Andrade, to teach Tagalog, the local language, to the family three evenings a week. Cathy was a very outgoing four-year old and got to know lots of people at the Gilarmi apartments. The apartment building had a ramp going up the seven floors of the complex as well as an elevator. Cathy would bounce her ball up and down the ramp and talk to people as they looked out of their apartments at her. Whenever our family rode on the elevator the other riders knew Cathy. The apartment was right next to a shopping center that had a small American-style café called Coffee Time. The family went there frequently for simple suppers of hot dogs and American milk shakes. We played cards and other games with the children after dinner.

We took our first trip within the Philippines while we lived in the apartment. One of our friends from the Bound Brook church was in the Peace Corps with her husband in Balayan. Mike had his company chauffeur, Fausto, drive the family on the trip. We visited the couple, Leslie and Steve Limon, in their home and they seemed very pleased to see people from her hometown. After we left the Limons, we stopped to see Crater Lake in an inactive volcano, then drove down to the China Sea and went swimming. The sand on the beach was black from volcanic ash. Peter dove into a big wave with his eyes open and came out with his eyes full of black sand. Luckily we had a roll of toilet paper with us and I picked out every grain of sand with rolled up tissue paper. The fact that the sand was black helped me to see it better and get it all out. We ate lunch overlooking another volcanic lake, Lake Taal.

From the day we arrived in Manila, the family was invited out for dinner almost every night for six weeks. The day after we arrived we were taken to the Union Church for services in the morning and to the Polo Club for dinner by the vice-president of Union Carbide Philippines, Bob Scheid and his wife, Sally. The next day we moved into our apartment. The Japanese couple who lived in the next apartment invited us to dinner. We became good friends of the Tanaguchis even though their two-year-old son, Etsu, bit Cathy after dinner. The following evening Union Carbide gave a dinner in our honor at the Plaza Hotel.

We located a house to rent within the first week after our arrival, but it was still under construction so we had to wait several weeks before we could move in. The house was in Makati, a suburb of Manila. A week later we bought a small green Toyota station wagon for the family car. On April 3rd we moved into our house. It was perfect for our family with five bedrooms and a spacious downstairs. We had been allowed to send essential furniture by airfreight so we could survive until the rest of our furniture arrived. At least we all had beds to sleep in. That night the Scheids invited us over for a cookout and the next day our new neighbors invited us over for dinner. On Saturday, April 5th we gave Cathy a birthday party in our new house. We invited seven children and ten adults. Etsu, one of the guests, was on his good behavior and did not bite anyone.

A week later we hired two maids, Seny and Lulu. Having live-in maids in the house was a new experience for me, but it was a way of life in the Philippines so I went along with it. I found it very stressful at first, but after a few days I set some ground rules, and this eased the strain. I told Lulu not to clean upstairs on Saturday until everyone was up so as not to awaken the family. I told Seny not to clean while we were eating breakfast and to stay in the kitchen until after Mike left so I could kiss him good-by in private. We had a number of problems with Seny. She thought that she was a playmate of Steve. They had water pistol fights and she would hide behind the door and let him have it right in the face when he came into the room. She would run around to get away from Steve and drop dishes that she was carrying. She broke all the cups of our everyday china set. She liked to sit on the roof and sulk. She also lied. The final straw, however, was when she started fighting with Lulu and biting her. I had never fired anyone, but after five months with Seny, I finally fired her and drove her home to her uncle's house. After we fired Seny, Lulu told us that she had invited her boy friend to stay at our house while we were away. We were all relieved when Seny left, including Lulu, who was afraid of her.

The rest of our furniture came early in May and we enjoyed watching the difference between the small Filipino moving men and the big husky movers that had moved our furniture out of the Bound Brook house. We brought our upright piano to the

Philippines because Cindy had been taking lessons for quite a while and was showing real promise as a budding piano player. In Bound Brook two hefty men carried the piano out to the truck. In Makati it took ten Filipinos to get the piano off the truck and into the house. We could hear them outside counting over and over again, "isa, dalawa, tatlow" (one, two, three) as they all tried together to get the piano off the truck. We were glad that we brought it, however, as Cindy did take lessons and became quite a capable pianist while she was in Makati. She was very fond of her teacher, Mrs. Hallare.

Having been persuaded not to bring our dining room furniture with us, we soon realized that we would have to buy a dining room set. We bought a beautiful set made of Philippine nara wood (known in this country as Philippine mahogany). We figured that we could sell it when it was time to leave the country. After the set was delivered, we gave a dinner for the outgoing treasurer of Union Carbide Philippines. This was the beginning of a succession of dinners and parties for the next two years. We gave a dinner for 12 to 14 people every month or two and gave big Christmas parties for Mike's employees both years that we were in Makati. It was easy with two maids to help clean and cook and we made many delightful Filipino and American friends. We played charades and other games after dinners and really enjoyed our social life in the Philippines.

Soon after we moved into our house we joined a country club called the Polo Club, so that the family would have a place to go swimming, play tennis and participate in other activities. The Polo Club also had charming restaurants where we could take visiting guests to dinner. Cindy had a nice group of friends whose families belonged to the club and Mike and Steve frequently played tennis in the evenings on their lighted courts.

Most social invitations during our first three months included the children. We played bridge and other games with the children in our evenings at home and also watched TV with them. Steve and I especially liked to watch the old Laurel and Hardy movies. Gloria Andrade, our Tagalog teacher, came for dinner sometimes and also sat with the children if we had to go to a party alone. Mike took the family to the Polo Club for dinner about once a month and we continued to go to the Coffee Time restaurant. Mike and Steve went running together early in the mornings before Mike went to work. We soon met another American family whose children were the same age as ours. We enjoyed going to each other's house for cookouts.

Mike enjoyed his work at Union Carbide Philippines. Being treasurer and chief financial officer gave him the advantages of responsibility and freedom of action that one gains as an executive of a small company without losing the advantage of security in working for a large corporation. He dealt with government officials and other industry executives and found his job both challenging and exciting. During his tenure the company constructed a new manufacturing plant in Cebu. The company grew in size and Mike had to increase the size of his operation, giving him the opportunity to hire several new managers. In the process he interviewed some of the brightest, up-and-coming young businessmen in the Philippines. He hired three of these young men: Ely Quaizon as head of accounting, Bobby Montalibano as head of finance and Danny Romero as head of insurance. They were all honest, intelligent and diligent and a pleasure to work with.

Mike found it challenging to learn the problems of different currencies. While he was in the Philippines, the company anticipated that the country might soon go through a serious devaluation of the currency, which could give Union Carbide some serious financial problems. Mike found this an exciting challenge. One of Mike's accomplishments concerned the debt of Union Carbide Philippines to Union Carbide headquarters in New York. Union Carbide Philippines had incurred a significant debt to Union Carbide in New York for the original establishment of the company. Thus Union Carbide Philippines had a large US dollar obligation when Mike first arrived. Mike was able to convert a large portion of this debt to pesos in Philippine banks during his tenure there. Mike was also able to arrange that the additional debt incurred for the new plant at Cebu was obtained from Philippine sources. Consequently when the devaluation of the local currency did occur, most of the company's debt was in pesos rather than in US dollars, which would have tremendously inflated it. Mike found it fascinating and challenging to deal with Philippine bureaucracy in securing permits and government approvals to construct the new plant in Cebu.

Union Carbide Philippines distributed batteries through a network of salesmen. The sales force covered all of the country and each salesman was furnished with a truck that served as a warehouse for the batteries. In effect there were thousands of mini warehouses throughout the Philippines. Keeping control of the inventory was a difficult job. One of Mike's employees, Sul Maniquez, was chief auditor of the company and it was his responsibility to stay on top of this difficult job.

When Mike started at Union Carbide Philippines, the company was under the direction of President Shafer who ran it in an autocratic fashion. Three months later Shafer retired and Vice President Scheid filled his position. Bob Scheid used a more collegial form of leadership as president. He held a management meeting every Friday morning that lasted all morning and sometimes into the afternoon. The meetings covered all the company's operations and made all of the major decisions affecting the company. Attending the meetings were the top management group consisting of Bob Scheid, President, Frank Godinez, Vice President of Marketing, Charlie Braswell, Director of Manufacturing and Mike Schuyler, Treasurer and Chief Financial Officer.

Prior to Mike's arrival the company had experienced a serious strike that had not only crippled production, but had soured relations between management and the workers. Scheid was determined to improve labor relations and avoid another strike. He relied on Godinez, as the senior Filipino in the company, to serve as the liaison between management and the workers. Godinez relished this role as the representative of management and the workers and used it effectively as a representative to both groups.

In addition to establishing Union Carbide Philippines, Union Carbide International had also created a joint venture with the Guevara family in the Philippines. Maria Christina Chemical Industries was created with the company offices in Manila and the manufacturing operation in Iligan on Mindano, the southernmost and largest of the Philippine islands. The company produced calcium carbide. The president and treasurer of Union Carbide Philippines were members of the board of directors of Maria Christina and also president and treasurer of the company. In his capacity as treasurer of Maria Christina, Mike visited Iligan several times and often took the whole family along. The resident director of the corporation in Iligan was Conrado (Rads) Guevara, who treated us royally every time we visited Iligan. We grew to know his family well and one of Mike's prize possessions from the Philippines is a sword that Rads gave him as an honorary "datu" (chief) of the local tribe. Rads also gave our family a magnificent kulingtang as a gift after one of our visits. It is a large ornate stand with colorful wings on each end and roosters' heads projecting from the front. The stand holds eight brass gongs of different sizes that make music when struck with playing sticks. The kulingtang still stands in a place of honor in our family room in Bound Brook.

The children began the fall term of the International School in Makati in July. Cathy entered kindergarten, Peter went into the fourth grade, Cindy started junior high in the seventh grade and Steve entered high school. For a long time I had promised myself that I would start work as a nurse after all my children were in school. Now was my chance. My Philippine visa did not allow me to earn a salary in the Philippines, but this did not deter me from pursuing my career. I knew a woman doctor at Children's Medical Center in Quezon City, so I asked her if the medical center would allow me to work pro bono. She asked the head of the medical center, Dr. Fey del Mundo, if this would be acceptable and was told that they would be delighted to have me.

A week after the children started school I began working at Children's Medical Center. I ran into a huge traffic jam on my way, then lost my way completely and ended up in Manila. I finally arrived at work two hours later at 10a.m. The supervisor was very understanding and took me on a tour of the center. On Tuesday I found my way with no problem and the trip took only thirty minutes. I decided to work on the maternity ward. I worked only in the mornings the first year as Cathy was in school for just half a day, but the second year I worked five full days a week.

At first the staff treated me like a celebrity. I was the only American working at the medical center and they didn't seem to know what to do with me. I decided that I would have to find some work to do, so I joined the student nurses, helping them make beds and care for their patients. By the end of the week the head nurse realized that I was serious in my intent to work, so she assigned me patients of my own. The next day the clinical instructors came to get me to teach a ward class for the student nurses, which I continued to do every week. I worked for a few months on the ward and then transferred to the labor and delivery center. The hospital had no electrical fetal heart monitoring, so I kept track of the fetal hearts by listening to them with a stethoscope. In one case I noted a drop in the fetal heart rate and immediately reported it to the doctor.

A caesarian operation was performed on the patient and the baby's life was saved. Later the patient presented me with an exquisite piece of embroidered material from which to make a dress.

After a year in obstetrics, I asked for experience in the operating room, which they readily granted. I worked as an assistant to Dr. Reyes, the chief of surgery. I bought a number of textbooks on surgical anatomy and studied them arduously to be knowledgeable about the types of surgery scheduled each week. The Tagalog lessons that we had at home helped me understand the staff when they spoke in the local language during the operations. I really liked the nurses and orderlies in the operation room. They were all very skilled in their work. The two orderlies, Teofilo and Jose, kept the supplies in excellent order and were very alert to the needs of the surgeons and patients. They were both extremely supportive to me. I ate lunch with the operating room staff each day. Their lunch consisted of a heaping platter of rice and a bowl of broth with fish heads and spices in it. They scooped up the sticky rice in a ball in their hands and dipped it in the broth and ate it. They knew that I did not like fish or rice, so they ordered a hamburger for me.

When there were no operations the nurses and I made dressings. One nurse told me about her family's experience during World War II, when Manila was taken over by the Japanese. There were five girls in her family and her father kept them hidden in the cellar as the Japanese soldiers frequently raped the Philippine women. She said it was a terrifying time for the Filipinos. Another friend told me of watching his father being shot along with all the men in his village when the Japanese took over. The other nurse that I worked with was the head nurse of the operating room. I had great respect for her capable management. These nurses, Becky and Norma, became good friends of mine and later visited us in Bound Brook during a trip they made to the U.S.

In my year working in the operating room I witnessed a number of fascinating operations and became good friends with Dr. Reyes. One custom that interested me was that families were involved with patients' operations and postoperative care. The whole family, including toddlers, was allowed to sit behind a glass partition to watch their mother undergo a caesarian operation. Children were also allowed to visit relatives who were newly post-operative patients. I saw children playing on the floor with their trucks in the rooms of their postoperative relatives.

The environment of the hospital rooms was also surprising, at times, when you saw lizards crawling on the walls over the beds of patients. There was a high incidence of parasites and tuberculosis in Philippine patients. In one operation, when the surgeon opened a child's stomach, it was full of white worms. Tuberculosis was easily spread between family members in the inner city of Manila, as the poorer families all slept together on one mat in one-room shacks. These shacks were crowded together with no running water or waste disposal facilities.

While I was working at the medical center, the staff gave a baby shower for one of the nurses. They invited me to come but didn't think I would. I went home, baked a cake and went back to the shower that evening. They were surprised and pleased that I came and we all had a good time. The Filipinos were fascinated by the skin color of new babies. The pregnant nurse who was being honored had medium brown skin and her husband had very pale skin. There was much discussion over what color the baby would be. Another case that interested the maternity nurses involved an American actress who was having a baby by a Philippine plumber. Again there was much speculation on the likely color of the baby.

At the end of July, Mike and I went to Hong Kong for four days. Another Union Carbide couple, the Hundorfs, offered to take our children while we were gone in return for our taking their children earlier when they went on a trip. We thoroughly enjoyed our stay in Hong Kong; I especially liked shopping there. Import duties were low in Hong Kong compared to the Philippines. I enjoyed shopping in the big air-conditioned quay next to the docks where wares from many countries were sold at bargain prices. I also found it intriguing to explore small shops on the narrow streets of the city. There were piles of china plates stacked in the corners of these shops and if I took the time to pore through them I could usually find a colorful plate that I liked.

In Manila we occasionally enjoyed a concert at the new Philippine Cultural Center. On one occasion we attended a special dinner and concert by Beverly Sills, who was visiting the Philippines with her family. It was a formal occasion and President Marcos and his wife, Imelda, sat right in front of us. Mrs. Marcos was a stunning woman. I was enthralled by Beverly Sills' singing, which was magnificent. She had a very powerful voice and charmed the audience completely.

In the fall we became active in church activities. We joined a Bible study class given on Wednesday evenings and I took on a Sunday school class. We considered joining a square dance class that was held in the church. Mike was against this at first, declaring that he did not come to the Philippines to take up American square dancing. I pointed out to him that half of the class was Filipinos and it would be a good opportunity to make new friends outside of Union Carbide. He relented and we began square dance classes in mid-September. It was one of the best decisions that we made in the Philippines. We met wonderful friends and thoroughly enjoyed dancing with them. At first the class met once a week, but later we were meeting two or three times a week, including dancing at individual homes.

In October we acquired a new maid who was superb! Anita had been the Hundorfs' maid and, when they went back to the United States, Anita came to work for us. She knew our children from the time that they had stayed with the Hundorfs while we were in Hong Kong. She was capable, intelligent, mature and very friendly. The children liked her and Cathy grew to adore her. She became a wonderful friend to me and we worked very well together. She and Lulu also got along well with each other. On October 3rd we gave a dinner for fourteen friends and, with Anita's help, it ran smoothly. After dinner we played games and everyone seemed to have a great time. A week later, Cindy gave a birthday party for twelve friends at our house and Anita was a big help to her too.

We entertained a number of foreign visitors while we were in the Philippines, some from Union Carbide and some who were friends of the family. A botanist friend of my father, Padre Raulino, visited us in October. I took him to an experimental farming station of the University of the Philippines in Los Banos, about an hour south of us. We met a botanist there who knew Father as a famous botanist. I liked Los Banos so much that I later took the wives of several visiting Union Carbide executives there to entertain them while their husbands were at meetings. Another old friend of ours, Rebecca Stickley, the mother of my maid of honor, came through Manila on a tour. She stayed with us for a night and we took her to a Chinese wedding that she enjoyed. Although we had a busy life in the Philippines, having friends from home visit us always lifted our spirits.

At the end of October, Sally Scheid had an operation for cancer that had metastasized. She looked to me for support and I visited her frequently both in the hospital and at her home. I took her homemade foods and listened to her expressions of anxiety about the future. I tried to assuage her fears and comfort her. She showed a brave outlook and when we returned to Bound Brook she visited us there to thank us for our support.

In November there was a national wrestling tournament at Clark Air Base in northern Luzon. The whole family went to see Steve wrestle and he won first place! We were bursting with pride. We celebrated at the cafeteria at the base and the children relished the American food there. At the end of November we were invited for Thanksgiving dinner to our next door neighbor's house. The Kuzs bought the dinner at the U.S. commissary and our children again enjoyed eating American food and sharing an American holiday with another American family.

At the beginning of December the family took a trip to Iligan where Mike had business at Maria Christina Chemical Industries. This company was owned jointly by Union Carbide and the Guevara family. The head of the Guevara family was Judge Guevara. He had four sons, Victor, Conrado, Ricado and Danny. Conrado (Rads) was the resident manager of the plant in Iligan. Whenever we visited Iligan, Rads and his wife, Medy, were very gracious to us. On our first visit we stayed in the local hotel where the water was turned on only at certain hours of the day. Being unaware of this, Mike got in the shower and soaped himself up when suddenly the water went off. I ran down to the front desk and told them of his dilemma and they turned the water back on for ten more minutes. While we were in Iligan, Rads and Medy invited us to dinner at their home and Medy took me sightseeing and shopping the next day. We invited them to dinner at our hotel the second evening, along with Rad's brothers Danny and Conrado (Cards). A week later they all came to dinner at our house in Makati.

On December 19th we gave a party at our house for Mike's employees and their wives, eighty people in all. Our guests ate heaps of rice, talked, laughed, played guitars, sang and played with our children. We had a gigantic buffet for them. We had plenty of food except for rice. We ran out, then quickly bought more rice and cooked it immediately. The Filipinos are small thin people, but they consume a great deal of rice. We continued our Christmas practice of taking home-cooked goods to people at Christmas time. Our Filipino friends were surprised and pleased by our custom. On Christmas day, Tonette and Consuelito Guerrero invited our family to spend our first Christmas away from home with their family. They made a delicious dinner for us and gave each of our children a lovely gift. Tonette was the chief engineer at Union Carbide and he and his wife became lifelong friends. We celebrated New Years Eve at the Polo Club with Mindo and Min Fajardo, also friends from Union Carbide.

January 1970 was an eventful month. On January 2nd, Cathy was invited to the birthday party of her school friend, Chaumi. Among our children, Cathy had the most international group of friends while we were in the Philippines. Her best friends from her class were Chaumi from Japan and Ricky from the Philippines. The next day, Colonel Guevara invited our whole family to visit Corregidor on a naval ship that he had leased for the day. Corregidor was fascinating and it was the setting of my favorite movie, *So Proudly We Hail*. The rocks on Corregidor had red circles on them and the Filipinos called them the "blood rocks" of Corregidor. Colonel Guevara brought a lunch for each of us and we ate it while sitting on the rocks outside the famous tunnel on the island. This was the tunnel where General MacArthur and his troops, as well as medical personnel caring for the American wounded, held out during the Japanese bombardment of Corregidor at the beginning of World War II. They held out there until April 1942. We felt very fortunate to have been invited on this fascinating expedition.

On January 16th we went to a formal dinner at the Hilton for United States Ambassador Byroade. It was a splendid affair. The next day we went to a square dance jamboree at the Polo Club for all the groups in Luzon. It was a festive gathering and each club came in costumes made out of the same material. Our group chose a bright purple and red material so we really stood out. The individual members of our group could chose any pattern they wished to make dresses and shirts out of the material. I chose a pattern with a white blouse and white ruffle sewed into the dress. Mike's shirt had a white vest to contrast to the bright colors of the material. I took the material to our dressmaker, Rita Vivas, who could make anything I wanted from a simple picture that I drew. Rita was a talented seamstress and I felt that I had found a replica of my Grandma Elsie. Rita was a lovely person and she made Cindy, Cathy and me lots of cotton dresses that I designed. Textile material in the Philippines was colorful and inexpensive.

On the last day of January, Mike took the family on a week vacation to Bagio, a resort in northern Luzon. Bagio was the one place in the Philippines that felt like home. It was high in the mountains and cool. There was a small United States Army base there, Fort John Hay, and the children loved the American food that they could purchase at the commissary. We went with two other families, the Lippincotts and the Ames. Both couples lived permanently in the Philippines. The men were American and their wives were Filipino. The first day we went to a cookout for lunch at the Ames' and then they took us to the Philippine American Life House for dinner. The next day we all played golf and ate dinner at the Officers Club. After dinner, we put Peter and Cathy to bed and went back to the Club for a sing-a-long and dancing. We played golf with Steve and Cindy in the morning, while Peter and Cathy played with the Ames children. In the afternoons the whole family played tag-football. We had dinners together and played cards with the children in our cabin in the evenings. On our last day in Bagio, Mike and Steve played 18 holes of golf, Peter went horseback riding and the girls and I went to the market. We all dressed up for our last evening and went to the Officers Club for dinner. We had a heavenly week at Bagio.

In February we were invited to Judge Guevara's birthday dinner. It was a lovely big party honoring his 85th birthday and we were the only Americans there. He was a highly respected dignitary in the Philippines and his family was very proud of him. The rest of the week I made cakes for a big dinner at our church for the minister and his wife. On Valentine's Day we had twelve guests to dinner and games. We wrote love sonnets and had a marriage quiz for the couples to test how much they knew of each other's backgrounds.

Our family played lots of games and watched movies on television together. Some nights after we put the children to bed we would go over to a lounge in the shopping center and listen to violin music over a nightcap. The Anito Lounge was our favorite spot to relax together. On February 28th we celebrated the anniversary of our first year in the Philippines. We invited Gloria Andrade, our Tagalog tutor, to dinner with the family and all played charades in the evening.

At the end of March we went camping for four days at Alligator Lake in southern Luzon. We joined our two favorite couples from the square dancing group, Jim and Katie Tennant and Doc and Dessie Adams, for this adventure. The Tennants brought their youngest daughter, the Adams brought their two sons and we brought our four children. We had a very relaxing time. We camped next to the lake and ate delicious home cooked meals of fried chicken, potato salad, spaghetti and Doc's stew for dinners, and eggs, bacon and pancakes for breakfasts. There was a man living near the lake in a star shaped house built on top of a tower. He was an American who had stayed in the Philippines after the war. His two teenage sons, Charlie and John, lived with him. He had built his house up in the air to keep out snakes and animals. He had spread the rumor that the lake was bewitched to keep others away from it. Thus we were the only people swimming in the lake. There was a rope hanging from a tree branch over the water and the children loved swinging out on the rope and jumping into the lake. We played games with our children and Charlie joined in. Charlie asked me how Peter got his scar on his stomach. I told him that Peter was born with a mal-rotated gut that had to be operated on when he was three days old. He wanted further explanation, so I told him that Peter's duodenum hung straight down and did not twist around like a normal person's. Charlie thought the story was funny and began to call Peter "duodenum Pete," which made Peter laugh.

We came home on Sunday night and went back to school and work the following day. A week later on April 7th we experienced our first earthquake, a big one. Mike was in a restaurant on the fourteenth floor of a building having lunch. He said that the building kept swaying back and forth. The waiters hid under the tables. At our house Cathy called downstairs to me saying, "There must be something wrong with my new desk, everything keeps falling off of it." Some children were killed in a school that collapsed, but most buildings in Makati had been built to withstand earthquakes and thus weathered the shock. There were after-tremors for several weeks.

6

Home Leave and Back to the Philippines

Union Carbide granted an annual vacation of four weeks plus travel time to its overseas personnel. The company paid for the round-trip airfare and there was no extra charge for stopping en route to and from the United States. The family was excited at the prospect of flying around the world and visiting interesting places on the way. We discussed the itinerary for many weeks before we decided on just what stops to make and then Mike bought the plane tickets. On our way back to the States we planned to visit Beirut, Vienna, Munich, Amsterdam and London. The spring semester of school ended in mid-April and we planned to leave the beginning of May.

In preparation for the trip we bought souvenirs to take to our friends in the States and went to one last square dance party at the home of one of our friends. The children asked their friends over for dinners and sleepovers, and Lulu arranged to visit her family while we were away. When we went on home leave we left Anita in charge of the house. Sally Scheid was critical of our leaving a maid in charge and told me that we should arrange for an American couple to watch over our house. I told her that I had complete confidence in Anita, who, in fact, took perfect care of our house.

We flew out of Manila on May 1st and arrived at our first destination, Beirut, at 5a.m. After some sleep we hired a taxi to take us on a tour of the city including the American University and the rug market. The Lebanese merchants were such shrewd salesmen that we almost bought a rug, but came to our senses before completing the transaction. The next day, Mr. Braiar from Save the Children Federation picked us up in two cars. He drove us to see Butrus, the child we were currently supporting through the organization. After lunch we drove to see Joseph, a young man whom we had supported for 15 years. He showed us the cave that he and his family were living in when we first started to send our monthly support. They had used the funds to build a house and buy a cow. Before they bought the cow their diet had consisted solely of almonds and figs from the trees on their land. After they got the cow they added milk and cheese to their diet. We were delighted to meet Joseph and his family in person. We were especially taken with his sprightly father. There were pictures of our family hanging on the walls of their home and they all thanked us profusely for our support that helped improve their lives.

After biding farewell to Joseph we flew to Vienna for two days. We took a city bus to Schoenbrunn Palace, which took our breath away with its splendor. After dinner we strolled to the park across from our hotel where people were waltzing on a platform in front of Johann Strauss' statue. We joined the dancers in the fast Viennese waltzes and had a wonderful time. We both love to waltz, the faster the better. What a wonderful evening it was! We did some shopping in Vienna and then flew to Munich. We celebrated my birthday in a restaurant next to the pension where we were staying. The children gave me beautiful gifts that they had purchased in Vienna—pretty violet earrings, a lovely flowered trivet, some miniature playing cards and a pretty pin. Late that evening we trudged up five flights of stairs to our $5 pension rooms. I think we woke up the whole building.

During our stay in Munich we drove to Salzburg and took a chair lift up the mountain, seeing gorgeous scenery all the way. We ate lunch at the hotel at the top and then visited the salt mines at Hallein in the afternoon. Everyone had to put on coveralls before entering the mines. We went through the inside of the mountain where we slid down slides to reach the salt mines. It was a fascinating experience. We had dinner in Salzburg and drove back to our pension in Munich for the night. The following day we drove to Garmish, a charming village near the Austrian border, and took the cable car to the top of the Zugspitze. In the afternoon we returned to Munich and had dinner at the Town Hall Rathskellar. By coincidence our old friend Tom Long was in town for a business conference and joined us at the Hofbrauhaus that evening. Everyone there was drinking beer out of 20-ounce mugs and singing German songs at the top of their lungs. We had a great time. We all went shopping the next day and Mike bought me a German dress that I wore out to the Hofbrauhaus that night. We had our final continental breakfast of cocoa, coffee and croissants in our pension before flying out of Munich.

On the taxi ride from the Amsterdam airport we were thrilled to see the colorful tulips along the road. In the afternoon we shopped for Delft china, ate dinner and went to bed early. The following day we rented a car to drive around the country. We drove to Nykerck where Mike's relatives emigrated from long ago and then to Spakenberg to see people in costumes. We visited the Ann Frank house in Amsterdam and empathized with the tragedy of her life. Later we went to Maduradam, a miniature village that fascinated the children.

One of my best friends from Columbia University, Maryann Marcus, was living in London with her family at that time. I had written to her from the Philippines asking her to find us an inexpensive boarding house for our stay in London. She found a clean inexpensive house near Kensington Gardens that had just enough rooms for our family. During our visit to London, we went to see the changing of the guard at Buckingham Palace. We rode on a double decker bus and visited the Tower of London, where we ran into our friends the Lippincotts from Manila. The next day we visited Westminster Abbey and then took the Lippincotts to lunch. After lunch Peter went off with the Lippincotts, Steve went shopping and Mike and I and the girls went to Charles Dickens' house. That night our family was invited for dinner at the Marcus' home in a charming suburb of London. Our children got along well with theirs. The following day we rented a car and drove to Windsor Castle and then on to Stratford-on-Avon. It was fun driving through Sherwood Forest and imagining that Robin Hood and his men were hiding behind the trees. We saw Ann Hathaway's cottage and Shakespeare's birthplace and ended up in a pub for dinner on the way back to London. Cathy bought a small doll in costume from each country that we visited on the trip. Her collection of dolls from many countries was becoming impressive.

When we arrived in New York Mike's parents met us at Kennedy Airport. Mom and Dad treated us to a night in New York City and gave us tickets to see the play, *1776,* while they stayed with the children in the hotel. The next day we returned to Bound Brook and checked into a motel. We spent only a few days in Bound Brook before resuming our vacation travels, but we managed to see all our friends and they were most gracious to us. Marion and Bruce McCreary gave a huge open house for us, our neighbors Ella and Jack Handen hosted a dinner party for us, Beverly Weber invited us to dinner with the Deipnos and we attended the monthly Congregates dinner at our church. Mike had to spend a couple of days at the Union Carbide headquarters in New York and, while he was in the city, Beverly drove me to see some of my favorite people, Sophie Mickolowski, Ann Kobezak, Gloria Cross and some neighbors.

On leaving Bound Brook, we drove to Rockport to see my parents, grandparents and other relatives. Tom and Simi Long flew up from Georgia and the other members of our book group drove up from New Jersey. We invited the relatives to join us for dinner and showed slides of the Philippines. We had a heavenly weekend with our closest friends and relatives. The following Monday we drove to Albany and stayed with Mom and Dad Schuyler for several days. The children were delighted to see our dog, Ginger, again. We then flew to see my brother Bunkie and his family in Columbia, Missouri and then on to Cody, Wyoming to visit my brother David and his family. Steve wanted to spend the rest of the summer working on David's ranch. David and Mary were agreeable, so we left Steve in Cody as we continued our journey back to the Philippines.

We arrived back in the Philippines on June 3rd and everyone in the family passed out from exhaustion in different rooms of the house. When Mike came home from work, it looked as if the house had been sprayed with sleeping gas as the children were lying on the floor, on a chair and draped over the piano bench, asleep. It took us a week to get back to a normal sleeping schedule.

Shortly after our return to the Philippines, we had a family party to celebrate Anita's birthday and that weekend we visited friends and gave them little gifts from the States. I wrote lots of thank you letters to our friends in the United States for all they did for us while we were on home leave. There was never another time in my life that I wrote as many letters as I did in our two years in the Philippines. Later we went to a square dance party and in the succeeding days we gave a couple of dinners for a number of friends. We were back to our old routine almost immediately. We went to Cebu for the opening of the new battery plant where there was a grand reception and dancing to celebrate the opening. On our anniversary we went to dinner and dancing at the top of the Hilton.

Steve returned from Wyoming in time for the beginning of the school year on July 13th. Steve had a difficult time adjusting to life in the Philippines after his return. He began associating with some American youngsters for whom the circumstance of a wealthy life style, with time on their hands, was an invitation for trouble. As parents, we were naturally concerned about the situation and discussed with Steve the advisability of attending a boarding school in the States. Steve agreed that this might be a good idea. During August he tried to find more wholesome activities to keep away from these friends. He attended the church youth group meetings and spent most evenings at home with the family. However, by the end of August he was agreeable to going to the States with Mike to look for a suitable boarding school. Mike and Steve left for the States on September 5th. They visited a number of schools and determined that Cushing Academy in Massachusetts would be best for Steve. He started the fall term at Cushing. His grandparents were nearby in Albany, New York in case he needed them. He joined the wrestling team, but pulled his shoulder out in practice and was unable to wrestle during the season. He spent Christmas vacation with his grandparents and also visited Bound Brook. People in the church, neighborhood and high school were good to him. I missed him and wrote to him frequently. I visited a couple of psychiatrists myself to get advice on how we could help him. The first psychiatrist I visited was quite negative, but the second one was supportive and helpful.

Cathy had a problem with her eyes while she was in the Philippines. She had strabismus as a toddler and had surgery on one of her eyes before we moved to the Philippines. The operation was a success at first, but then her eye went back to being crossed. We found an excellent eye surgeon in Manila, Dr. Gloria Lim, who told us that both of Cathy's eyes would eventually need to be operated on. But first her vision had to be improved. Cathy would have to wear a patch over the eye with better sight to force her to use the eye with poorer vision

and regain good vision in that eye. The patch was put on a pair
of glasses to cover her good eye, but Cathy hated the glasses
and the patch and managed to lose them or break them "by
accident". We finally bought cheap glasses from the drug store
so the accidents were not so expensive, and Cathy learned to
accept wearing the glasses with the patch.

Family life went on even though Steve was not with us. Cindy
gave a surprise birthday dinner and slumber party at our house for
her best friend, Laura Forbes, at the end of September. We had a
party for Cindy's birthday on October 12th. The next week we
invited our whole square dance group to a birthday dinner for one
of the members. We pushed back our furniture so that we could
dance in our family room. At the end of October, Union Carbide
hosted a big dinner dance at the Hilton that we really enjoyed.

We went on another camping trip with the children and our
friends, the Tennants, early in November to the Hundred Islands
in the Lingayan Gulf of northern Luzon. The scenery was
beautiful. The islands are made of coral and look like giant
mushrooms sticking up out of the water because the ocean has
eaten away their coral base. We stayed in little wooden shacks
and swam in the surf on the Lingayan beach the first day we
were there. On the second day we took a boat to one of the
islands. We took a picnic lunch and ate it in a little cove with
pure white sand. We swam in the warm turquoise colored ocean
and I dove down and brought up some pieces of coral. We
were the only people on the beach and enjoyed the privacy. On
our way back to the mainland our guide took us to see a cave
on another island. The cave was full of bats that gave me an
eerie feeling. After dinner that night we built a bonfire on the
beach and sang songs. The next morning we left and I took
some coral back in the trunk of the car. I did not realize that
coral is a living thing and soon it began to smell. We had to
take it out of the trunk and leave it on a beach on the way back
to Makati.

In mid-November the Manila area was hit by a severe typhoon. We were given warning ahead of time so that we were somewhat prepared. We followed the instructions on the radio and filled our bathtubs and other containers with water before the storm hit. We were told not to go out in the storm and to leave glass doors ajar so that they would not blow out from the pressure of the wind. When the storm hit it blew over airplanes on the runways, shacks, gigantic trees, rows of telephone poles and roofs off of people's houses. Sheets of galvanized metal were commonly used as roofs, and these roofs flying around the Manila area were very dangerous for anyone who ventured outside during the storm. The typhoon washed huge ships up on the shore and uprooted majestic palm trees that lined the main boulevard through Manila. There were floods everywhere and the electricity and water supply were cut off.

Our lifestyle changed dramatically. With no air conditioning or television, we opened the windows and played card games by candlelight every evening. We used the water in the tubs and trashcans to flush the toilet and we went to bed earlier than usual. The family learned to enjoy games and socializing without television. The electricity was cut off for over a week. We had a gas oven so we could cook and we ate by candlelight at night. We had not purchased a turkey for Thanksgiving because turkeys were expensive. Our next door neighbors, the Kuzs, had the privilege of shopping at the United States commissary, so they had bought a turkey at American prices. On Thanksgiving morning Mr. Kuz knocked on our door and handed us his turkey as he had an electric oven and could not cook it. We of course invited their family to come to Thanksgiving dinner and share the turkey cooked in our gas oven. Two Union Carbide executives from New York had just arrived in Manila, so we invited them to dinner also. As we held hands and were saying grace around the candlelit table the lights suddenly came on. We all cheered.

For the remainder of the Thanksgiving weekend we took the family on a trip to Zamboanga and Jolo at the southern tip of the Philippines, near the equator. One of our neighbors in Makati had parents living in Jolo and they invited us down for a visit. On the airplane the stewardess spilled a cup of hot coffee in my lap. Mike reacted quickly by throwing a glass of cold water on my lap and ripping the skirt off of my dress so my body was not burned. My hand was burned and the stewardess bandaged it. Then the steward crawled into the baggage area of the plane and retrieved my suitcase so that I could put on another dress. Tootsie, our neighbor from Makati, met the plane and took us to her parents' house. They treated us to a steak dinner and in the evening we played cards with the children at the motel. The next day we swam at the pure white sandy beach lined with towering palm trees and lush jungle growth. We limited Cathy to an hour in the sun, but even this was too long for her fair skin and she was badly sunburned. We flew to Zamboanga in the afternoon and stayed at a big hotel that reminded us of an old Sidney Greenstreet and Peter Loree movie. Little boys dove into the water and brought up conch shells that they sold to the tourists. We flew to Cebu next and visited the new Union Carbide plant there. We played water tag with the children in the hotel pool before dinner. Next we flew to Iligan and stayed again at the hotel with limited water. We visited Maria Christina waterfalls and shopped for brass in the town. The Guevaras invited us all to dinner and the next day we went swimming with Rads Guevara at Costa Bravo beach. We had dinner again with the Guevara family that night.

When we got home, we wrapped and mailed Christmas gifts to Steve. We celebrated Peter's eleventh birthday with a family party and then made an audio-tape for Grandma Elsie for Christmas. She was losing her eyesight so we made her a number of tapes while we were in the Philippines. Each member of our family would talk to her on the tape and tell her about his or her life and interests. She told us that she really enjoyed receiving our family tapes.

On Christmas Eve, Cindy joined the Union Church. We had a lovely family Christmas the next day with a beautiful artificial tree and lots of gifts. Santa left Cathy a giant, bright red, papiermache water buffalo that she named Timothy. Timothy has had a long life for a water buffalo. Cathy's daughter now loves to ride on Timothy's back, thirty-four years later. Two days after Christmas we gave a party for 80 of Mike's employees and their spouses for the second year in a row. It was another success and everyone ate lots of food and sang and laughed together. After dinner we did the tinikling, a local dance in which the participants have to keep hopping back and forth over long sticks that are clapped together by people at each end of the sticks.

At the end of December we took the family to Pagsanan Falls and stayed at a nice hotel there. We went up the rapids of the river in boats paddled by local young men. Mike, Peter and Cathy rode in one boat and Cindy and I rode in the other boat. On the way down the rapids Mike's boat filled up with water, but no one was hurt. After warm showers and hot cocoa, we ate dinner at the hotel and watched native dancing. The hotel staff held a contest for the best tinikling dancers and Mike and I won the prize. The next day we drove to Paete, a small town that was famous for woodcarvings. Each child bought a carving and then we went swimming. We came home in time to go out for New Years Eve with the Fajardos again at the Polo Club.

In January we gave three dinner parties for Philippine and American friends. At the end of the month another big square dance jamboree was held at the Polo Club. We continued square dancing regularly until we left the country. In February we felt honored to be invited to Judge Guevara's birthday party again. On Valentine's Day we hosted a dinner party to celebrate the holiday. We played some fun games and the couple who won the marriage quiz received a big red heart-shaped pillow as a prize. Our Filipino friends told us that our dinners were the only American affairs where they met Filipinos that they had not met before.

On February 22nd, Dr. Lim told us that it was time to operate on Cathy's eyes as she had regained her vision in the lazy eye. I was glad that the operation would be done in the Philippines where hospitals are lenient in their policies on letting families stay with relatives after they had surgery. Dr. Lim operated on both of Cathy's eyes at the same time. Her expertise enabled her to perform a highly successful operation on both eyes and restore them to perfect vision. The fact that I could stay with Cathy night and day after the operation helped her recovery. The hospital provided a bed for me in her room and, although both of her eyes were bandaged, her emotional state was excellent. I read to her, talked with her and took her for walks around her floor in the hospital so that she could talk to other patients. We were so thankful that we had found Dr. Lim.

Early in March 1971, Steve returned to the Philippines. Cushing Academy had not worked out for him. He returned to the International School until the end of the term. In April we celebrated Cathy's sixth birthday and had a visit from Colonel and Mrs Kreuter, old friends of Mike's parents. They had lived in the other half of the duplex that Mike's family had lived in at Fort Monroe, Virginia in the 1930's. They were a delightful couple. We took them out to dinner at a nice restaurant with the children. Peter was going through a sullen stage at the time. When we ordered our dinners, Peter requested a bacon sandwich, which was not on the menu. Mike told him to order something on the menu. He was very stubborn and insisted on a bacon sandwich. Mike finally ordered him a hamburger, but he did not eat it. A few days later the Kreuters invited us to the Manila Army Navy Club for brunch after church. As we came in the door, Colonel Kreuter put his arm around Peter and said, "I checked with the waiter and he says that they have bacon sandwiches." Peter grumbled, "I hate bacon sandwiches." Fortunately Colonel Kreuter had a good sense of humor.

At the end of March, Mike's two-year tour of the Philippines was up and he was reassigned back to New York City. We began to prepare for our departure. We wanted to take something special back to the Deipnos. We designed an oblong block to be made out of Philippine nara wood. We arranged to have DEIPNOSOPHISTICAL SOCIETY carved on one side and a quotation from Saint Augustine carved on the other side. The quotation had been chosen for a group motto, as we felt it typified the philosophy of the society. The Philippines have many excellent wood carvers and labor is cheap, so beautiful woodcarvings are a bargain. We had five carvings produced, one for each couple in the group. We have all treasured these souvenirs over the years.

We gave one more big dinner party and were taken out for a farewell dinner by Union Carbide executives. The staff at Children's Medical Center gave a reception for me and Dr. Fey del Mundo presented me with a silver pin in appreciation for my work at the medical center. We attended Cindy's graduation from junior high school, where she received an honors award. She went to a dinner dance that night to celebrate with her classmates.

The last few days were a whirlwind of activities. Our minister's wife gave me a surprise party for my birthday on May 5th and on the 10th we took the Guevaras out to dinner. The next evening, 70 of Mike's employees and their spouses gave us a farewell party at our house. Everyone brought delicious Philippine food and lovely going away gifts. The party was very festive. On the 13th our square dance gave us a farewell party and on the 14th the movers finished packing all our belongings, including the

Philippine dining room set that we could not bear to part with. Our neighbors took us out to dinner on our final night.

We said good-by to Manila on May 16th. We decided to take our vacation on the way home and made stops in both Asia and Europe. We flew from Manila to Hong Kong where we shopped for two days. Then we flew to Bangkok and stayed at the Royal Hotel. We visited Timland, a Thailand cultural center, where we saw native dances and cockfights. The children rode on an elephant and Steve held a big python, with trepidation. We toured the Bangkok floating market where hundreds of small boats loaded with fruits, vegetables, flowers and fishes bring their products to be sold each morning. The people who live on houseboats or in shacks at the water's edge used the canals for washing and bathing. We saw the walled city of the Grand Palace and the Temple of Dawn with their ornate exteriors and marveled at their splendor.

After two days in Thailand, we flew to New Dehli where Mr. Lippincott had arranged for a local businessman, Mr. Mohen, to meet us and be our guide. The next morning we were driven to Agra to see the Taj Mahal, which is made of gleaming white marble, a majestic and inspiring sight. On the way back we saw some commotion on the side of the road. A man was exhibiting a fight between a mongoose and a cobra, a chilling sight. He stopped the fight before its conclusion so that he could use the mongoose and the cobra for the next show. While we were stopped an Indian woman who seemed somewhat crazed, grabbed Cathy's arm. She appeared to have lost a child of her own and she would not let go of Cathy. Mike talked calmly to her and gradually pulled Cathy away. It was a scary moment.

The following day we shopped in the marketplace, which was jammed with people. Mike was afraid that we might lose one of the children as we pushed through the crowds looking in the shops, so he insisted that he and I each hold one of our children firmly in each hand. We flew to Bombay that evening and spent the night. We were horrified to see people sleeping and dying in the streets. Our next stop was Beirut, which we had visited the prior year. We went back to Beirut because Joseph had written to Mike and asked him to be his best man in his wedding. He told Mike that he would arrange the date of the wedding according to our schedule so that we could be present. The wedding was a lovely affair and Joseph's wife, Jeanette, was a beauty. She and Joseph were both schoolteachers. There was a nice luncheon in Joseph's house before the wedding and a reception in Jeanette's village after the wedding. We went to Sidon where pictures were taken by the castle, and then we drove Joseph and Jeanette to Beirut for their honeymoon. We were scheduled to leave the next day, but I came down with a severe case of intestinal flu and we had to change our plane reservation. I stayed in the hotel the next day while Mike and the children went sightseeing in Beirut with Joseph and Jeanette, who insisted on postponing their honeymoon for a day. Mike took them all out to dinner. The next day I was able to travel and Joseph and Jeanette saw us off at the airport.

We flew to Zurich, rented a van and took off for a week's trip around Switzerland. Soon after we left Zurich, the gearshift broke. We pulled into the tiny village of Rapperswill on the Sea of Zurich. We had dinner at the only restaurant in town and walked around the village. There was only one bedroom available in the town's only hotel. However it was a big room on the top floor. The hotel manager brought in some quilts for the children to sleep on the floor and we slept in the bed. The room had a scenic view of the water and mountains. In the morning we all went peddle-boating while the van was being fixed. We left Rapperswilll that afternoon and drove through the Julier Pass to Silverplana, where it was snowing. The next day, while driving to Chiavennia in Italy, the van broke down again. The local garage was able to fix the van while we ate lunch, then we drove along Lake Como to Lugano in northern

Italy. We had an early dinner looking out on beautiful Lake Lugano and stopped at a sidewalk café in the evening to listen to romantic music.

We continued our trek through the beautiful Swiss countryside. From Lugano we traveled over the St. Gotthard Pass to Andermatt and on to Lucerne. The scenery was absolutely beautiful on the drive along Lake Lucerne. We stayed at Hotel Johannemitterhof and went to dinner and dancing at a nearby restaurant to celebrate our last night in Europe. Cathy had continued to buy small dolls dressed in the costume of every new place that we visited. She had quite a collection by the time we arrived home. She still has this collection in a glass case in her home today.

On the last morning while we were packing, I couldn't find my purse. I realized that I had left it in the restaurant the night before. It was Sunday, the restaurant was closed and we had to drive to Zurich to catch our plane to the States at 3:00 p.m. Mike finally found the home phone number of the restaurant owner and called him in desperation. The owner met us at the restaurant and we found my purse with our six passports in it. We drove to Zurich, turned in the van, ate a quick bite of lunch and rushed to the airport. All six of us ran through the airport and boarded the plane just five minutes before it took off. We arrived at Kennedy Airport in New York City at 9:00 p.m. Mike's parents and the Webers were there to meet us. It felt good to be back in the United States.

7

Deipnosophistical Society

Our life in the Philippines was a two-year break in what was one of the most important aspects of our adult life—our book discussion group. I started the group when Peter was a baby. The original three couples were Dick and Beverly Weber, Tom and Simi Long and Mike and I. We asked the Webers and the Longs to each invite another couple to join the group, so that the group would be diversified. The Longs brought their neighbors, Jerry and Edie Stern, to the third meeting. The Webers brought their neighbors, Bruce and Marion McCreary, to the fourth meeting. We then had a reading group of ten interested members.

The rules that we agreed on for the group included a monthly meeting for which all members would read the same book and come prepared to discuss that book. Each month a different member of the group would chose a book and lead the discussion. Another member of the group would host the meeting at his or her house. Beverly chose the first book and the Longs offered to host the first meeting.

Beverly chose *An Essay on Population,* by T. R. Malthus. It was a two-volume treatise on the problem of overpopulating the world, published in 1798. The author made two postulates:

"First that food is necessary to the existence of man, and secondly that the passion between the sexes is necessary and will remain in its present state." He concluded, "Assuming my postulates as granted, I say that the power of population is indefinitely greater than the power of the earth to produce subsistence for man." He severely criticized the existing poor law system in England for its indiscriminate doles to large families that encouraged an excessive increase in births among the poorest families and made poverty even worse than before. This message, of course, is relevant to modern times and the discussion of the book was lively.

Beverly had an interest in examining the writing of social philosophers in different periods of history. Her interests were varied, however, and she also chose classic novels and biographies of famous people in history and philosophy. Other books that she chose for the Deipnos to read early in their history included: Saint Augustine's *Confessions*, James Boswell's *Life of Samuel Johnson,* Franz Kafka's *The Trial,* a nightmarish novel of an almost hallucinatory trial, and Henry Thoreau's *Walden*. Thoreau was a brilliant writer from Concord, Massachusetts, who chose to live alone in a hut at nearby Walden Pond for two years. During that time he watched and wrote about his natural surroundings and pondered the problems of mankind.

In *Walden,* published in 1854, Thoreau minutely describes his observations in the woods adjacent to Walden Pond. The Deipnos were enthralled with his descriptions of nature such as the way that a mother bird attracted danger to herself to keep predators away from her babies. His description of the fierce resiliency of ants was amazing to read. He watched the combat between black and red ants and painted it as a raging internecine war. He described the vicious engagement between two types of ants as a "conquer or die" battle of the red and black ants. Thoreau took a wood chip on which two red ants and one black ant were fighting and put it under a tumbler so he could continue to watch the fight under a microscope. He commented, "They struggled half an hour longer under the tumbler and when I looked again the black soldier had severed the heads of his foes from their bodies, and the still living heads were hanging on either side of him like ghastly trophies."

Although Thoreau was described as a rugged individualist, his self-sufficiency in the woods seemed somewhat compromised when we learned that his family members did his laundry and brought him supplies. He borrowed much of the equipment he needed for survival and made frequent trips to town during his two years in the wilderness. However he was a free thinker and disliked the restrictions of society such as alarm clocks and schedules. He was also a pessimist, and is often quoted for his comment, "The mass of men lead lives of quiet desperation."

Beverly, an attractive brunette with the chiseled features of her Germanic background, is an energetic and resourceful person. Her dry wit always enlivened the group. She was involved with numerous community activities and, in every organization that she was involved with, she always felt obliged to do more than anyone else. Beverly was talented in many areas and contributed creatively in whatever area she worked. As a librarian in an elementary school she continually came up with creative projects for the children and as an adjunct college faculty member she kept her students enthralled with the subject at hand. She is a talented musician, playing the piano and organ in churches, schools and community concerts and at times has accompanied opera singers. For all her accomplishments she was very modest and never mentioned the accolades and tributes that she had received. She attended the Peabody Academy of Music and graduated from Johns Hopkins University. She has graduate degrees in music and library science from Rutgers University and has been active in both of these areas, as well as later becoming President of the Board of Trustees of the Middlesex Library.

Beverly had a wide background of knowledge and experience, which she contributed to the book group discussions. She was one of the more active participants in the group but was never strident in her remarks. She frequently reminded the group of other books that we had read that were relevant to the discussion. The group chose Beverly to be our archivist in our first meeting. We decided that we did not want our group to become encumbered with the appurtenances of most organizations with their officers, bylaws and procedures. But we did recognize the need to keep track of whose turn was coming up for a book or to host a meeting, so we decided that an archivist could take care of all administrative functions. The obvious choice for the position was Beverly. Her administrative skills were apparent from the beginning and she became by acclamation the only officer in the group, our archivist. She has faithfully and conscientiously exercised this function throughout the groups' existence, scheduling the discussion leaders and hosts for the meetings, corresponding on occasion with authors of books that we had read and making other arrangements concerning the group.

In addition to all these talents, Beverly was a superb hostess. She provided an elegant dinner for the group whenever it was her turn to entertain. Her dining room was papered in dark blue velvet and her china was ribbed in the same rich blue color. The table setting was always impeccable, with fine china, Waterford crystal, sterling silver place settings and accouterments. The table floral arrangements were tasteful and colorful. In this rich setting she provided delicious gourmet meals with several scrumptious homemade desserts.

Dick Weber, a tall, slender, handsome, redhead of Scotch Irish descent, was a pivotal force in the group. He continually offered opinions that motivated discussions. Dick would interpret a recent statement by a public figure in a completely different way than other members of the group did. Most of the time his opinions were contrary to the opinions of the rest of the group, so discussion never lagged or was boring. His opinions about economics and the nature of man were almost always pessimistic, but he was never gloomy in nature. He felt that people were basically aggressive and he never ceased to talk about man's "killer instinct." No one in the group was ever offended by Dick's comments, but occasionally he disturbed a guest at a meeting by his unpopular opinion. When he heard that someone had been upset, he was always amazed that people could be offended by views that were contrary to their own. Another of his favorite comments about his opinion on most subjects was, "It is perfectly obvious."

Over the years many of the members of the group modified their views as a result of discussion, but Dick always remained true to his original opinions, never wavering from his singular view of the world and mankind. Dick was the libertarian of the group, believing in the minimum of government regulation and the lowest possible taxation. He was a Christian, but with an agnostic bent, always searching for other approaches to religious understanding. He was interested in Buddhism and other contemplative religions, searching for a better understanding of man's relationship to God. He was also very concerned about his health and was sensitive to many ills, real or imagined. He was physically fit, but had no interest in athletics. He kept in shape by doing Yoga exercises and a lot of physical work on his home and yard.

Dick had a marvelous sense of humor. He loved to hear and tell jokes, especially if they were somewhat raunchy. His comments were sometimes interspersed with words or phrases that might not be well received in finer society. At such times Beverly would grimace and give him a gentle reprimand. Dick and Beverly had met in a church youth group in Baltimore when they were in high school. They were married when Beverly was eighteen. She went to college after they were married and often recalled how she took exams when she was about to deliver a baby.

In the beginning Dick chose books about psychology such as David Riesman's *The Lonely Crowd,* Sigmund Freud's *Beyond the Pleasure Principle* and C. G. Jung's *The Undiscovered Self.* Dick agreed with Jung's view that, "the individual human being should be in the measure of all things." Jung wrote, "Man is the one important factor and the salvation of the world consists of the salvation of the individual soul." He wrote, "man must be aware of his instincts and inner self as well as of the outside world . . . if he is to exercise an influence on his environment." He concluded, "Happiness and contentment can be experienced only by the individual and not by the State . . . which is nothing but a convention of independent individuals." As time went on Dick also chose books on history and sociology. His favorite history book that the group read was William Shirer's *Rise and Fall of the Third Reich.* Mike chose the book early in the group's history, but it was so long that we used it for the book for a second month and Tom Long led the discussion for the second half of the book. Another favorite book of Dick's was his choice of Karl Menninger's *Crime of Punishment.* It was a critique of the penal system in this country showing why it doesn't work and what should be done to improve it.

Simi Long was the "lady" of the group. She was always concerned with being polite to everyone. She had definite viewpoints, but offered them in a calm, modest manner so as not to offend anyone. She was an excellent listener and seemed genuinely interested in what everyone said. She often complemented others on their thoughtful and cogent analysis, even if she disagreed with the opinion being expressed. She was interested in people's personal lives and was complementary about other members' accomplishments and families. She always asked me about my children and expressed delight at their progress and achievements.

As members of the group entered into discussion many felt the
natural impetus to express their own views. Simi, on the other
hand, gave the impression of being far more interested in hearing
the views of others than in expressing her own opinions. She
had the rare quality of making the speaker feel that his or her
view was important to her. She argued in a reasoned manner,
but we felt that her opinions came from her heart.

Simi was a striking blonde. Her personality was reflected in
her cheerful countenance and gracious manner. She was well
read on current affairs and had an interest in politics. She was
an active member of the League of Women Voters and often
brought their opinions to bear on the discussion. She had a
conservative attitude about government and an interest in the
South. One of her book choices was *The South and the
Southerner* by Ralph McGill. Simi's father was a minister and
religious issues were important to her. She recently wrote to me
that there were five books she read in the group that were
foundational to what she was. The books were *The Gospel of
John*, *Meditations* by Marcus Aurelius, *Essays on Freedom and
Power* by Lord Acton, *Worlds in Collision* by Immanuel
Velikovsky and *The Time of our Lives* by William Saroyan. She
commented on the *Gospel of John*, "I loved it when we read it
and the Love principle was certainly important to me at that
time. It has grown more important to me as I have grown. Now
it is the cornerstone of my life." As to Aurelius' *Meditations*,
she says, "This book was my first excursion into introspective
writing and these were fascinating disclosures to me." Of Lord
Acton's essays she states, "This book established a foundation
for my political beliefs. I had already studied his writings in
college in my major, Political Science, but it was wonderful to
discuss them with such thoughtful minds." And of *The Time of
Our Lives* she commented, "Here was the perfect counterpart
to all the depth of thinking that the Deipnos get into. No matter
what is going on, what terrible anxieties or disasters, we can
still have the time of our lives. Isn't it great?" Simi told me that

of all the books that she read in her years with the Deipnos, her two favorites were the *Gospel of John* and Aurelius' *Meditations.*

Tom Long met Simi when they were students at Ohio Wesleyan University. Tom was the scientist of the group. He had a Ph.D. in physics. He had the most secure job in the group, at AT&T Bell Laboratories, which colored his outlook on life. He was a tall, handsome and fit young man who was justly proud of his education and achievements. He approached discussion topics in a scientific manner—hypothesis, analysis and then conclusion. He often found it difficult to accept conclusions based on intuition or emotion. He had a good sense of humor and was intrigued that Dick could express a unique and unexpected viewpoint on almost every issue. He always treated the other members of the group with respect and expected similar treatment in return.

Hobbies were more important to Tom than to other members of the group. He enjoyed building and flying model airplanes and was also fascinated with automobiles. He purchased a DeLorean automobile when it was first produced. He never sold it and became active in the National Association of DeLorean Owners. His book choices were varied, but his favorite was Velikovsky's *Worlds in Collision.* The author was teaching at Princeton University when we were reading the book, so Tom called him on the phone to discuss a few points during our meeting. Other books that Tom enjoyed reading in the group included *Doctor Zhivago* by Boris Pasternak, *Life of Samuel Johnson* by Boswell, *Lord of the Flies* by William Golding, *The Trial,* by Kafka, and *Letters and Papers from Prison* by Dietrich Bonhoeffer.

The fourth couple of the original group was Jerry and Edie Stearn. Jerry presented one book, but after a year they decided to drop out of the group, as they did not like being committed to reading a book every month. They were replaced soon after they left by Mahlon and Esther Merk, The Merks moved shortly after they joined, but not before Esther picked the most unpopular book in the history of the group, Dalton Trumbo's *Johnny Got His Gun.* The book was maudlin and sickening to read and the group was unanimous in its condemnation of it.

The fifth couple to join the group was Bruce and Marion McCreary. Marion was the only member who did not attend college, but she was no less educated, as she was a voracious reader and always read several books before choosing the one for her selection. She came from a family of three girls and one boy and her parents had only enough money to pay for one child's college education. Her parents sent their son to college. Marion was a beautiful woman who had come to terms with an extensive birthmark that covered most of her body. She wore heavy makeup on her face, long sleeves and dark stockings to cover the birthmark. She had a forceful personality and was loved and respected by the group. I especially revered her as she encouraged me to be more assertive in some areas where I was hesitant. Bruce worshipped her.

Marion was always well prepared when it was her turn to present a book and lead the discussion. The books that she chose exemplified human life rather than philosophy, economics or science. Many of her books were about unusual challenges to individuals. An example of a physical challenge that she chose was Alfred Lansing's *Endurance,* about Shackleton's harrowing journey to the South Pole. It turned out to be the favorite book of three members of the Deipnos. She also liked books about interesting places such as Mark Twain's *Life on the Mississippi.*

Marion's favorite author was David McCullough. She chose his first book, *The Johnstown Flood* early in the Deipnos existence. It was typical of McCullough's writing, the story of a sensational occurrence, which he reported, with vivid yet scholarly writing. As with all his books, McCullough had carefully researched his subject and presented it in an exciting and absorbing manner. The book is the story of a coal and steel town in Johnstown, Pennsylvania in 1889, where an old dam above the town burst, sending a torrent of water crashing down the mountain, violently destroying the town and killing 2,209 people. After presenting the book, Marion and Bruce visited Johnstown to see it first hand. Marion refused to stay in the town and, understandably, insisted on staying on top of the mountain.

The Johnstown Flood was the beginning of David McCullough's gift for writing well-researched sympathetic social histories. He would write six more detailed volumes about fascinating events in social history and become one of the most respected historians of our time. Our archivist, Beverly, wrote to him to tell him how popular he was with the Deipnos and that only three other authors had been represented in our readings as much as he had at that time: Plato, Mark Twain and Thoreau. He wrote back, "I am delighted to learn of your society's interest in my books and to discover that I have been included with such company." He asked Beverly for the derivation of the group's title and they carried on a brief correspondence on the subject.

Bruce McCreary was a true gentleman. He was tall, handsome and soft-spoken. He was the sleeper of the group in more than one sense. In the beginning he was relatively quiet during the discussions, but over the years he became more confident of his opinions and more voluble in expressing them. He was a very thoughtful, caring person to the group and to his family. He was devoted to his children and comforted the babies when they cried during the night. Many times he took naps in the middle of the group discussions for lack of sleep the night before. He frequently would wake up with a start and join the discussions as if he had never left. One of his major contributions to the group was his ability, with a wry comment, to puncture a high minded statement of one of the other members and bring the discussion back down to the real world.

Bruce was an engineer by education and experience and many of his selections reflected his scientific and technical bent. He was also a conservative and the first book that he chose was Barry Goldwater's *Conscience of a Conservative.* He came from a farm in the mid-west. His family was religious and he was the only teetotaler in the group. He and Marion met in the church choir in their youth. His favorite book that he read in the group was Lansing's *Endurance,* an early choice of Marion's.

I was the founder of the group. I was also the most idealistic. I had been searching to understand the nature of human beings and what our purpose in life should be. My favorite topic was philosophy and I introduced the group to some of the great thinkers of the Western world. The members of the group were tolerant of my choices, but they drew the line at my choice of Baruch Spinoza's *Ethic.* It wasn't my favorite book either. Some of the philosophers that I chose during the first decade of the Deipnos were Plato, Aristotle, Augustine, Aurelius and Bonhoeffer. I also chose books on history and biography. In discussing people in history, their character was far more important to me than their achievements. I always believed that people could be improved and I was a firm believer in the nineteenth century philosophy of progress.

Truth and goodness were my standards for evaluating writers and people in general. Dick and I had endless arguments over whether people were governed by love or the killer instinct. I was a disciple of Plato's absolute truth and a strong believer in the Johannine philosophy as found in the *Gospel of John.* My favorite book that I chose and read in the group was the *Gospel of John.* I also enjoyed cooking and entertaining, and the members of the group were always complimentary of my dinners.

Mike was the generalist of the group and had a greater variety
in his book selections than anyone else. His book choices
covered history, economics, literature, the Bible and philosophy.
He was by nature soft-spoken, but in the heat of discussion
with the book group he raised his voice and at times drowned
out the others. He never failed to rise to a comment of Dick
Weber whether it was relevant to the discussion or not.
Frequently the two of them would be drawn into a heated
discussion that was far afield of the topic of the book selection.
At times he would repeat his view, each time with more vigor
and careful reasoning, attempting to persuade others to his point
of view without realizing that their opinions might not be based
on the same line of reasoning as his own. He was an enthusiastic
supporter of the group. Mike majored in engineering in college,
but chose a college that also gave him some background in the
liberal arts. His interest in the liberal arts grew after college and
was stimulated by his participation in the book discussion group.

Mike chose some of the most provocative books for discussion.
His first book choice was William James' *Varieties of Religious
Experience*, which engendered much discussion on how people
relate to God and how various religions stimulate different
feelings and actions. One of the most fascinating characters
that James described was St. Augustine as an example of the
divided self. In his autobiography, *Confessions,* Augustine was
torn by the struggle between his baser self and his yearning to
be chaste. He was ashamed of his weakness of will that led to
the licentious behavior that prevented him from rising to a higher
level of living. Then one day he heard a voice in the garden
that said, "Take up and read." He interpreted this as a command
from God. He seized the Bible and read the section on which
his eyes first fell: "not in rioting and drunkenness, not
chambering and wantonness, not in strife and envying; but put
ye on the Lord Jesus Christ, and make not provision for the
flesh, in concupiscence. Instantly at the end of this sentence,
by a light as it were of serenity infused into my heart, all the

darkness of doubt vanished away." James' comment on this passage was, "Augustine has given an account of the trouble of having a divided self which has never been surpassed."

Another character in James' book, that fascinated the group was St. Suso, an ascetic, who had a garment made with strips of leather into which 150 sharp brass nails were driven with the points of the nails always turned toward his flesh. He wore this night and day for sixteen years. Such aesthetic practices were seen as indispensable pathways to perfection of the soul.

Another book that Mike chose, Nicolo Machiavelli's *The Prince,* generated quite a different type of discussion from the group. Mike asked questions such as, "Do you agree with Machiavelli that 'the ends justify the means?' If not, how can you justify the United States participation in World War II?" Another of Mike's questions was about Machiavelli"s belief that "A prince cannot observe all those things which are considered good in men, being often obliged to act against faith, against charity, against humanity and against religion." Mike asked the group, "Can a man be a good ruler and still follow the Christian and Hebrew principles?" A third question that Mike asked concerned Michiavelli's statement, "When a people goes so far as to commit the error of giving power to one man so that he may defeat those whom they hate, and if this man be shrewd, it will always end in his becoming their tyrant." Mike asked the group, "Does the degree of support given a leader lead to a degree of tyranny of the individual? Think of examples such as Napoleon, Hitler, De Gaulle." There was no dearth of discussion on these topics.

Mike's favorite books that we read in the early days of the group were William James' *Varieties of Religious Experience,* Benjamin Franklin's *Autobiography,* Machiavelli's *The Prince,* Robert Heilbroner's *The Worldly Philosophers* and Miguel Cervantes' *Don Quioxote.*

In February 1962, Bruce and Marion McCreary introduced John Sheehan to the book discussion group. He was a widower of many years, with a Ph.D. in chemistry. He was the only Catholic in the group and the most liberal in his political views. He had been educated by Jesuits and could out-argue any member of the group in discussions about religion. John was learned and articulate with an excellent vocabulary. He was passionate, but never strident, in discussions and always respectful of others' opinions. He was a sincere and cheerful person. He was the most ardent supporter of the group, which probably played a more important part in his life than in any of the other members. He was always grateful to me for starting the group and recognized my role as the founder frequently in poems and speeches that he dedicated to me.

John was a free thinker in political thought, but a firm conservative in regard to his religion. He claimed to be a champion of women's rights, but his concepts of women were rooted in those of an earlier generation. His devotion to the Catholic Church, however, was unassailable, thanks to his upbringing in the Jesuit training. He was a romantic by nature and was influenced by the philosophy of the age of progress. He viewed his profession in scientific research as a vehicle of progress. He was an admirer of the Platonic philosophy that truth was revealed through the Socratic method of discussion. The first book that John chose was Lord Acton's *Essays on Freedom and Power.* A quote from that book that we all remembered was, "Power corrupts and absolute power corrupts absolutely." It was one of his favorite books along with Pierre Teilhard de Chardin's *Phenomenon of Man* and Alexander Pope's *Essay on Man.* Pope wrote that everyone had an overruling passion. The group had a great time trying to figure out what was the overruling passion of each of its members. John also chose Mark Twain's *Huckleberry Finn,* which everyone enjoyed.

John loved movies and was a supporter of this art form. He served on a board of film critics in New York City and attended their annual film festivals. He was a natty dresser and looked like an Irish professor with his tweed jackets and ascot ties. He kept fit playing golf. He had been a widower for a number of years and didn't seem interested in remarrying. He had adored his wife, Natalie, a charming English woman who had died of ovarian cancer, leaving him with the care of four small children. With the help of his sister Anna he tried to raise them, but the children also found solace with Beverly Weber, whom they looked on as a substitute mother.

After the Merks left the group there were nine members who would remain in the group for the next forty years or until they died. Early in 1964, Dick suggested a name for the group, The Deipnosophistical Society. The archivist recorded "The Deipnosophistical Society was incorporated March 20, 1964, upon incontrovertible evidence presented by Richard Weber (said evidence found under 'Encyclopaedia' in the *Encyclopaedia Britannica)* that 'deipnosophistica'—the art of philosophizing while feasting—was indeed a word." The name was immediately converted to "Deipnos" to refer to both the group and the individual members.

The Deipnos did more than read and discuss books. We also socialized. In the summers we got together for picnics in backyards and at the New Jersey shore. We sometimes attended a special movie or play together. In March of 1964 we drove into New York City to see the movie, *Tom Jones.* I was nine months pregnant and had to go to the ladies room frequently. Each time I went my big stomach would bump into the heads of the people in the row in front of us. After the movie we came back to the Webers house for dinner. In 1965 we celebrated the reading of our fiftieth book by dining at a fancy restaurant and then seeing another movie. I chose the movie after reading a

favorable review. The movie, *A Stranger Knocks,* was terrible
and we all joked about it afterwards.

In 1967, we invited the Deipnos to my parents' summer home
in Rockport, Massachusetts for the book discussion on Labor
Day weekend. We all had a great time and this became an annual
tradition for the next sixteen years. In 1968 AT&T Bell
Laboratories transferred Tom Long to Columbus, Ohio and
subsequently to Atlanta, Georgia. We were devastated to lose
two of our dearest friends who were charter members of the
group. But we never really lost them as they came back
periodically for special occasions and we always kept in touch.
They remained our cherished friends. In March we put on a
farewell dinner for the Longs and presented them with a silver
bowl on which was inscribed a quotation from St. Augustine
that the group had adopted as its motto:

> All kinds of things rejoiced my soul in their company—
> to talk and laugh and do each other kindnesses; read
> pleasant books together; pass from lightest jesting to
> talk of the deepest things and back again; differ without
> rancor; teach each other or learn from each other—
> these and such-like things kindled a flame which fused
> our very souls and of many made us one.

After the Longs left we invited a series of guests to attend the
meetings. No couple measured up to the Longs, but we did
have some interesting people attend our meetings and a few
actually joined the group for a short time. Neighbors and friends
were among the guests, and in the summer of 1968, a friend of
John Sheehan named Rita came to Rockport for the Labor Day
weekend meeting. We all liked her, and her carrot recipe became
a favorite of the group. The women in the group used her recipe
frequently in preparing dinners for our meetings. She only came
to one more meeting of the group, but she volunteered to present
a book at that meeting. She chose a six-hundred-page book,

Henry James' *Portrait of a Lady*, and did a fine job of leading the discussion.

When we went to the Philippines, the Deipnos observed an hiatus for the two years we were overseas. When we came back to the States for home leave in May, 1970, the Deipnos, including the Longs, gathered in New Jersey for a big open house at the McCreary's and then drove to Massachusetts for a special meeting of the group at the Rockport house. Beverly chose Thomas' *Under Milk Wood* for a group poetry reading. When we came home for good the next year, the Deipnosophistical Society resumed monthly meetings in July 1971. We presented to each couple the Philippine mahogany blocks with St. Augustine's quotation carved on them. They were delighted with the gifts.

When we returned from the Philippines, Mike and I rented a house near the Webers until our tenants moved out of our house in Bound Brook. One summer day, John Sheehan and an elegant looking woman walked by our rented house while we were standing in the yard. He introduced the woman to us as Mildred Moore, a friend from Squibb, where they both worked. We could tell they were in love. Millie came to her first Deipno meeting in August and became a lifetime member. She was a divorced Protestant who had been married for five years in her youth. John was a strict Catholic and asked the archbishop to annul Millie's former marriage so that he could marry her in the Catholic Church. It took over a year for the annulment to come through.

In early 1972, John came to the Deipno meeting and announced that we were approaching our one-hundredth book. He suggested that the group take a cruise in July to celebrate reading one hundred books together. The group was delighted with the idea. Beverly found a brand new cruise ship that was going on its maiden voyage to Bermuda in July. She and I drove to New

York City to check out the ship and found it a splendid, sparkling clean vessel. We decided that the Webers and we should reserve extra large rooms where we could hold our meetings. The cruise ship sailed on July 15, 1972. Millie's annulment had not yet been granted, so she and John stayed in separate staterooms.

None of the group had ever been on a cruise before so we were thrilled with all the festivities on board. We decided before we left that each couple would bring copies of a short story or article for the group to read each day. Then after dinner each evening we discussed one of the articles and the couple who chose it would lead the discussion. We only discussed for a short time each evening before going to the ship dance or movie. The crew may have thought that we were some subversive group, but no one ever investigated us. The topics chosen for the mini-discussions were:

> Goheen's *Mind and Spirit* by the Schuylers
> Gage's *Mafia is not an Equal Opportunity* by the Longs
> Stockton's *Lady or the Tiger* by John Sheehan
> *Amnesty for Vietnam Deserters* by the McCrearys
> Roche's *To Make Democracy Work, End Inherited*
> *Wealth* by the Webers

We limited the sessions to an hour but the discussions were very lively. At the last meeting of the Deipnos on the ship, John Sheehan presented me with a beautiful wooden tray with a painting of Bermuda on it. He read a poem that he had written in my honor as the foundress of the Deipnosophistical Society.

The accommodations on the cruise were luxurious and the meals were magnificent. There was dancing every night, movies and other activities for guests. We took four children on the cruise: Billy Weber, Peter and Cathy Schuyler and Amy McCreary. The two girls were eight and ten years old and were angelic on the ship. They loved going to the children's activity sessions and enjoyed dressing up for dinner each evening. The boys were twelve and felt that they were too old for planned children's activities. They were unruly and spurned the sumptuous food that was served at meals. They insisted on asking for food that was not on the menu. Billy always asked for canned peaches and Peter wanted bacon sandwiches. Sometimes they were obstreperous and were reprimanded by one of the ship's staff. Mike was called to the chief steward's office one evening during cocktails where he found Peter with a gash in his forehead. He and Billy had been spinning each other on tabletops in an empty lounge and Peter flew off the table and hit his head on the corner of another table. The application of a butterfly bandage fixed the gash and a stern reprimand from Mike subdued the boys for the rest of that evening.

When we got to Bermuda the boys' behavior improved as Dick took them sightseeing. They especially liked going on the glass-bottom boat and diving with Dick. The first day in Bermuda, Mike and I and the Longs took a bus with the girls to go swimming at Horseshoe Beach. The next day we all took a bus to the Elbow Beach Resort and went swimming again. The women in our group enjoyed window shopping at stores in town with displays of beautiful English china. Mike and I rented a motor scooter and toured the island. The scenery was exquisite with sparkling white buildings, white sandy beaches and turquoise water.

On the final night of the voyage there was a gala farewell dinner. The menu included elegant appetizers, lobster, pheasant and filet mignon for entrees and baked Alaska for dessert. Most of us chose both lobster and filet mignon and when dessert time arrived all the lights went out and the waiters marched in with flaming trays of baked Alaska. We really enjoyed the spectacular dinner, but the boys still asked for canned peaches and a bacon sandwich. After dinner there was a formal dance and we posed for a group picture in our dressy clothes. The cruise was a marvelous celebration for having read one hundred books together.

John and Millie were married two months after we returned from the cruise. The archbishop had granted an annulment of Millie's former marriage, so they could be married in the Catholic Church. They were married on September 16, 1972 in the local church in Middlesex, New Jersey. The reception was held in Millie's apartment in Highland Park. It was a joyous occasion. The Deipnos were thrilled at the joining in marriage of these two wonderful people whom we all loved dearly.

8

Back to School

In June 1971, right after we returned from the Philippines, we bought a big new station wagon and drove to visit parents and relatives in New York, Massachusetts and Maryland. When we returned to Bound Brook, Union Carbide paid for us to stay in a motel for a few days. Many families invited us for dinner and we enjoyed socializing with old acquaintances. On June 25th we attended the wedding of the Weber's daughter, Barbara (affectionately known as "Mitey"). The next day we drove to Rockport for four days and had a wonderful time.

We had leased our Bound Brook house until September and the tenants wished to stay in the house until the lease was up. So we rented a house in Middlesex near the Webers for the two months and moved in. The house belonged to Professor Hamilton and his wife, who spent summers at their vacation home. It was fun living near Beverly Weber who came over to chat almost every day. Mrs. Hamilton was very gracious to me before she left on vacation and told me that I could use her best china and silver to entertain social gatherings. I especially liked her large soup tureen, so I decided to fill the tureen with pancit molo soup and invite some friends for a Filipino dinner. The soup contained pieces of chicken, pork and onions in broth and special meatballs made of ground pork, veal and beef wrapped in home made noodles. I also made pancit with shrimp, chicken and pork in sauce over hair thin pasta. I roasted a fresh ham and served it with applesauce and pineapple and cottage cheese salad. The guests really enjoyed the special dinner and the games after dinner.

Before the end of June we met with the principal of Bound Brook High School, Joseph Donnelly, to talk about what Steve could do to make up some of the material he had missed in his sophomore year. Mr. Donnelly suggested that Steve attend summer school at Somerset Community College to make up what he had missed. Steve went to summer school for six weeks.

At the end of July I received a call from the emergency room at JFK Medical Center telling me that Steve had been in a car accident. I was told that they could tell me nothing about his condition over the 'phone, I had to come there in person. I started to panic and asked if he was alive. I was again told that they could tell me nothing, and that I would have to come to the hospital to find out how he was. I was terrified. During the thirty-minute drive to the hospital I imagined the worst. When I arrived at the hospital I was so upset that the nurse made me sit down and take deep breathes to calm me down before I saw Steve. Steve had been thrown through the windshield from the passenger side of the front seat. He had a huge gash down his forehead and there was a flap of skin from his scalp to his cheek. The gash ran down next to his right eye and his eye was full of glass. The doctor said that he could not give Steve anesthesia because he had a head injury. The nurse held his arms while the doctor took out numerous glass splinters from around his eyes with tweezers. I called our family doctor, Dr. O'Brien, for a recommendation of a plastic surgeon to sew up Steve's face. The best plastic surgeon in the area, according to Dr. O'Brien, was Dr. Arkoulakis, who was on the staff of JFK. He did an excellent job of stitching Steve's face. Within a couple of years there was almost no visible scar. Steve continued at

Somerset Community College and passed his exams, but showed no interest in going on with school.

I was very worried and anxious about Steve and became almost obsessed with my inability to help him find the right direction to pursue. Mike urged me to find an outlet from my worry about Steve. In July I arranged for an interview at Middlesex Community College to see if they would hire me as an instructor in their nursing program. I was under the impression that a bachelor's degree in nursing was sufficient to obtain a teaching position. I learned that my Bachelor of Science degree did not qualify me to teach, and that I would need to go to graduate school and obtain a master's degree to teach in their associate degree program.

I looked into available graduate programs in nursing in the area and found that only Columbia University and New York University (NYU) had such programs. After investigating both universities, I decided to apply to my alma mater, Columbia. Columbia turned out to be the perfect choice for me as the graduate program there was far more flexible than the NYU program. It gave me the opportunity to take a number of courses in philosophy, literature and history as well as in nursing. I began the application process at once. In August I took the Miller Analogy Test for entrance into Columbia's graduate school.

The tenants moved out of our Bound Brook house on August 28th, and Beverly Weber volunteered to help me paint the kitchen before the movers came. The tenants had painted our kitchen bright pink, which we didn't care for. I had always wanted a yellow kitchen as a background for my blue and white Delft collection. Beverly was a super painter in addition to all her other talents and we got the job done in jig time. I spent two days cleaning first the Hamilton house before we moved out and then our Bound Brook house before we moved in. The

movers arrived on September 1ˢᵗ and moved our belongings
into the house. It took us two weeks to unpack everything.

Our church asked us to talk to the congregation about our life
in the Philippines. Our sermons were well received and people
were most interested in the Filipinos. Later the Women's
Association of the church asked me to give a slide presentation
on the Philippines. I presented a program on the contrasts
between the wealthy and the poor in that country and I also
showed slides of the beautiful scenery.

The children started school in early September. Steve started
eleventh grade, Cindy ninth grade, Peter sixth grade and Cathy
second grade. Cathy was a world traveler and her teacher was
amazed at her breath of knowledge and experience. Her teacher,
Mrs. Eutsler, asked Cathy to tutor another second grader who
needed help with reading. Cathy loved Mrs. Eutsler and the
feeling seemed to be mutual. Peter was a handful in the sixth
grade and got into more than his share of battles with classmates.
However, Peter soon found an outlet that would change his life
dramatically for the better. He joined the wrestling team in the
community recreational program. He had a natural talent for
the sport, which enabled him to excel even though he was small
for his age. Cindy started high school and joined her old friends
from elementary school. They were a wholesome group of girls.
She was an excellent listener and other people liked to tell
her their troubles. She was popular with her classmates as
well with her teachers and she was successful with her
studies. Steve, however, found school boring and did not
seem to be challenged by his classes. By the end of the
school year when he became sixteen he could legally drop
out of school and he chose to do so.

On September 25ᵗʰ I registered at Columbia University for
graduate studies. I had been out of school for sixteen years and
this was an exciting new experience for me. I took a train into

New York City and then took the wrong subway to Columbia. I came out of the subway station and found myself in the middle of Harlem. A kind black woman asked me where I was going and when I told her I was looking for Columbia University, she informed me that it was on the other side of Morningside Park. I thanked her and said I would walk through the park. She looked horrified and said, "Go right down those stairs, take the subway back to 59th Street and take the local to 116th street." I did as she directed. After I finally got to Columbia, I was so overwhelmed by the registration process that I went home before I finished the final steps and had to return the next day to finish registering. I registered for five courses my first semester, one on Mondays and four on Wednesdays, signing up for courses in history, aesthetics, research, statistics and nursing. I took the train into the city two days a week and scheduled the rest of my time for reading and writing papers, while the children were in school. Mrs. Kobezak cared for the children after school on Wednesdays and Cindy cooked dinner for the family those evenings.

The semester did not end until January, but we had a break for Christmas. I made cakes and brownies and we delivered them to shut-ins before Christmas. Then I prepared for our own family celebration. I cleaned the house, shopped for Christmas dinner and wrote a paper for school before Christmas. Christmas Eve we made cookies and the children decorated them and pinned them on a Styrofoam tree, as was our tradition. Mom and Dad Schuyler arrived at 4:00 p.m. and we served them cocktails while I made dinner. After dinner we wrapped gifts and went to the midnight service at church. After that we filled the stockings and went to bed. On Christmas morning, I made coffee cake for breakfast and then we gathered in the family room to open the gifts under the tree. We had a big rib roast of beef for Christmas dinner and Cindy made a cake for dessert. In the evening we invited the Webers and both their mothers over to socialize with Mike's parents. This was another of our traditions.

After everyone left at midnight, I wrote in my diary, "This was the best Christmas ever!" We went to church the next day (Sunday) and Mom and Dad took us out to lunch before they left for home.

The new year did not begin well. Two days after Christmas, I came down with the worst case of flu I ever had. I was sick for a week and could not go out for New Year's Eve with the Webers or go back to school on January 3rd. I had a lot of reading and papers to write for my classes at Columbia so I had to get up and tackle my work. We had the Deipno meeting at our house in January so I had to prepare the dinner for this meeting, which lasted until 2:30 a.m. I also attended my morning bible class each week. I took my last exam on January 26th and then came home and slept for two days.

In February I registered for five more courses in the spring term: curriculum, teaching strategies, philosophy and two areas of nursing. I soon discovered the thrill of taking a philosophy course taught by a superb professor. I took Philosophy 3601 with Dr. Robert McClintock. He was a brilliant teacher and his subject matter was fascinating. I learned in graduate school what I was too inexperienced to understand as an undergraduate, that when you find an outstanding professor you should take every course you can that is taught by him or her. I took six of McClintock's courses during my graduate studies and loved every one of them. In Philosophy 3601 he covered eighteen classic texts including ones by Rousseau, Goethe, Stendhal, Dickens, Tolstoy, Turgenev, Flaubert, Butler, Hardy, Maugham, Fournier, Mann, Joyce, Bronte, Eliot, Woolf, Burgess and Hesse. He told us to choose six of the books for our papers. I chose Rousseau's *Confessions*, Flaubert's *Sentimental Education*, Dickens' *David Copperfield,* Butler's *The Way of All Flesh,* Hardy's *Jude the Obscure* and Mann's *The Magic Mountain.* I wrote a five-page paper on each book and received an "A" on each one. I thoroughly enjoyed reading the books, writing the papers and participating in the discussions in the seminar-type class. That semester I also wrote a paper for my Maternal Childcare nursing course on hyperactivity in children. I did a mock case study on one child with this problem and found it helped me understand Steve and his problems in regimented classroom settings. In later years, I used the paper many times in teaching nursing classes on pediatrics.

That spring we were involved in some other activities. We flew to Puerto Rico to our niece's wedding early in March. We missed our plane at Newark and just made it to the church in time from the next flight. As we were ushered into our pew, the pew in front of us collapsed with everyone sitting on it. Luckily no one was hurt. The wedding finally began and afterwards we danced all evening at the reception. It was an exciting weekend.

Two months later my mother's heart stopped. Fortunately she was in the hospital for tests when it happened and the doctors were able to start her heart again. She had ventricular fibrillation and was told she would have to stay on a strict regime of medications, proper exercise and no salt in her diet. She adhered to this regime which prolonged her life considerably. I visited her in the hospital in Maryland until she went home.

My spring term ended on June 1st. During June, Mike took Steve and Pete on a camping trip to give them some special attention. They enjoyed being together in the forest, setting up the tents and cooking meals on the campfire. They went canoeing down the rapids of the Delaware River and hiked through the woods. In July we went on our cruise with the Deipnos and, when we returned, we spent a week in Rockport visiting relatives, swimming off the rocks, playing round-robin ping-pong, charades and board games such as *Trivial Pursuit*. It was fun and exciting to be together in a place that we all loved so much. In September, John Sheehan and Millie were married and the Deipnos attended the ceremony and reception. It was a festive affair and they were glowing with happiness.

In my third semester, in the fall of 1972, I took eight courses and earned all "A's" except for one "B+" in a course on junior colleges. The other courses that I took were in research, fundamentals of nursing, crisis intervention, history of American social thought, and philosophy. The theory of crisis intervention was new to me and I was to use it frequently in my future teaching in nursing. The philosophy courses that I took that fall were three one-credit courses with Dr. McClintock, one on Plato, one on Dante and one on Francis Bacon. I received an "A" in each course and thoroughly enjoyed writing papers on two of my favorite authors, Plato and Dante. When I became a college professor myself, I used both of these papers frequently as background material for my courses.

In January, after my final exams, we gave a buffet dinner for eighteen of our friends. It was a gala affair that ended at two in the morning. The next day I went to New York City and registered for my fourth and last semester of the masters program. I signed up for five courses in the following areas: mental health, curriculum development, nursing education administration, practice teaching and philosophy. My professor in curriculum development, Dr. Margaret Tyson, was my favorite nursing professor and would later become my doctoral studies advisor. In her class we worked in teams to develop curricula for hypothetical nursing programs. This course proved valuable to me in my later teaching career when I developed a new graduate curriculum, and also when I taught a course in curriculum development in that new program.

I discovered another wonderful professor of philosophy that spring, Dr. Philip Phenix. He was the chairman of the philosophy department and he taught a course entitled, *Educational Classics of the West*. The reading list for the course was outstanding, covering major works of the following authors: Plato, Augustine, Erasmus, Locke, Rousseau, Franklin, Emerson, H. Adams, W. James, Dewey, Whitehead, Russell and Ortega y Gasset. The requirements for the course were active participation in class discussion (no problem for me), and a final paper comparing the writings of all thirteen authors concerning a specific theme. I enjoyed reading all the books, writing the paper and participating in the class discussions. I received an "A" for the final paper and the course.

The environment at Columbia was warm and friendly. The dining room resembled an old fashioned aristocratic club with a high ceiling, paneled walls and heavy oak furniture. I ate dinner there when I had evening classes. After my first class with Dr. McClintock, I met him in the dining room and he called me by name. I was amazed that he knew my name after just one class. I was so impressed that I made a point in my future teaching career to always learn the name of every student in my course by the end of the first class. I finished the course work for my sixty-credit Master of Education degree in May 1973. During May and June I did practice teaching at Essex Community College in Newark, New Jersey. Mike talked to me about going on in my graduate work to earn a doctorate. He encouraged me to keep going to school because I was doing so well and I really loved my course work. He reasoned that it would be important to have the top degree before starting my career. He said it would be difficult to still be in school when I took on the responsibilities of teaching. As usual he was right and I was delighted to keep on with my studies.

To obtain a doctorate required thirty more credits of course work and writing a well-researched dissertation. To get a head start on this endeavor, I decided to attend summer school. During July and August I took the first two courses toward my doctorate: *History of Education in the United States,* taught by Toni Thalenberg and *The Arts and American Education,* taught by Dr Maxine Greene. Dr. Greene was one of the most popular professors at the college and I thoroughly enjoyed her course. She had great personal magnetism and approached her subject matter with enthusiasm and keen analysis. She assigned ten books for required reading and two long papers. The professor in the other course required us to read seven books and write six papers. All this reading and writing in five weeks time was almost overwhelming, but I made it through and received an "A" in both courses. However, I resolved not to go to summer school again.

After summer school was over we invited a number of friends to Rockport for different weekends including the Handens, the Deipnos and Cindy's boyfriend. We had picnics on the rocks with each group that visited, and a lively discussion with the Deipnos when they were there. Cindy's friend, George, was a tall handsome teenager, who had never been away from home before and his mother was somewhat anxious about his going to Massachusetts. Beverly Weber visited us while George was at Rockport and George enjoyed her wit. George went home on the bus from Boston, but he was uneasy about taking a bus alone. We all drove him to Boston and put him on the bus. Beverly kept him amused on the way to Boston to assuage his nervousness.

At the same time that I was finishing my masters program in May, Mike finished working for Union Carbide and was hired for a new job at Pan American World Airways. Earlier in his career, he had decided that he wanted to work at more than one company, but he wanted international experience first, so he went to the Philippines for two years. When he came back to Union Carbide in New York, the job that he took over was not exceptional. This experience reinforced his decision to work for another company. Soon after he returned to the States, he started keeping his eyes open for other opportunities. He became aware that Pan Am, which had serious financial problems, was looking for financial management people to try to improve their financial organization. One area that they were particularly interested in improving was their budgeting process. Mike wrote to the senior vice president of finance to express his interest. After a series of interviews with financial management people at Pan Am, he was hired as director of corporate budgets with a department of about fifteen people.

One of the most delightful perquisites of his new job was the opportunity to fly on any Pan Am flight free of charge on a space-available basis. Because of his position in the company, this perk allowed him to take his whole family free of charge and entitled them to travel first class if space was available. We took full advantage of this opportunity. Mike and I flew to Paris for our nineteenth wedding anniversary in June. We only went for one night, but we lived like royalty. We stayed at the Hotel International in Paris for half price as it was owned by Pan Am. We walked around the city and went to the apartment where Mike's parents had lived when they were in Paris. We visited the Louvre, saw a special Van Gogh exhibit and ate at a charming restaurant on the left bank in the evening. We flew home the next day after a spectacular anniversary.

Over the Labor Day weekend, Mike and I visited Copenhagen, which we loved. We saw the statue of Hans Christen Anderson's little mermaid sitting on a rock in the harbor and we shopped in Stroget near the Town Hall Square. We spent a day at Tivoli, a world-famous amusement park, a magical experience. We drove north to the Viking Museum stopping along the way for true Danish pastry at a sparkling clean farm. The pastry in Denmark is not the heavy pastry that we see in our country, but rather, it is light and puffy with delicious custard in the middle. For our last evening in Copenhagen we took a taxi to an inn on the outskirts of the city where we had dinner and danced to beautiful waltzes all evening. We loved every minute of that evening and flew back to the States elated.

For our third free trip on Pan Am we took the children to Portugal for a four-day vacation over the Thanksgiving holiday. The first day we toured the city. When we came back to the hotel to dress for dinner, we realized that we had left the key in our room. The landlord did not have a spare key, so Mike suggested we call the police to help us get into our room. The landlord became agitated at that suggestion and said he would take care of the problem. He fetched a long plank and stretched it across the courtyard to the windowsill of our room from the room opposite ours on the fourth floor. Then he walked across the plank to our window and climbed in to get the key to our room. We took the children out to a nice restaurant that evening and everyone was in a good humor.

The next day we rented a car and took a two-day tour of northern Portugal. We drove to Estoril for a morning snack and then went on to Boca de Hades where we climbed on the rocks at the bottom of a big cliff. We drove to Sentra to see a Moorish castle, where we climbed the wall around the castle, and then drove to Cascais, a small fishing village on the ocean. We stayed in the only hotel in town in a room with a balcony overlooking the beach. After dinner we walked around the town stopping at the fish market and a souvenir shop. Later Mike and I went to the John Bull Pub. In the morning we all ate breakfast on the balcony and looked at the fishing boats lined up along the beach. After breakfast we packed our bags and checked out of the hotel. We drove to Queluz and toured a palace there before returning to Lisbon airport and flying home. I finished writing a philosophy paper on the trip home and typed it the next morning before taking the train to school.

While I was attending graduate school, Mike gave the children special attention, especially Cathy. He read all eight of Laura Ingalls Wilder's "Little House" books to her and they became her favorite books. She read and reread them herself and could cite quotations from different books by exact page numbers. I found a copy of Howard Pyle's *The Wonder Clock* in the Columbia bookstore and brought it home to Cathy. My mother had read it to me as a child and I loved the stories in it. Pyle begins the preface of the book with the statement: "I put on my dream-cap one day and stepped into Wonderland." At the conclusion of the preface he says to the reader: "Now if you would like to go into Wonderland, you have only to hunt up your dream-cap (for everyone has one somewhere about the house), and come to me and I will show you the way to Time's garret." Mike and Cathy found funny old caps in the hall closet and put them on each night before Mike read to her in the big white chair in the living room.

When Mike started at Pan Am he thought that it was an exciting opportunity because the company's existing budget system was very poor. In the first few months that he was there he implemented a number of changes. However, the senior management was fighting a losing battle trying to maintain a viable company. They would make a decision in one month and the next month give up on that decision and try another direction. There was no consistency in the direction that the company was going. After Mike had been there eight months the company decided to reduce costs by eliminating the corporate budget department. Mike was notified that his job was being discontinued in December. The company managed to hobble along for the few remaining years of its existence but eventually went out of business in the late 1970s.

During Mike's short term at Pan Am, I was working on my doctoral degree. I applied for the certification examination for eligibility for doctoral study. Dr. Tyson offered to be my doctoral advisor and I readily accepted her offer. Studying for the certification exam was one of the most arduous chores I encountered in the doctoral program. I studied the history of nursing over the sixteen years that I had been out of school. I took careful notes on all the current theorists in nursing and made a file of all the key issues in nursing over the last decade. The exam was on October 26th from 1:00 to 5:00 p.m. I was so tense before, during and after the exam that I could not wind down until the next day. Mike took me out to dinner to celebrate

the exam being over but I could not relax enough to go to sleep
at all that night. I passed the exam and was then eligible to
continue in the doctoral program.

Earlier in the fall I had met two students from Greece, Vasiliki
Lanara and Afrodite Reyes. Vasiliki and I were both interested
in doing philosophical dissertations. We decided that we needed
the backing of both the philosophy and the nursing departments
in order to do such a study. We discussed our ideas with the
chair of the nursing department, Dr. Elizabeth Mahoney. She
was agreeable to our suggestion and went with us to see the
head of the philosophy department, Dr. Philip Phenix, who was
also willing to allow this innovation. I asked Dr. McClintock to
be my dissertation advisor and he agreed. Vasiliki and I
supported each other as we prepared our dissertations. I ended
up writing an intellectual biography of Florence Nightingale
and Louisa Schuyler and Vasiliki wrote her dissertation on
heroism in nursing. Vasiliki and Afrodite became my good
friends and I invited them to Bound Brook for Thanksgiving
dinner before we took off for Portugal with the children.

I took four courses during the fall of 1973 in preparation for
writing my dissertation. One of these courses, *Religion and
Education,* was given at Union Theological Seminary, an affiliate
of Columbia University. In this course I was given the
assignment of writing an in-depth research paper on an
individual or topic. I chose Louisa Schuyler, the founder of the
first nursing school in the United States at Bellevue Hospital in
1873. I conducted extensive research in New York City where
Schuyler had lived and worked. I found valuable bits of
information about Schuyler at the New York Public Library,
the New York Historical Society, the Russell Sage Foundation,
the State Charities Aid Society, Columbia University's Butler
Library and Union Theological Seminary Library.

Louisa Schuyler was born into one of New York's most
distinguished families. She was the great-granddaughter of

Alexander Hamilton and Betsy Schuyler, the daughter of General Philip Schuyler of Revolutionary War fame. She possessed the intellect, commitment and zeal of these famous ancestors and had the additional attributes of tactfulness and compassion. She was a woman with a religious mission and an outstanding administrative ability. In the Civil War she organized and ran the Women's Central Association for Relief in New York State. This organization was one of the largest branches of the United States Sanitary Commission, which was responsible for providing supplies and medical care for the sick and wounded Northern soldiers. In later years, Schuyler's sense of mission drove her to establish the first training school for nurses in America and to bring about extensive reforms in the care of the poor, the insane and the blind. With the wealth of information that I discovered in New York City institutions, I was able to write a sixty-page comprehensive biography of Louisa Schuyler for my course and earn an "A" for my effort.

Another course that I took that fall was a seminar on conducting historical research, taught by Professor Kershner. He not only instructed the class how to perform historical research, but also how to avoid the pitfalls that can occur in doctoral study. A third course I took was a colloquium in philosophy and education with three wonderful professors, Maxine Greene, Philip Phenix and Jonas Soltis. It was a very small class of doctoral students and the discussions were fascinating.

The toughest class that I took in the fall of 1973, TN 6000 *Research Project Seminar,* was the class in which students proposed the plan for their dissertation research. According to the catalogue, "Students had to remain in the seminar until their research problem was clearly stated." This course was a roadblock for many doctoral students, some of whom repeated the class five or six times before having their proposal accepted and others who never found an acceptable research topic. Early in the semester I presented my proposal to the faculty and students in the class and it was promptly shot down.

When I first discussed topics with my dissertation advisor, Dr. McClintock, he told me that my ideas were too global and asked if there was any narrower topic that I was interested in. I told him of my admiration for Florence Nightingale. He had written an intellectual biography of Ortega de Gasset for his dissertation and suggested I do the same for Nightingale. Dr Tyson knew that I was taking a course at Union Theological Seminary where I was writing a biography of Louisa Schuyler as my class assignment. She suggested that I take my finished paper on Schuyler to the TN 6000 class as an example of an intellectual biography to prove that I was capable of doing the same thing on a larger scale for Nightingale. This strategy worked and I was cleared to go on to the next course in the spring, TN 7000 *Dissertation Seminar*, which involved presenting one's dissertation project for approval.

At Christmas time, we took the family to my parents' house in Kensington, Maryland. My brother Bunkie and his family were also there. We had a very enjoyable holiday opening gifts, eating sumptuous home cooked meals and playing charades together. The hit of the game was my father loudly imitating a truck, when it was his turn to act out a quotation. We chuckled at his performance on the way back to Bound Brook and this episode became one of our family's favorite reminiscences. When we returned home, Cindy's cousin, Susie McDowell, visited us for a few days. She was fourteen, charming and very attractive. Cindy's boyfriend's older brother was smitten with Susie and sent her a huge bouquet of roses. Susie was swept off her feet and we had to closely chaperone her until she left for home a few days later. We were relieved when she left even though we missed her. On New Year's Eve we hosted a party for twenty-four friends at our house. We decorated the cellar and served a big dinner on the ping-pong table which looked elegant covered by a linen tablecloth. We danced in the family room and had a wonderful evening.

9

Doctoral Dissertation

When I returned to Columbia in January 1974, Dr. Tyson suggested that I go to London to conduct research on Nightingale's original documents. No American historian of nursing had inspected the original Nightingale writings. Dr. Tyson was aware that I could travel to London for free because of Mike's position at Pan Am. She signed me up for the first session of TN 7000 in the spring term of 1974 and the group accepted my proposal. The class met on February 11th, and in anticipation of passing, I had made all the necessary preparations for going to London that very night. Mike met me after the class and drove me to the airport.

Although Mike's position at Pan Am had been terminated in December, the treasurer of the company asked him to take on a short-term assignment to reorganize the insurance claims department. Consequently, he was retained on the Pan Am payroll until the end of April 1974 and was allowed free flying privileges through the end of May. This situation allowed me to fly to London three times for free before he lost the free-flight privilege. I left for my first visit to London on the night of February 11th and arrived in London at 6 a.m. the next morning. I went to the information desk at Heathrow Airport and asked about hotels. The man at the desk asked me for my price range and I told him the cheapest room available. He started suggesting hotels at one hundred dollars per night and I kept on saying no until he reached eight dollars per night. He sent me to Haddon Hall, one block from the British Museum where I was to do my research. When I arrived at Haddon Hall it seemed clean and hospitable. I rented a room with a single bed, a bureau and a straight chair. The bathroom was down the hall. There was a small living room on the first floor with a TV.

I walked to the museum and went to the manuscript room where I told the curator that I was there to do research on Florence Nightingale. He asked to see my reference. I was dumbfounded. Had I come all the way to London to be blocked in my attempt to conduct research? Then I remembered that Dr. Tyson had given me the name of a friend, Miss Fawkes, who was the Director of the Visiting Nurse Association of London. I took a taxi to Miss Fawkes office and she filled out the museum's reference form. That evening I walked around Bloomsbury Square and saw a little china figurine of Walt Disney's Winnie the Pooh, which I bought as a gift for Cathy. I put him on the bureau in my room and every time that I opened the door to my room I saw him smiling at me and it cheered me up. I really missed Mike and the children.

For the next two weeks my daily routine was the same. I ate breakfast in the tiny breakfast room at Haddon Hall, then walked to the British Museum by 10 a. m. when it opened. I sat in the manuscript room taking notes until dinnertime. For the first couple of days I ate dinner at Wimpys or a small restaurant, but I disliked eating alone. I asked one of the guards at the museum if he would recommend a small, friendly, inexpensive restaurant nearby. He suggested a tiny Italian restaurant half a block from the museum. It had one cook and one waiter and the customers sat together at three picnic tables. I loved the place and ate lunch and dinner there from then on. After dinner I worked until closing time at the museum. I dieted during the times that I was in London, rationalizing that if I had to be away from Mike, I could at least return to him looking sleek and beautiful.

I learned to cope with the museum rules. The curator brought me the original writings of Nightingale, but they were in volumes that had to be placed on special stands on the desks. Only pencils, no pens, could be used to take notes. However, the pencil sharpener in the museum was broken, so every noon after lunch I rushed back to Haddon Hall and sharpened twenty pencils to take notes in the afternoon. Taking notes all day was tedious, so I raced myself to see how many pages of notes I could take each day. I increased my output of notes markedly in the weeks that I spent in the manuscript room. Another problem in the museum was the toilet paper, which was like waxed paper, with "British Museum" stamped on every piece. I brought my own toilet paper in my purse each day. In order to enter the museum, everyone had to have their bags checked for explosives. The guards used to chuckle over the toilet paper in my purse.

The museum was closed on Sundays so I decided to visit one of the sailors that my parents entertained during World War II in Winchester, Massachusetts. Horace and his wife, Elsie, lived in Leicester, England about an hour by train from London. I called Horace and he was delighted to have me come for a visit. I took the train to Leicester after I finished at the museum on Saturday afternoon and he and Elsie met me at the station. They served me high tea when we reached their home and then took me with them to their dance club for the evening. The members of the club were doing line dancing so I was able to join in the fun.

Horace and Elsie put me up in their guestroom and in the morning gave me a delicious breakfast of eggs, bacon and tomatoes. Then we visited their son David and his family. David

was the baby that was born while Horace was staying at my
parents' house during the war. Horace named the baby after
my brother David. David and his wife, Ann, had two adorable
children, Tracy and Gary. Tracy, age 5, had red curly hair and
lots of freckles and Gary was a cute little two-year-old. We ate
lunch at the local pub after we left David and his family. Then
we visited their daughter, Pat, her husband, John, and their
children, Guy and Zoe. We also visited Pat's in-laws, Florie and
Ted, who were members of the dance club that Horace and
Elsie belonged to. We returned to Horace's house so that Elsie
could put the roast beef in the oven. While the one pound roast
cooked for two hours we went to the park and played with David
and his children. After a delicious dinner, Horace and Elsie
drove me to the station and I took the train back to London.

The next week was a repeat of the week before, conducting
research all day in the museum and watching TV in the Haddon
Hall living room each evening. I called Mike every night at
midnight when he would be home from work. Some evenings
I would go to a nearby store and get little gifts for the children.
As I gathered more notes from the museum, I would spend
evenings sorting out my research findings. I began to understand
my father's obsession with research, as I became fascinated
with Nightingale's writings. She was a brilliant woman who
wrote 147 books for publication and thousands of memos. The
British Museum contained 125 volumes of her handwritten
letters and notes, as well as all her 147 published works. I was
extremely challenged in my efforts to gain a realistic picture of
her life and character. She carried on an extensive
correspondence with many famous people of her time including
Benjamin Jowett, John Stuart Mill, Harriet Martineau, Lord Ripon
and Queen Victoria. She discussed Plato and Hegel at length
with Jowett in letters over a thirty-year period. John Stuart Mill
critiqued her thousand page philosophical work, *Suggestions
for Thought to Searchers After Truth Among the Artizans of
England,* which she claimed had been influenced by Mill's *A*

System of Logic. She and Queen Victoria had a close relationship and mutual respect for each other.

Florence Nightingale was born into a wealthy English family, but in spite of her family's wealth she showed an early concern for the sufferings of others. She developed into a deeply religious person and came to believe that she was personally called by God to help others. She recorded her calls from God in her notes from childhood on. She believed that God wanted her to work with Him to improve the well-being of mankind. She was driven throughout her life by an intense commitment to help humanity. She devoted her life to the mission of improving the misery and unhealthy living conditions of people all over the world. Two powerful forces shaped her life: ideals and a need to act on those ideals. She commented, "The most practical way of living for God is not merely thinking about Ideals, but doing and suffering for Ideals." Her commitment to carry out her religious ideals helped her achieve far-reaching reforms in her lifetime.

Nightingale was an accomplished statistician. She used statistics to demonstrate the need for improvements in sanitation and health care. During the process of collecting data on certain hospitals she recognized the need for uniform statistics on hospitals and she prepared model hospital statistical forms. She presented these forms at the International Statistical Congress and suggested setting up uniform hospital statistics throughout the world. The Congress approved of her proposal and wrote a resolution that it be communicated to all governments represented there.

Nightingale first became concerned for improving health conditions when she was a sent with a group of nurses to care for the wounded soldiers of the Crimean War. When she arrived at the Barracks Hospital in Scutari, she witnessed the horrifying sight of wounded and dying soldiers in the filthy environment of a hospital with liquid sewage on the floors from clogged drains. More men were dying of cholera and typhus than from wounds received in battle. She and her nurses cared for the sick and tried to clean up the hospital. Nightingale wrote many letters to government officials in London urging them to investigate the situation. Finally a Sanitary Commission was sent to Scutari which mandated action to clean up the hospital and subsequently the mortality rate dropped dramatically. Nightingale's concern for the health of others was not limited to soldiers. In the ten years following the Crimean War, she worked to reform civilian hospitals and workhouse infirmaries in England, to improve health and sanitation in India and other British colonies and to establish the first professional schools for nurses and midwives. She was also instrumental in developing an army medical school.

Among her many services in health care improvement, Nightingale's greatest contribution is undoubtedly her reform of nursing care. She recognized a crucial need for educated nurses who would be both committed to serving others and qualified to perform that service. In 1860 she used the Nightingale Fund, which she had received for her work in Scutari, to establish the first professional nursing school at St. Thomas Hospital. Her goal was to educate nurses who could act intelligently to prevent illness as well as to care for the sick. She taught nurses to collect empirical data on patients' conditions through careful observation so that they could make wise judgments about their care. She envisioned the Nightingale School as the germinating source from which a modern profession of nursing would grow. In the first twenty years after her school opened, the graduates became superintendents in many hospitals in Europe, Asia and the United States. These superintendents often took staffs of nurses with them, thus introducing a whole new system of nursing to other areas of the world. Nightingale's interest in nursing and health reforms continued to the end of her life. She developed District Nursing in England and a system of health missioners in India to educated the poor in their homes about hygiene and sanitation. In 1887, in her fiftieth year of reign, Queen Victoria gave the prestigious Women's Jubilee Gift, a large monetary award, to support District Nursing in England.

Nightingale was influenced by the reigning ideas of her time. One of the characteristics of the Victorian era was faith in progress. Enlightenment thinkers such as Isaac Newton had come to believe that the human intellect was capable of discovering and using scientific principles to improve human existence. Francis Bacon had described the empirical method and John Locke had popularized it in England. Nightingale was strongly committed to the empirical method. In the 19th century a spirit of reform grew out of the combination of renewed religious dedication and scientific knowledge. This spirit of reform was given added momentum by idealistic philosophies that filtered into England. The German philosopher Immanuel Kant argued that people should work toward perfection morally as well as physically and that it was God's plan that they should use their reason to work out their perfection. Georg Hegel wrote that the human mind has the potential for perfection and must develop by stages until it reaches that apex. August Comte, the father of Positivism in France, advocated using empirical research to discover the social and moral laws to perfect society. Nightingale agreed with the Idealists and Positivists that God had a plan for people to use their reason to understand the social and moral laws that would lead them to perfection. She wrote, "Hegel and Comte are men who . . . have a grasp of absolute truth never before equaled."

Nightingale's beliefs were also influenced by Unitarian ideas. She was brought up in a Unitarian family and agreed with Unitarians that religion should be concerned with actions to help others. She supported the Unitarian belief that education was essential for preparing people to understand God's laws for the perfection of mankind. Nightingale believed that people could only move toward perfection by letting God's will take over their hearts and minds. She felt that she was a co-worker with God carrying out his mission to perfect mankind. At age fifty-two she wrote, "O my Creator . . . Thou knowest that through all these twenty years I have been supported and only supported by the belief that I was working with Thee who wert bringing everyone to perfection."

The writers whose ideas Nightingale referred to most in her personal writings were Plato, St. John, Dante, Bacon, Locke, Newton, Kant, Hegel, Comte and Mill. I had read all of these authors in my courses in graduate school or in the Deipnosophistical Society and had a liking for them similar to Nightingale's. I could readily relate to her ideas and therefore found her a fascinating subject for my dissertation. I firmly believe that doctoral students must have a passion for the topic of their dissertation if they are to generate the drive to finish it.

After two weeks in London on my first trip, I flew home to Mike and my family. It was wonderful to be with them all again. Peter was becoming a highly successful wrestler and winning a number of tournaments. We went to a tournament on the day I arrived home and watched Peter win the gold medal. The Webers invited the family over for a big roast beef dinner on Sunday night. On Wednesday, February 27th, I returned to Columbia, noting in my diary, "Its great to be back at school."

At the beginning of February I had registered for my last four classes in the doctoral program. They were TN 7002, a continuation of *Dissertation Seminar,* TN 6601 *Colloquium in Philosophy and Social Studies,* TS 4107 *Human Reproduction and Sexual Development,* and TF 3601, a course that I had taken before with Dr. McClintock. McClintock frequently rewrote his courses so that they were completely different from before. I went to the registrar to ask for permission to take TF

3601 again as it contained all new content. The registrar granted my request and labeled the course D 3601 so that I would get credit for it. The reading list for the revised course included many authors whom I would be reading for my dissertation such as: Bentham, St. Simon, Fitche, Hegel, Owen, Comte and Mill. It was a great course to take as a finale to my doctoral course work. I thoroughly enjoyed the readings, papers and class discussion.

On March 10th I flew to London again to continue my research at the British Museum. The daily routine was the same as on my first visit. My mother had contacted some friends in London who invited me to dinner at their homes. One of these friends was the director of Kew Gardens who knew my father as a fellow botanist. He and his family lived in a mansion on the site of the gardens. There was no central heat, however, so each room had to be heated by a fireplace or electric heater. The family was very friendly to me. We ate high tea in the family room with a blazing fire in the fireplace. Then at dinnertime we crossed a cold hall to the dining room, which had a heater. The maid brought the dinner down the cold hall in covered serving dishes to keep it warm. The meal was delicious and my hosts were most gracious. I was invited back to their house the next month and enjoyed seeing the rhododendrons in full bloom in the gardens before dinner.

At the museum I had a number of manuscripts photocopied. This was expensive but worthwhile to shorten the time I would have to spend in London away from my family. I bought more gifts for the children in my spare evenings as I was missing them so much and feeling guilty for being away. When I flew home after this visit, Mike and Cathy came to JFK to meet me at 9:00 p. m. when the plane was due in. However, the plane was unable to land, and after circling the airport for nearly an hour, the pilot flew to Dulles Airport to refuel. The plane flew back to New York and was finally able to land at 1:00 a.m.

Boy, was I glad to see Mike and Cathy! They were both very chipper after their long wait and we all slept late the next morning.

I returned to my classes for two weeks and then flew back to London for my last visit. The daily routine was the same as before, but by this time I had really increased my output of daily notes. I managed to go through forty-five of the volumes containing Nightingale's personal notes, letters and manuscripts. The richest sources of her philosophy were the five volumes of her letters to Benjamin Jowett and several volumes of her letters to John Stuart Mill and her Aunt Mai. Her *Suggestions for Thought to Searchers After Truth Among the Artizans of England* gave the clearest picture of her philosophy of life. The three volumes of her diaries were also very enlightening. Her philosophy of nursing education was spelled out in seven volumes containing her comments on The Nightingale Nursing Program at St. Thomas Hospital and her letters to her students, which she continued to write well into her eighties. I found time during this visit to research another collection at the museum that contained the manuscript for Nightingale's book, *Letters from Egypt.* This manuscript gave me an excellent understanding of her religious beliefs as she compared them to those of the early religion of Egypt. I was also able to photocopy a number of her published pamphlets about health care problems in other countries. I brought home a fairly comprehensive collection of Nightingale's writings, which helped me immensely in writing her biography.

I had tickets to fly home from London on Friday, April 16th. The taxi came to pick me up in plenty of time to make my flight. However, on the way to the airport, we were stopped by a parade that lasted two hours. When the parade finally passed us it was too late to make my plane. The taxi took me back to Haddon Hall and I stood in the middle of the living room and cried. I called Mike and he was very comforting. I could not get a seat on another plane until Monday, so I went back to the museum for one more day on Saturday. I finally got back to my Mike at 9:00 p. m. Monday night. The children were waiting up for me at home and it was wonderful to be together again. The children all liked the gifts and told me the news of what had happened while I was gone.

I returned to school on Wednesday and the next day Cathy came into the city with me on the train. After my appointment with Dr. McClintock at Columbia, we took a bus down Riverside Drive to the Museum of the City of New York to see the dollhouses and the toys. We had lunch and took another bus down 5th Avenue before coming home on the train with Mike.

Grandma Elsie was worried about us because Mike had been unable to find another job, so in May she sent us $500 to help us out. Pan Am had given Mike an additional thirty days of free flights after he finished the insurance claim job, and we had about a week left to use that privilege. I told Mike that the best use of Grandma's gift would be to raise his morale by going on a trip to Italy. He was easily convinced and we used the last free flying privilege for a four-day trip to Rome. The trip really did improve the morale of both of us.

We loved Rome. Our hotel was near the Spanish Steps and after seeing them we ate lunch in a cute little restaurant. Mike tried to order in Italian, but the waitress turned the menu over and showed him that the other side was in English. In the afternoon we visited the Trevi Fountain, the Pantheon, the Colosseum and the Victor Emanuel Forum. We ate dinner at a sidewalk café and went to bed early. The next day, Friday, we visited the Vatican. We walked through St. Peters and were thrilled with the beautiful statues, especially the Pieta. We visited the Vatican Museum and the Sistine Chapel. As I gazed at the ceiling in amazement, Mike read to me about each of the paintings. After lunch we returned to St. Peters where Mike read to me about each statue. We ate dinner at another sidewalk café and then found a place to dance.

On Saturday we rented a car and drove to Tivoli, a magnificent garden. We ate lunch there and then drove to Spoleto, a walled town at the top of a small mountain. We walked around the town and then tried to go into the castle by the town square. The officer at the entrance shook his head no to Mike, but Mike kept insisting in pidgin Italian that we wanted to go in. Finally someone sitting in the square came over to Mike and explained that it was a prison not a castle. We returned to Rome and ate dinner at another sidewalk café. We left on Sunday and flew back to the States. The trip really did boost Mike's morale and he went back to his job search with renewed vigor. Grandma Elsie was a bit taken aback when she learned how we spent the $500 as she thought we might need it for food, but when we explained how much it helped Mike's morale, she took it gracefully.

On June 6th we went to Mike's twentieth reunion from Princeton. It was the first time he had been to a Princeton reunion even though we lived only forty minutes away. The experience took us back to college days with dinners in the club and dancing in the evening. Each reunion class had a band playing under a huge tent. In our class's tent Lester Lanin played all the old fox trots and jazz numbers that we had danced to in college. We had a great weekend at Princeton. We went out to dinner and dancing ten days later to celebrate our twentieth wedding anniversary.

I did a lot of reading in the summer as background for my dissertation. I had decided that my dissertation would be about both Nightingale and Schuyler. Nightingale had developed the first modern nursing school at St. Thomas Hospital in London and Schuyler had created the first nursing school in the United

States at Bellevue Hospital in New York City. I gave my dissertation the title: *Molders of Modern Nursing: Florence Nightingale and Louisa Schuyler.*

In order to gain an in-depth understanding of the ideas of leading thinkers of their time I used Mike's alumni card to take books from Rutgers University libraries. Rutgers' Alexander Library was near our home, had an open shelf policy for taking out books, and had no limit on the number of books that could be taken out. I especially liked the open shelf concept, as Columbia did not allow students to enter the stacks. At Alexander Library I could look up a book on a subject and then go to the area of the library where the book was located. Once there I could find many more books on the same topic and decide which books were best. I took out about 200 books on the history and philosophy of the 19th century and brought them home as resource material. I piled them around the edges of the floor in our bedroom, but Mike didn't care for that. He bought me two bookcases with five shelves each in which to arrange all the books by subject matter.

Cathy came to the library with me to help carry all the books to the car. I skimmed through these books noting good supporting passages for my dissertation. I took out books by and about the philosophers that Nightingale and Schuyler had read and liked. I read many nineteenth century philosophers, as both women were products of that century and were influenced by their ideas. I read several books on Unitarianism, the religion of both of them, and I read books by and about the women themselves. I read books on the history of the nineteenth century and the centuries that led up to it. Two of my favorite books on nineteenth century ideas were *The Victorian Frame of Mind* by Walter Houghton and *The Idea of Progress* by J. B. Bury.

In July I outlined my biography on Nightingale and started to write. The children were busy with summer activities or visits to grandparents, so I had whole days for writing. I started at 9:00 a. m. and wrote until 11:00 p. m. every day. I took a two-day break to read the book that I had chosen for the Deipno meeting. It was Kant's *Lectures on Ethics,* one of my favorite books. I presented it at the McCreary's house at the group's August meeting. Then I went back to writing my dissertation for another month. I took another break at the end of August and we spent a week at Rockport with Dick and Beverly Weber. The Deipnos came up over Labor Day weekend and we had a lively discussion on the pros and cons of state-sponsored gambling, led by Beverly. We had delicious meals including our annual turkey and ham dinner in the big dining room. We also had our annual picnic on the rocks, enjoying a beautiful sunset.

At the end of August Mike finally secured a new job with a shipping company, United States Lines. We were all relieved and thrilled. Mike had been job hunting for nine months. After the insurance claim project was finished, the treasurer of Pan Am had provided Mike with an office and secretarial help while he was searching for another job. He continued to commute to New York City daily while he was job hunting. He wrote hundreds of letters during his search, usually to the top financial officers of every major company in the New York-New Jersey area. He had almost forty interviews and he remarked that, were it not for the tension and concern of being out of work, it would have been a fascinating experience learning about these companies and talking to their senior management officers. In August 1974 he received a call from the chief financial officer of United States Lines, and after several interviews with him and other officers, he was offered the job of manager of financial analysis.

Mike began his job at United States Lines at the beginning of September. He was responsible for analysis of financial results of the company, analysis of proposed business opportunities and direction of the company's budget process. He was in charge of a department of seven people. Mike's experience at both Pan Am and U.S. Lines revealed to him that the system of cost control in the transportation industries, and, he suspected, of other service industries, was not nearly as well developed as in the manufacturing industries. He saw the opportunity to institute a system of cost reporting and cost control that would be far superior to the one currently in use at U.S. Lines and other steamship companies.

Mike spent several months of his spare time developing a comprehensive proposal for a new system based on standard costs. He presented his proposal to the president and other senior officers. They were interested and asked many questions, but in the end they decided not to accept Mike's proposal. It was just too radical a change in the system they were used to. Mike told me that this experience taught him a lesson that he had apparently not learned well enough in the past, that is: proposals for change are rarely accepted at one meeting, or even at a series of meetings. He said that support for a change must be developed over a period of time, convincing one person at a time through a series of discussions on the value of the proposal. He concluded, "Only when you have developed the support of a sufficient number of key individuals should you present a formal proposal to a decision-making group."

U.S. Lines was located at One Broadway in Manhattan. Mike had a beautiful office overlooking the Hudson River and the Statue of Liberty. He enjoyed working at the company and developed a great deal of respect for his fellow workers there. Bart Wilcox was his first boss at U.S. Lines. He was a very polished urbane gentleman. Mike enjoyed working for him and respected him for his intelligence and ethical integrity. Wilcox had lived in Europe for several years and had married a beautiful French woman. He and his wife came to dinner at our house and were very charming guests. Mike's department was made up of bright young men with M. B. A.'s. Mike liked the men in his department, especially Joe Sacardi, an energetic young manager who had grown up in Brooklyn and was determined to succeed. He was intelligent and capable and almost always accomplished whatever he set out to do. When U.S. Lines relocated to New Jersey, Sacardi asked for an increase in his salary to cover the cost of his commute to New Jersey. Mike denied his request, so he requested permission to ask Mike's boss, who also denied it. So Sacardi then went to the president of the company and got what he wanted. Mike admired his determination and business ability. Another member of Mike's department that Mike respected was Angelo D'Alia. He was the only member of the group without a graduate degree, but he was conscientious, reliable and loyal. He took care of most of the clerical work of the department. Mike was well respected by his superiors and the men under him and he enjoyed working for U.S. Lines.

I spent all of September 1974 writing about Nightingale. Dr. McClintock had told me to finish the whole dissertation before giving it to him to read. At the end of September I took the first draft of over 300 pages to Dr. McClintock. He stunned me by announcing that he was about to go on a sabbatical and would not be able to read it. I was shocked. I informed Dr. Tyson of what had happened. She took me by the hand and marched over to Dr. Phenix's office to solicit his help. He was very supportive, telling me that he would find me a replacement for Dr. McClintock. He arranged for Dr. Douglas Sloan of the Philosophy Department to take me on as an advisee. Dr. Sloan took my dissertation home, read it in a couple of days and then returned it to me with very few suggestions for revision. I made the revisions in a week and he gave me his approval of the finished product. I was eternally grateful to him.

During October and November, I re-typed the whole dissertation and gave copies to my doctoral committee: Drs. Phenix, Sloan,

Tyson, Mahoney and Rines. There were two philosophy professors and three nursing professors reading my dissertation in preparation for my oral examination. Cindy was a great help to me in preparing the bibliography for the dissertation. We made piles of books on the floor of her room by authors whose names began with each letter of the alphabet. She hand wrote each author and book in bibliographic form in alphabetical order so that all I had to do was copy her list on the typewriter. The bibliography was 35 pages long, so her help was truly appreciated. She was also one of my proofreaders, along with my mother, Beverly Weber and Mike. When we finished the bibliography Cathy helped me take the two hundred books back to Alexander Library.

Late in November the Webers asked us out to dinner. They picked us up at 7:00 p. m. and we drove over to their house to pick up something. Then Mike announced that he needed to go back to our house for something that he had forgotten. He told us all to come in the house while he found what he needed. As we walked into the house, there was a loud shout of "Surprise!" I was flabbergasted. I couldn't grasp the situation. I kept repeating, "I don't believe this." Mike and the children had arranged a surprise party to celebrate the completion of my dissertation. There were nine adults and twenty young people who had all managed to get into our house in the ten minutes that we were away. Cindy had organized the party and secured the food with the help of the guests. Everyone was exuberant and, when I finally came out of shock, I was thrilled and excited.

A few days later, Cindy was crowned the Bound Brook High School Homecoming Queen at the Thanksgiving home football game. Our minister's wife, Helen Ann Bower, was a real fan of Cindy. She jumped up screaming with joy, ran down the bleachers and chased the car with Cindy in it around the football field. We were so proud of Cindy. Her popularity was due not only to her looks, but also to her personality. She was a good listener and truly interested in the problems of others. After the game we had Thanksgiving dinner at the home of our next door neighbors, Jack and Ella Handen.

December 5th was the big day of my oral examination, the final step in the doctoral process. It seemed that having two departments represented on my oral committee brought harmony to the group. The professors from both departments were very polite to one another and to me. Before I went into the orals, Dr. Tyson told me to be calm as I was the true expert on the subject of my dissertation. She was correct, everyone deferred to my knowledge of Nightingale and Schuyler. Dr. Phenix commented that he might have questioned Nightingale's sanity after hearing about her notes to God, but when he considered that she had 147 publications, he ventured that he wouldn't mind being crazy like that. The committee voted unanimously that I had passed the orals. The only suggestion for revision was from Dr. Phenix who thought that the introduction could be shortened. I finished the revision and the doctorate on December 10, 1974. On December 20th Mike and I gave an open house for sixty friends to celebrate.

10

New Ventures

I began to look for a college teaching position at the beginning of 1975. In January, I submitted the abstract to accompany my dissertation and met with Dr. Tyson. She informed me of a temporary position at City College to replace a nursing faculty member on maternity leave. I met with Dr. Hosford, the Dean of Nursing at City College, that afternoon and received an offer of employment that evening. I began my new job, my first experience as a college professor, early in February. The nursing major at City College was an upper level program. Nursing courses did not begin until the junior year, after the students had taken two years of background liberal arts courses. The nursing faculty members at City College were divided into four teams, one for each semester of the junior and senior years. I was placed in Team I where I taught Nursing I. This course included content on Fundamentals of Nursing and Maternal Child Health Nursing. Nursing courses included both classroom learning and clinical experience. In the classroom, faculty taught theoretical knowledge of their specialty to prepare students to function intelligently in the clinical areas. Nursing I lectures were given at the college on Mondays and Wednesdays. Clinical teaching for the course was scheduled for Tuesday and Thursday at Mount Sinai Medical Center, where students worked in the prenatal clinic, the labor and delivery section and the postpartum unit.

Before the spring term began, the Webers talked us into joining them for a three-day weekend at the Concord Resort in the Catskills. We had a great time skating, sledding, eating gourmet meals and dancing every night. Dick Weber signed up for every dancing and craft class that was given at the resort and we all went to an auction on the last day. At the auction we bought a small Oriental rug for our downstairs bathroom, which has been there ever since. It was a welcomed break for all of us and we thoroughly enjoyed ourselves as we always did when we went on a trip with the Webers.

In the last week of February I gave my first lecture as a college professor and was I nervous! There were 120 students in the class and I learned all of their names by the third class. By the end of the term I had caught on to college teaching. The Dean of Nursing called me into her office and offered me a permanent position as an assistant professor and gave me a raise to go with it.

During my first semester, Steve was in another serious automobile accident He was driving on an icy road and the car skidded into a lamppost. Luckily the post snapped in half and the car lurched into a ditch. Steve was cut up but not seriously hurt, thank God! Steve was having a difficult time during this period. He went from one job to another and came to the conclusion that he was not going to get the kind of job that he liked without a college education. He asked if we would send him to college, and, of course, we agreed that we would. Lacking a high school diploma, he took the high school equivalency exam and passed with flying colors. He was accepted for the fall term at Middlesex Community College.

This was Cindy's senior year in high school and she applied to a number of colleges. She decided to go to Bucknell University, as she had not yet heard from her first choice, Princeton University. She did not think that she had a good chance of getting into Princeton, but she held off accepting any college until after April 15th when Princeton replies would be mailed to applicants. Princeton did accept her and she was amazed and thrilled when she read their letter of acceptance. Fortunately Mike had been given a promotion at U.S. Lines with a substantial raise that would help us finance two children in college.

Peter joined the Bound Brook High School wrestling team in his freshman year and was becoming the star of the team. His coach was quoted in the local paper as stating, "Pete Schuyler has the greatest potential of any wrestler I have ever coached." At the first meet of his freshman year, Peter defeated a senior district champion on the Roselle Park team. He continued to win every match and was undefeated in dual meets at the end of his freshman year.

Cathy had skipped the fifth grade in the fall of 1974 and was worried that she would not make new friends easily in her new class. However by the spring she had made a number of new friends and she invited ten girls to her eleventh year birthday party. Mike put clues for a treasure hunt at well-known buildings around town. The girls were given their first clue at our house, and then they rode their bikes around town to find subsequent clues that finally led to the discovery of the treasure. They were enthusiastic in their searches and came back ready for dinner and birthday cake. After dessert they played charades and other games.

Towards the end of April, Cindy gave a sermon at our church as part of the Youth Sunday program and I gave a lecture at Columbia University on Florence Nightingale as part of their Research Day. Early in May, Mike and I went to my twentieth undergraduate reunion from Columbia and we had a great time with my friends and their spouses at a barbecue following the reunion.

May 14, 1975 was a big day for me. Although I had completed my doctorate in December, the official graduation ceremony was held in May. My mother had heart problems and could not drive up to New York City. She did not want to miss the ceremony so she took a train to the city and stayed at the Sheraton Hotel across the street from Pennsylvania Station. Mike, the children and I took the train into New York City on the morning of the graduation, picked up Mother at the hotel and rode the subway to Columbia University. There was a special ceremony at Riverside Church for the doctoral candidates in the morning before the regular graduation in the afternoon. Mother told me how proud and cute I looked marching up the church aisle with the other candidates who were all taller than I was. After the regular graduation there was a reception and Mother gave Dr. Tyson some rare books as a gift. They had a lot in common and liked and respected each other immediately. That night the McCrearys hosted a dinner in my honor where the Deipnos gave me a Lladro figurine of a nurse that I have treasured ever since.

At the end of the month, Peter took a train to New York City to participate in a wrestling tournament. He won first prize in his weight class of 101 pounds and received a large trophy. On his way back to Pennsylvania Station on the subway, he sat across from some older rough looking teenagers. One of them asked, "Hey kid, what's that trophy for?" Peter replied, "Wrestling." The fellow that had asked the question turned to his friends and said, "Wow, we better not mess with him." That was one of the family's favorite anecdotes for years.

At the completion of her senior year in high school, Cindy and her friend next door, Debbie Handen, asked if they could have a class graduation party in the two adjoining back yards and serve beer. We agreed on the condition that only seniors were allowed at the party. The Handens and we were worried that younger teenagers might crash the party and drink beer. Dick and Beverly Weber volunteered to help the Handens and us chaperone the party. Dick took his responsibility seriously and paroled the yards frequently. Close to 150 seniors came to the party and they had a glorious celebration.

July was a busy month for the family. Cindy offered to paint the inside of the house to earn some money for her college expenses. What a worker she was! I would never have attempted such a tremendous job, but she just pushed the furniture to the center of each room, covered it with plastic sheeting and painted each room in short order. Beverly Weber and I took Peter and Bill Weber to Rockport later in July. My mother had invited us and we had a great time with her. The boys went fishing, swimming and biking. We found a used tandem bike for the boys for $15.00 and they had a great time riding it all over Cape Ann. On the last day of July, Mike and I took Cathy to the Jersey shore where we enjoyed swimming, the amusement park and a delicious dinner.

Dick and Beverly Weber found an article in the paper about "pub crawling" in the British Isles. They brought it to our attention and we agreed that it sounded like an interesting and fun thing to do. We decided to take a two-week pub-crawl to England and Scotland in August to celebrate the completion of my doctorate. What a great time we had! We flew out of Kennedy Airport late in the evening and arrived at London's Gatwick Airport early the next morning. We took a train to Victoria Station and then a taxi to Haddon Hall, where I had stayed while researching Florence Nightingale at the British Museum. Mike and Beverly were itching to begin sightseeing at once, but Dick and I were too exhausted, so we napped in our rooms while they walked around the Bloomsbury area. That night after dinner we set out on our first pub-crawl in Soho. We chose Victorian pubs full of customers to get the flavor of Charles Dickens' time. We went to two Soho pubs and ended up at the White Swan.

Monday morning Dick and Beverly went to see the changing
of the guard at Buckingham Palace, while Mike and I went
shopping on Oxford Street. I took Mike to lunch at my favorite
little restaurant near the British Museum where I had eaten my
meals during my earlier visits to London. I introduced him to
the waiter that I liked so much and Mike thanked him for
cheering me up while I was alone in London. After lunch we
rented a small station wagon for our trip around England and
Scotland. We met the Webers at Haddon Hall and set out for
Cambridge to see the university. We were pleased to find that
there was an outdoor market in the town with wonderful fresh
fruits and vegetables. Dick, a great fruit lover, bought several
large oranges, which he enjoyed on our trip to Leicester to visit
Horace and Elsie Callis that afternoon. I had visited them when
I was in London the year before, and they had also visited us in
the States.

Elsie cooked us a marvelous roast lamb for dinner and served
English trifle for dessert. It was our first experience with trifle
and both Beverly and I asked Elsie for the recipe, which we
have used on numerous occasions since. After dinner they took
us to the Free Trade Inn, their local pub. It was a small brown
building with a thatched roof. Inside was a cozy room with a
fireplace and a dartboard on the wall. It was full of local people,
many of whom knew Horace and Elsie. When we went back to
their house, Horace and Elsie very graciously put Mike and me
in their bedroom while they slept on an inflatable mattress in a
backroom. They put the Webers in the guestroom.

In the morning we called a garage for someone to come and
look at our rented car. It had been stalling on the way to Leicester
the day before. It was a brand new car, but the garage owner
felt it needed new spark plugs and points. While the car was
being fixed, Horace and Elsie took us to see Warwick Castle, a
medieval structure filled with old relics. Next we drove to
Coventry Cathedral. It was a moving experience to see the new

cathedral built next to the ruins of the beautiful original cathedral that had been bombed in World War II. We ate at a restaurant next to the statue of Lady Godiva riding naked on a horse. That night we went back to the Free Trade Inn for a nightcap with Horace and Elsie and their son David.

The next day the car still wasn't functioning correctly, so we took it back to the garage and then toured the town of Leicester. There was an outdoor market and Dick again headed for the oranges. Mike and I surveyed the china stalls, as we both like English china. I managed to buy several large pieces to carry back to the States from our trip. The car was finally fixed by the end of the afternoon and we drove back to Horace's house. That night Horace and Elsie's daughter, Pat, invited us all to an elegant dinner at her home. We ended the evening together at the John Smith pub.

Thursday morning we had breakfast with Horace and Elsie and thanked them profusely for their hospitality. We drove to the Bronte family home in Haworth. We toured their home and then walked out on the moors. We could feel the loneliness that Charlotte and Emily Bronte expressed in their novels *Jane Eyre* and *Wuthering Heights*. That night we drove to York, ate dinner and visited the local pub. We asked the bartender to recommend a bed and breakfast lodging in the vicinity. He directed us to the home of Mrs. Robinson right next to the local church. Her home was large and charming; the only drawback was the bong of the church bell every hour throughout the night. In the morning she served us a typical English breakfast of juice, cereal, eggs, bacon, sausage, broiled tomatoes, toast and marmalade along with our coffee and tea. This was the first of many bed and breakfast establishments that we visited on our trip.

After breakfast, we walked around the city of York and visited the magnificent cathedral. We were awed that it was built 800

years ago. At this time America was making plans for a big
celebration for its upcoming 200th birthday while in England
the people accepted as a routine matter that their buildings and
cities were so old and well preserved. We visited the York
museum and wandered through the shops and out-door market.
After lunch we drove to Edinburgh along narrow winding roads.
There were sheep along the wayside that periodically wandered
into the middle of the road. For a while Mike followed a car
pulling a trailer (a "caravan" as the English called it). Mike
kept leaning out his window to see if he could pass. Dick, who
was sitting beside him in the front seat, exclaimed, "There is
absolutely no reason for you to pass that caravan," but Mike
did it anyway. Dick was so horrified that he stayed in Edinburgh
an extra day as he refused to get back in the car. When he
finally did get back in the car two days later he rode in the back
seat for the rest of the trip.

In Edinburgh we spent two nights at Mrs. Meeks' home and
were served breakfast on beautiful Spode china each morning.
Edinburgh is a lovely city. We climbed the hill to Arthur's seat
and went to see Holyrood Palace. The next day Dick was not
ready to travel again, so he and Beverly stayed in Edinburgh
while Mike and I drove to St. Andrews to see the famous golf
course and the lovely beach on the North Sea. We watched
children playing in the sand and I walked in the water and
climbed on the rocks. We met the Webers for dinner and
afterwards we decided to visit the Deacon Brodie Dance Hall
for an evening of dancing. We took a taxi and were warned by
the driver that we would find a "rough" crowd there. However,
we found the hall enjoyable and danced in a circular path around
the edge of the hall as the locals did.

On Sunday we started out for Oban in the Scottish highlands. A
couple on the plane from New York had told me how enthralling
the resort town of Oban was. They highly recommended that
we visit it and their advice was excellent. We had a full evening

after we reached Oban. We went to the evening service at the Church of Scotland (Presbyterian denomination). The hymns were familiar and the sermon interesting. After church we went to a show about Scottish culture at the MacTavish Restaurant. We saw highland dancers and heard bagpipers and Gaelic singing over a delicious dinner. After dinner we hurried back to our boarding house as our landlady, Mrs. MacFee, had told us she locked the door at 11:15 sharp. Mrs. MacFee was the quintessential Scottish woman. She was suspicious, terse and tight with her money. She posted a sign in the bathroom stating, "BATH BY ARRANGEMENT ONLY—EXTRA CHARGE."

We spent the next morning in antique shops. Beverly bought two huge platters, which made us wonder how she would get them back to the States. We left Oban and drove to the ferry to the Isle of Arran. While we waited for the ferry we ate a picnic lunch on the rocky shore. The rocks were like those at Rockport and I decided to take a couple of pretty ones home with me. Mike kept admonishing me not to use packing space for rocks. I took them anyway and those rocks still look beautiful in my rock garden in New Jersey. The ferry to Arran was small and the trip was a short ride. After our visit, we took a larger ferry from Arran to Dumfries on the mainland of Scotland. We checked into the Balmoral Hotel in Dumfries and went to Bruno's for a delicious dinner. After dinner we visited the Coach Horse Pub. We were surprised to find that pubs in Scotland closed at 10:00 p.m., so we ended the evening at the Balmoral Lounge in our hotel.

We headed down to England the next day. It rained all day, but Mike insisted that we go out in the rain to walk on Hadrian's Wall. We all trudged along the wall, actually enjoying the experience. We stopped for lunch in Penrith and browsed in antique shops again. This time I bought a two-quart china pitcher and wondered how I would get it home. We drove through the English Lake country and on to Blackpool, a resort on the western coast of England. We loved Blackpool and went to its famous dance hall at the Tower. The décor of the ballroom was rich scarlet and gold and everyone there was dressed to the nines. There was a large orchestra playing and the dancing was exhilarating. We danced around the ballroom moving in one direction with all the other couples like figures on a giant carousel.

We spent the night at the home of Mrs. Finney and, after a substantial breakfast, we shopped at two outdoor markets before leaving for our next destination. We drove south to Wroxton, the school that John Weber would be attending on a semester abroad the following spring. Wroxton was located in a charming little village right out of a Thomas Hardy novel. All the houses and town buildings were thatched and we saw a man re-thatching the church roof. Mike insisted that I sit for a photo on a bank in front of a thatched house. Unfortunately he sat me down on a thistle and, boy, did it sting! My whole upper leg turned bright red and continued to sting for quite a while. We visited Wroxton, a former home of Lord North, and marveled at the elegance of the place, including the furnishings, the chapel and fifty acres of gardens and lakes. One room was called the "King's Room", as both James I and Charles I had slept there. The building had originally been an abbey in the seventeenth century.

After touring the school, we walked across the lane to the Wroxton Inn for lunch. We were informed that lunchtime was over and we could only get tea as it was late in the afternoon. We told them that we were really hungry, so the innkeeper brought us tea and a large platter of cheeses and crackers. He left us to enjoy our repast in the cozy living room of the inn. When he returned he was horrified to see that we had wolfed down almost the entire platter of cheese. He promptly removed the platter and we thanked him and went on our way somewhat abashed.

Our next stop was Compton Wynates, a magnificent Tudor mansion with splendid gardens and grounds. For years afterwards we saw this manor in movies that needed a large Tutor mansion as background for the plot. We drove on toward Oxford, stopping on the way to see Blenheim Palace, the residence of Winston Churchill. It was too late to go inside, but we admired the beauty of the palace and its grounds. When we reached Oxford we found bed and breakfast lodging at the home of the Olivers. They had a cute two-year-old son named Simon, who was very friendly. We ate dinner in town at the Chinese Palace and then went pub crawling at The Grapes and The Black Swan.

In the morning, we toured some of the colleges at Oxford. Christ College is the most famous as it encompasses the cathedral. My favorite college was Baiol, where Florence Nightingale's friend Benjamen Jowett had been the dean. As we were leaving Oxford, we noticed a sign over the entrance gate to another college that stated, "Might Makes Right". This set off quite a discussion among us that continued on our drive down to the Cotswolds. We ate lunch in the town of Cirencester and visited a Roman museum there before driving on to the city of Bath. We found lodgings at Mrs. Millburn's home and took off for dinner and pub-crawling. We ate at The Walrus and the Carpenter restaurant and then visited four pubs: The Grapes, The Garrick, Bier Keller and the Roundhouse.

When we awoke the next morning, we toured the city and found Bath a fascinating place, with its cathedral, Roman buildings and charming open market under hanging baskets of flowers. There were many wonderful shops to explore with beautiful china and other treasures. Beverly wanted to go to the hairdresser and Dick wanted to sit and study the Roman baths, which he did for over three hours. Mike and I decided that it was a good time and place to buy gifts for the children and souvenirs of the trip. We spent the morning in the marketplace and had a great time. We bought models of a country church and two thatched houses in Coalport china, which we have treasured ever since. At noon we left Bath with the Webers and drove to see Stonehenge in Salisbury Plain. We were appalled to see a fence around the ancient stones and a cheap souvenir shop next to it. How sad that such an awesome monument to ages past should be so commercialized.

We returned to London during rush hour and left Beverly and Dick at Haddon Hall while we returned the rented car. For the first time on the trip Mike became flustered and drove on the wrong side of the street. We approached Oxford Street, the busiest street in London, and Mike turned right onto it. There were no cars in sight as they were all stopped at a red light a block away. Without realizing it Mike drove down an eight-lane highway going in the wrong direction. When the light ahead turned green we suddenly saw a mass of cars headed right at us. Mike quickly turned off on a side street and saved the day, and our lives.

We ate dinner at Fornecellos and then managed to visit seven pubs on our last night in London. First we went to the old city and stopped in at Ye Old Cheshire Cheese, a haunt of Samuel Johnson. Then we walked from St Paul's Cathedral to the Thames River, stopping at some of the best pubs that we had seen on the trip. We visited Ye Old Bell Tavern, The Horn Tavern, The Albion, The First Edition, The Butterfly and the Charles Dickens. Just to put the reader's mind at ease, we did not drink alcohol in all these pubs, but mostly mingled with the other patrons. At the last pub a man came over and offered us a homemade newspaper. We politely declined, but he persisted. Finally Beverly asked him how much it cost. He said, "nothing." Her pert repartee was, "The price is right, I'll take it."

At breakfast in Haddon Hall on our last day in England, the manager sat down at our table. He said how nice it was that

Mike could be there with me. He told Mike how homesick I had been there without him while I was doing my research. He was very gracious to us and Mike thanked him. After breakfast we tried to do all the things we had missed. We went shopping at Harrod's where we bought a Royal Dalton figurine of Alice in Wonderland reading a book that reminded us of Cathy. We visited Buckingham Palace again and went to see the Elgin Marbles at the British Museum. I showed Mike the manuscript room, where I had read Nightingale's handwritten correspondence and the magnificent domed reading room, where I had also studied. After lunch we took the train to the airport and flew home. All the china that we had purchased on the trip made it back to the States without breaking.

Later that summer, after we returned home from England, Bill Weber and Peter asked if they could ride their bikes to Rockport. We were reluctant to permit this trip, but they were restless fifteen-year-olds aching for something exciting to do and anxious for the opportunity to show their independence. We finally gave them permission and it turned out to be a great adventure. They rode their bikes to the Tappan Zee Bridge and began to walk the bikes over the bridge. They were stopped by bridge officials and told that they could not walk or ride their bikes over the bridge. Soon a man in a truck stopped and picked them and their bikes up and drove them over the bridge. On the rest of the trip they traveled on local roads and did not encounter any more troublesome bridge crossings. They slept in sleeping bags in fields and in a cemetery one night and completed the trip in four days and nights. We joined them in Rockport later that week and brought them back with their bikes in our station wagon.

The first week of September, I started my second semester as a faculty member at City College. My team had five faculty members on it. We were a compatible group and our team leader, Lucy Kennedy, was very supportive to me as a new faculty member. During the fall semester I was busy researching, writing and rehearsing new lectures that I gave on Mondays and Wednesdays. On Tuesdays and Thursdays I supervised a small group of students in their clinical experiences at Mount Sinai Medical Center. Clinical groups were limited to ten students so that faculty members could give more individual attention to each student as he or she worked with patients. Well-known philosophers on education claim that the best way to learn about something is to teach it to others. I found this to be true, as I felt driven to become an expert on the content that I was teaching, both in the classroom and in the clinical area.

My students worked in the obstetrics clinic at Mount Sinai, where they interviewed, educated and cared for maternity patients from low-income families. During the semester we spent one month each in the prenatal clinic, the labor and delivery unit, the postpartum unit and the newborn nursery. It was a fascinating time for me, and my students also seemed to thoroughly enjoy the experience. Many of the patients in the prenatal clinic were unmarried teenagers, some of whom had been sexually molested by their stepfathers. The very young patients did not have the knowledge and maturity of adult pregnant women who could accept the responsibility of caring for their babies. Mount Sinai employed an obstetrician whose specialized in caring for pregnant teenagers. She worked with the very young patients, some as young as ten and eleven years of age. Sometimes these young girls asked her to care for their babies while they went to parties; other times they just left their babies alone at home. Many young mothers let their own mothers raise their babies. My students frequently interviewed these young patients and taught them about pregnancy, labor and delivery and about postpartum and newborn care. The clinic provided a valuable experience for my students and they learned a great deal from teaching these patients at different stages of pregnancy and postpartum.

During my second semester at City College, Cindy started her first semester at Princeton University. She made new friends at college, but felt overwhelmed by her classes at first. She called home and told us that she was no longer at the top of her class, as everyone at Princeton had been at the top of their high school class. She felt unsure of herself, and was afraid that she would not be able to take adequate notes in her lectures or keep up with her assignments. A month later she had settled down and seemed more comfortable in her studies. Steve began his college experience at Middlesex Community College and felt quite comfortable there. We helped him find a room near the college. He did well in his studies and joined the wrestling team at the college, which he enjoyed immensely.

At home Mike and I kept busy with our jobs while Peter and Cathy were busy with school activities. Peter was engrossed with sports—cross-country in the fall, wrestling in the winter and track in the spring. Cathy was active in glee club and school plays and also in the church choir. She loved to sing and continued to be active in singing groups even as an adult. Mike's parents, his sister and his brother-in-law came down from Albany for Thanksgiving dinner and, on Christmas, we enjoyed a warm and wonderful celebration with the children and Mike's parents at our house.

We decided to end 1975 with a gala New Year's Eve party at our house. We invited many of our friends for a formal dinner dance at our home. Peter offered to paint the basement so that we could have an elegant sit-down dinner for twenty-four guests at one large table, which we set with all our fine linens, china, crystal and silver. I prepared a gourmet dinner, which we served buffet style on the dining room table from which the guests proceeded to the basement to dine together. The dinner included seafood supreme, roast ham with raison sauce, peasants' mignon, sweet potato casserole, broccoli au gratin and snow pudding. The evening included games, dancing in the family room and champagne at midnight to celebrate the arrival of the new year. The affair concluded with a decorated sheet cake and coffee at one in the morning. It was a very festive occasion and everyone seemed to enjoy the celebration.

The first months of 1976 were taken up with Peter's wrestling meets. The family attended ten meets in January and February to cheer Peter on as he continued to win every match. At the end of February, Peter won the district championship in his weight class and went on to take third place in the regional competition. Bound Brook fans came by the carloads to cheer him on at every meet. He was becoming a well-known wrestling star in the community.

I enjoyed teaching in my second year at City College, but a change in the leadership of our team began to make life difficult for me there. Lucy Kennedy, the first leader of Team I, left the college and a new leader for our team was appointed who was to make life miserable for the members of the team. Her name was Louise Grimoldi and she was a bitter and vituperative person. She hated her parents, her ex-husband and many people around her. Her method for evaluating students was to ask team members to tell her everything negative about the students in their clinical groups. She seemed to be very negative in her attitude toward me and I discussed this problem with Mike. He told me how he had worked out a similar relationship with a person he had worked with. Mike suggested that I ask Louise if we could discuss the tension that I was feeling in our relationship and try to work it out together. I arranged to meet with her and told her that I felt some antagonism from her and perhaps we could discuss the problem and try to work it out. When we met she looked me straight in the eye and said, "My psychiatrist says that I resent everything about you." I was stunned, but figured that she resented me because I had a loving husband and children, an earned doctorate and now was on the same level as she was even though I had not worked for twenty years as she had. She had many years of professional experience, but had no husband, no children and had not yet earned a doctorate. She didn't even have a close relationship with her parents. I concluded that Mike's method was not going to work in this case.

For the rest of the semester I put up with her caustic remarks and negative attitude toward everyone. I let out my frustrations each evening by punching Steve's punching bag a number of times before preparing the family dinner. Fortunately, at the end of the semester, Dean Hosford made Louise the leader for Team IV and gave me the leadership of Team I so I no longer had to deal with Louise on a daily basis.

In July of 1976, we went on our last family camping trip. Cindy and Steve were busy with summer jobs, so we took only Peter and Cathy with us to Lake Sebago in Maine. We did not take the camping trailer, only two small tents. We were therefore able to camp in the woods right next to the lake, which was crystal clear and wonderful for swimming. We went sightseeing, ate lots of lobsters and rented a boat for water skiing. Mike and Peter mastered the water skis and Cathy almost made it up on them. I didn't even try. We stopped at Rockport on our way up and back from Maine and visited my mother there.

We left Cathy with my mother, "Grandma Ruth", for a week and she had a wonderful time. She spent another ten days with Grandma Ruth in Kensington in August and loved every minute of her visit. Grandma Ruth spoiled her royally, feeding her whatever she craved and allowing her to read in bed as late as she wanted every night. Peter went to wrestling camp in August and Steve came up to Rockport with us for the last two weeks of August, when Beverly joined us with her boys.

At the end of the summer Steve decided that he would like to transfer to a four-year college. He and Mike researched a number of colleges and decided on Tampa University, which had a wrestling team, and Steve liked the prospect of living in the Florida climate. He applied and was accepted by Tampa University, which accepted all of his credits from Middlesex Community College. He was excited at the prospect of living in Florida where he could scuba dive occasionally and he decided to major in marine biology. Unfortunately the wrestling program was discontinued after he arrived at the college.

I started the fall semester at City College as leader of Team I. The other faculty members on the team were very supportive of me and we became a tightly knit group who worked most cooperatively with one another. The team consisted of five full time faculty: Tom Nolan, Sonja Liggett, Karen Lee, Diane Rendon and me. We also had two excellent adjunct clinical instructors, Ellie Lundeen and Lucile Belgrave. It was such a pleasure to work with all of them. In the spring term, City College decided to upgrade the clinical laboratory of the nursing program. I was appointed to the committee to develop our new laboratory. The committee visited a number of colleges with state-of-the-art laboratory centers to see some models that would help us revamp our lab. We visited the University of Delaware, Hampton Institute and the University of Maryland. We also asked the director of the nursing resource center at Wagner College to come to City College to tell us about their center. It was a fascinating project and we met many dynamic deans and lab coordinators from the different colleges. We came back with some excellent ideas on how to improve our own laboratory center

Peter was the star of the Bound Brook Wrestling Team in the spring semester of 1977. There was a great camaraderie among the parents of the wrestlers on the team. The adults used to meet at each other's homes for refreshments after the meets while the wrestlers went to the Riverview Diner to binge on their favorite treats. This was Peter's big year as a wrestler. He had grown in height and was having a difficult time getting down to his assigned weight of 122 pounds for the team. He was always hungry and irritable. Mike decided that 122 pounds was too low a weight for Peter's health and he informed the coach that Peter must go up to the 129-pound spot on the team. Peter was the best wrestler on the team and undefeated in dual meets for the past two years, so the coach agreed to let him wrestle at 129 pounds. He continued to be undefeated through the season and his fan club was growing. At the end of the season he won the district and regional championships and was eligible to go to the state competition.

We drove down to Princeton University to watch Peter wrestle in the New Jersey High School Wrestling Championship tournament. Jadwin Gymnasium was packed with fans from all over the state. After the first two days Peter was still in the running. On the last day, he wrestled Ray Belleran from Madison Center High School in the semi-finals. It was a very close match, but Peter won one to nothing. In the finals Peter was slated to wrestle Dave Tennez from Westfield High School. The suspense was nerve-wracking as two closely matched wrestlers battled. Peter defeated Tennez by a score of six to four. We were stunned. The fans went wild, as did his parents. The previous state champion from Bound Brook had been Mario Gentile in 1959, eighteen years before. Peter's reign as the latest state champion from Bound Brook lasted for twenty-seven years.

When Peter was declared the state champion at 129 pounds, Mike and I decided on the spot that we would ask all his fans to our house to celebrate. It was a great party and no work for me, as we bought ready-to-eat food. We bought Kentucky Fried Chicken, fruit cup, snack foods and many flavors of ice cream and sauces, along with soft drinks, beer and champagne, all of which we picked up on the way home. I didn't have to worry about cleaning the house, as it was a spur of the moment affair and everyone was too excited to notice the dust. Sixty people came to Peter's victory party. The coaches, parents of wrestlers and other faithful fans came and Peter invited wrestlers from the Bridgewater and Basking Ridge teams as well as all the Bound Brook wrestlers. A number of girlfriends also came. It was an exhilarating evening! The Bound Brook wrestlers elected Pete and Pat Gleason as co-captains of the team for their senior year. In the fall of 1977, Peter was elected president of his senior class.

Early in May, Mike and I took Cathy with us to Charleston, South Carolina to attend our nephew's wedding. We drove down the day before the wedding and had dinner with his parents, Mike's sister, Shirley, and her husband, Ed Saxby. It was a nice family gathering where we visited with Shirley and Ed's children, whom we seldom saw. On the way home we visited Myrtle Beach for the night and went swimming with Cathy the next day. Farther on we spent a night at Cape Hatteras and again went swimming the following morning. The trip was fun and we enjoyed sharing it with Cathy.

I met with my boss at City College, Dean Hosford, at the beginning of the fall term. I asked her for a raise as I was making a pittance of a salary. She was a woman who talked in circles to avoid coming to closure on any issue. She skirted the question of increasing my salary by telling me that I did not have any teaching experience, even though I had a doctorate. Whenever I left her office I was baffled as to what she had actually told me. She was very good at keeping me at bay and not giving me a definite answer. Her solution to avoiding a financial raise for me was to change my position to Team III where I would be teaching senior nursing students. The leader of Team III was Dr. Georgie Labadie, a charming person and a delight to work with. The faculty members of Team III were fine people and I enjoyed working with them. We found the senior students both challenging and talented.

The entire nursing faculty spent the year working on a comprehensive report for the upcoming National League of Nursing accreditation visit. Dean Hosford had hired a consultant to help the faculty develop a new conceptual model for the curriculum. The consultant died soon after she came to the college and her assistant tried to carry on for her. However, the assistant did not understand the model that the consultant was introducing. The assistant had a huge map of the model that she used to bring to the faculty meetings, but she never really explained the model. She told us privately that she was trying to avoid a meeting with the dean, because if the dean asked her to explain the model and saw that she couldn't do it, she would fire her. That is exactly what happened. After she left, the faculty continued to meet and had lengthy discussions on what should be included in the report.

Mike and I gave another open house at the beginning of 1978. Sixty guests came and we all enjoyed the evening festivities. I prepared 200 turkey sandwiches on party rolls, five loaves of date-nut bread, 200 Swedish meatballs and a couple of hams. There were cheeses, dips and other snacks and the affair ended with a sheet cake and coffee. On January 21st we gave a big dinner for Dick Weber's fiftieth birthday. We set up a table for twenty in the family room and had a rip-roaring party for "King Richard", who seemed very pleased at being so honored.

The Bound Brook wrestling season was very exciting for Peter in his senior year. He was really pumped up as the first New Jersey wrestling champion from Bound Brook High School in 18 years. He had previously been more reticent in his attitude as a team member, but now his confidence was at its height. His enthusiasm was catching and the team was on a winning streak. Peter continued to be undefeated and again won the district and regional wrestling championships. The New Jersey High School Wrestling Championship tournament was held at Princeton University in the middle of March. The event that everyone was excited about was the match between Pete Schuyler and Darryl Burley, a wiry athlete with an extraordinary sense of balance. Wrestling came as a natural skill to Darryl, while Peter got to the top through extensive training and conditioning. Peter had amazing control when he was on top of an opponent, in fact, it was almost impossible for a wrestler to get out from under him. Peter was a defending state champion, but Darryl had fantastic balance and skill. Darryl defeated Peter in an extremely tense match and took the state championship title with a seven-to-five score. Darryl won the outstanding wrestler award for his win over Peter. We took Peter and his coaches to dinner at the Nassau Inn after the tournament, but it was a very somber meal.

Both Peter and Darryl went to Lehigh University that fall and vied for the same weight class on the wrestling team. They became best friends and roomed together for the first three years at college. The coach was able to juggle their weight classes so that they were both able to wrestle on the team while they were at Lehigh. Even though they were rivals on the team, they became such good friends that each one was in the other's wedding party after they finished college. Darryl's natural wrestling skill enabled him to win first place in the National Collegiate Athletic Association (NCAA) wrestling tournament in his freshman year at Lehigh and again in his senior year. Peter won third place at the NCAA tournament in his senior year.

In March of 1978, Mike and I visited Florida for the first time in our lives. We went to see Steve at Tampa University and found him enjoying his life there. He took us on a tour of the college and the surrounding area. There were lovely homes built on lagoons in Tampa and we thought it a beautiful place to live. We spent one day at Disney World with Steve and we felt like a bunch of kids trying all the rides in the park. My favorite exhibit was a history of all the Disney cartoon movies starting with the earliest Mickey Mouse cartoons. We rode over London in Captain Hook's pirate ship and visited Treasure Island. We marveled at how real the talking mannequin of Abraham Lincoln was and enjoyed seeing the sparkling parade at the end of the day. We had a wonderful visit with Steve and felt that he seemed content at Tampa University. After leaving Tampa, we visited my foster sister, Donna Hoffman, in Tallahassee, Florida. We had never seen her home and it was nice to be with her in her cute little house.

The final destination of our trip was New Orleans, another place we had never visited and had longed to see. We loved the jazz music and the dancing in the street and cafes on Bourbon Street. We took the trolley out to a big old home for Sunday brunch where a jazz band marched through the rooms playing wonderful music and handing out balloons. We also browsed through the antique shops on Royal Street and found a magnificent statue of Saint George slaying the dragon. It was the largest and most expensive figurine that we had ever considered owning, but we rationalized that we couldn't pass up this opportunity of a lifetime. We bought the statue and I carried it in my lap back on the plane going home. It is our prize possession and always elicits wonder and praise whenever people see it for the first time. Even the grandchildren are impressed by it and love to hear the story of Saint George and the Dragon.

In April the Bound Brook wrestling team held an awards dinner. Peter was presented an award for being the first Bound Brook wrestler ever to be undefeated for four years in high school dual meets. He also won Most Valuable Player for both cross-country and wrestling at the final sports dinner of the year and he won the Scholar Athlete Award for the senior class.

Peter had no trouble being accepted to each of the colleges to which he applied. He first decided to apply to the United States

Military Academy at West Point. He befriended New Jersey congresswoman, Millicent Fenwick, by volunteering to help restore the historic cemetery next to the Bound Brook Library and she appointed him to West Point. The head wrestling coach there was delighted when Peter was accepted to the military academy. The coach became such a fan of Peter that he and his family came to dinner at our house several times. We were pleased with Peter's interest in West Point as his grandfather was a graduate of the academy and the cost would be free. However, in Peter's senior year he received a number of acceptances to other colleges, some of which offered him full scholarships, including Syracuse University and Louisiana State University. He was also accepted at Princeton and Lehigh Universities. The factor that decided Peter on which college to attend was his evaluation of the head coach of its wrestling team. Through attendance at summer wrestling camps, Peter became a great admirer of Coach Thad Turner at Lehigh University. Coach Turner visited Peter at our house twice and Peter was sold on having him for his coach. Lehigh, however, offered no athletic scholarships.

When Peter entered college, we would have three children in private colleges, none of whom would be on a scholarship. Many people advised us to push Peter into going to a college with a "free ride", but Mike argued that we would not penalize Peter just because he was offered full scholarships for his outstanding wrestling record. We believed that Peter should have the same open choice as Cindy and Steve had and he chose Lehigh University and Coach Turner. We never regretted our decision to let him go to Lehigh. Coach Turner was one of the greatest role models that Peter could have had. He was a man of great integrity who inspired his wrestlers rather than driving them to win. He had a wry sense of humor and loved to kid Peter who was so naïve that he made a perfect foil for Turner's jokes. Peter adored Coach Turner and kept up his association with him long after he graduated from Lehigh. Mr. Turner helped him find career positions in succeeding years and wrote many fine recommendations for him. Mrs. Turner was also very supportive to Peter and his wife, Dorianne. They named two of their four children after Thad Turner.

By the end of the spring 1978 semester, I was having serious doubts about staying at City College. I loved the students there, but Dean Hosford continued to be evasive about my salary. Louise Grimoldi was also becoming more of a problem. She was obsessed with gaining power and, once she completed her doctorate, she set out to push Dean Hosford out of her position and take over as dean herself. I could see what was happening and knew that if she became the dean, life for the nursing faculty at City College would be miserable. I decided to look for another job. I went for interviews at Bloomfield College and Rutgers University in New Jersey and Columbia University in New York City. I was accepted at all three places and then I saw an ad in the paper for a director of a new graduate program in nursing that was being developed at Wagner College in Staten Island, New York. Mike urged me to apply for the job, but I was afraid that I couldn't handle graduate education. Mike said, "nonsense, your doctoral education has prepared you well for such a position."

With Mike's encouragement, I went to Wagner College for an interview on June 12th and the nursing department called me three days later to offer me the position. I had a big decision to make about the next step in my career. I decided against taking the offers from Bloomfield College and Rutgers University. The salary at Bloomfield was low and the position at Rutgers was funded by a two-year grant, which did not seem propitious for my future there. The final decision was between Columbia University and Wagner College. Columbia was my alma mater and Dr. McClintock, my doctoral advisor, was on the search committee there. These two facts made Columbia look attractive to me. However, Columbia was in Manhattan and meant a long commute for me, neither of which circumstances appealed to me. Also, the nursing department was an independent unit that was isolated from the rest of the college, just as it had been at City College. Therefore, it would be difficult to be a part of the wider college community as a nursing professor at Columbia.

Wagner's offer seemed challenging and the college, itself, appealed to me. Wagner was a small college where I could be involved with all the departments, and become a member of college-wide committees. My old friend from college, Ellie Zuckerman, advised me to revisit both Columbia and Wagner, walk around each campus and decide at which one I felt more comfortable. I followed her advice and felt that Wagner had a beautiful campus where all departments seemed to work together for the good of the college. Wagner was also an easy commute for me with ample parking in a suburban setting. I went for a second interview at Wagner and was immediately charmed by the chairman of the nursing department, Dr. Mildred Nelson. She was eager for me to come to Wagner and she became my best friend there for over 23 years.

On June 23rd, I went to City College, handed in my resignation and cleaned out my office. Dean Hosford called me at home and offered to match the salary of any college that made me an offer. I thanked her, but replied that I had made up my mind to leave. A few days later I accepted the position at Wagner College and wrote to the other colleges to thank them for their offers.

11

Career Shifts

Before I started my new job at Wagner College, I spent the month of July visiting the National League of Nursing headquarters in New York City on weekdays to research models of graduate programs at other colleges. These models gave me information on how to construct a masters program in nursing at Wagner. The College hired me on August 1st, six weeks before the fall term began, so that I could prepare for the new masters program. I spent much of my time in the college library ordering new books and periodicals that were necessary for graduate study in nursing. I developed good relationships with the library staff, who were most accommodating in procuring the materials that I ordered. I also used the time to market the new program. I sent letters and brochures to over 200 hospital administrators and nursing deans in the New York metropolitan area. Our first graduate class was made up of forty students from Staten Island, Brooklyn, Manhattan and New Jersey.

Early in September I worked with the nursing faculty to complete the masters program requirements and develop the individual courses for the new program. We decided that students would have to complete 42 credits, including a thesis, to earn a master's degree in nursing. The program would include a base of liberal arts courses and opportunities for students to develop expertise in both a clinical area and a functional area of practice. In the clinical area students could choose either *Advanced Nursing Care of the Adult* or A*dvanced Nursing Care of the Child and Parent.* In the functional area students could choose either *Administration* or *Teaching and Curriculum.*

The program began in the fall of 1978 with 37 part-time and three full-time students. The first semester consisted of four core courses, one on theory, one on health assessment, one on advanced human physiology and one on management. Professor Kathleen Ahern developed and taught *Health Assessment,* Dr. Mildred Nelson developed and taught *Advanced Human Physiology* and the Economics Department taught a management course. I developed the first theory course, *Theoretical Components of Nursing I* and thoroughly enjoyed the experience. I reviewed my reading assignments from college and our book group selections and came up with a required reading list of books by both classical and modern authors. These authors dealt with the four key concepts of nursing: human beings, environment, health and nursing. I conducted my class in seminar style. Students were expected to read the weekly assignments and be prepared to discuss and analyze the content of the readings. In the first three weeks of the course they were assigned readings reflecting theories of classic writers on human nature, including St. Augustine's *Confessions,* Locke's *On the Conduct of Human Understanding* and Rousseau's *Emile.* Next, students were given a list of modern writers on human nature and told to choose one book to report on to the class. Each student gave a five-minute report on his or her author in the next two classes and brief discussions were held on each writer's theory. During the sixth and seventh weeks, students were assigned readings of two famous nursing theorists, Florence Nightingale and Martha Rogers. Both nursing theorists wrote of the effect of nursing and environment on patients' health. At this point in the course, students were required to write a paper on the nature of human beings, including what constitutes health for them, how the environment can affect their health and how nurses can promote their health.

In the second half of the course, students read books by modern nursing theorists. The second paper assignment required the students to compare two nursing models in relation to a nurse and patient situation. Students were to describe the nursing process for the patient within the framework of the two nursing models. Most of the papers were well written with excellent references and perceptive analysis. The papers were a delight to read. The course ended with a final exam. I was very pleased to see how diligent and thoughtful the students were, even though most of them were working, supporting families and going to school all at once.

For the second semester of the program I developed and taught *Theoretical Components of Nursing II*, which allowed students to expand their knowledge of the key concepts of nursing systems. Creative nursing practices were explored in light of theories of change and leadership. Political, social and ethical factors that influence nursing practice were studied and emphasis was placed on how nurses could influence local and federal legislation concerning nursing and health care practices. Reading assignments for the first half of the course were books on theories and models of change, group process, communication, leadership and decision making. In class students divided into groups to debate or role-play case studies, using a variety of models. The first paper assigned was on the topic of leadership. Students were required to read a biography of a leader and to analyze the leader using the theories and models that they had studied in the first half of the course. The papers were well written and interesting. The second half of the course dealt with nursing leadership in a variety of situations. The goal of the second paper was to identify a problem in nursing practice and develop an innovative plan of intervention and evaluation using specific theories and models to analyze the situation. Again the papers were excellent and again there was a final exam. These two courses were very interesting and stimulating both for the students and for me.

In the second semester students took *Advanced Nursing Research* and the introductory courses in their chosen functional and clinical areas of the masters program. I developed and taught *Teaching and Curriculum Construction in Nursing* and I also taught in the *Advanced Nursing Care of the Child and Parent* course. Dr. Edith Schmidt developed and taught *Administration Principles Applied to Nursing Settings* and Dr. Nelson developed and taught *Advanced Nursing Care of the Adult.* Dr. Mary Yanni developed and taught *Advanced Nursing Research.*

In the third semester of the program graduate faculty supervised students in teaching and administrative practice at various nursing schools and hospitals. Students were required to make their own arrangements with the agencies where they carried out their practice. The graduate faculty members were also advisors to individual students who were writing their theses in their last semester of the program. I grew very close to students as I observed them in practice teaching at other institutions and counseled them while they were writing their theses. Our three full-time graduate students graduated at the end of the second year and we had a party for them. The number of graduate students enrolled in the nursing masters program increased each year and the college considered the program a success. Our students came from different backgrounds and areas and brought a great variety of clinical, theoretical and personal experiences to the program. The masters program is still flourishing 26 years later. Several years after its inception, we added a nurse practitioner specialty to the program, which became the most popular area of concentration.

Less than a year after my arrival at Wagner College, the nursing department elected me as chairperson. Mildred Nelson had been the chair for five years and decided to step down, so the nursing faculty asked me to run for her position and they elected me as chair of both the undergraduate and graduate programs at the end of May 1979. My term began at the end of July. That summer I invited the nursing faculty and their families to a picnic in our backyard. We put up a tent and supplied plenty of food and games. It was a good way to build closer relationships with the faculty and everyone seemed to have a good time.

Mildred Nelson graciously offered to be my mentor when I took over as chair of the department. She advised me to make a pile of items that I did not know how to handle and once a week we would go over the pile together. As time went on the pile grew shorter until I could handle all the problems that came to my office. The nursing faculty members were very cooperative and supportive and I enjoyed being the chair. There were a number of department committees and everyone carried out their assignments willingly and responsibly. The nursing faculty worked together as a team and we socialized in our department lunchroom over lunch and coffee breaks. We felt that food was a stimulating asset and always had refreshments at our department meetings and workshops. We held annual workshops for a week at the end of each academic year to review the curriculum and prepare periodic reports for New York State and the National League of Nursing accreditation. We also gave a review course for the State Board Examinations each summer.

In early 1980, several faculty members were fired by the College, causing many of the faculty to become more active in the union. Meetings were held in a local church and I observed how the union leaders pushed faculty to strike in order to enhance the union's power, with little regard for the individual faculty members and how they would be affected by a strike. The union leaders managed to get the faculty agitated so that they voted to strike. I voted against a strike and refused to take part in it. The rest of the nursing faculty formed a solid block in support of the strike. They demonstrated and blocked non-strikers from entering the campus, but they asked me to come on campus and talk to the nursing students to reassure them that we would make it possible for them to graduate and take their state board examinations. The strike collapsed when the court decided that faculty members were part of management and therefore ineligible to organize.

As chair of the nursing department I participated in a number of professional organizations. My favorite organization was the Deans and Directors of the Greater Metropolitan Area. It was a group of nurses who were college deans and hospital administrators. They worked together to coordinate the education and practice of nurses. I was elected treasurer of the association and, as such, served on the executive counsel during my membership. We met once a month to discuss various issues concerning nurses. One of my favorite programs that we presented was a panel on *Bridging the Gap between Nursing Education and Practice.* I was the moderator of the panel and the program was well received. Other professional groups that I belonged to included the New York State Deans of Baccalaureate Nursing Programs, of which I was the secretary, Deans and Directors of Staten Island and the American Association of Colleges of Nursing, which met periodically in Washington D.C. I remained on these committees during the five years that I was chair of the nursing department.

During the 1980's I was frequently asked to speak at Wagner and other colleges and organizations. Soon after coming to Wagner, I spoke at the college's Faculty Forum. I spoke on *The Mission of the University* and I was very nervous about talking in front of my colleagues. I gave several more talks at the Faculty Forum over my years at Wagner and became more comfortable in succeeding years. In 1981 I spoke on Florence Nightingale at the inception at Wagner of Sigma Theta Tau, nursing's national honor society. I was also asked to speak on *Historical Studies in*

Nursing at Columbia University that same year. In 1983 I was invited to be the key speaker at Emory University School of Nursing Research Day, the theme of which was Florence Nightingale. I gave two long lectures during the day: *Nightingale: Paragon of Reformers* in the morning and *Nightingale: Philosopher with a Mission* in the afternoon. Mike came with me for moral support. In 1986 I spoke to the American Association of University Women (AAUW) Legislative Committee on *Dr. Mary Belle Harris,* a reformer of conditions in women's prisons; to the New Jersey Historical Society on *Women of Newark's Past;* and to Muhlenberg Hospital School of Nursing on *The Integrated Curriculum.* The next year I spoke to the Medical History Society of New Jersey on *Supreme Sacrifice*, a biography of Clara Maass, the nurse who lost her life as part of an experiment to find the cause of yellow fever.

One of the reasons that I chose the position at Wagner was that I wanted to become involved in the entire college, working on committees and projects that included faculty from many different disciplines. Soon after I arrived at Wagner, I heard about the Interdisciplinary Studies (IDS) program that all students were required to take in their first three years at the college. There were five courses in the IDS program: *The City; Shaping of the Modern Mind; Self and Society; Work; and Science, Technology and Human Values.* A sixth course was under construction. A dozen or more faculty from different disciplines worked on the creation of each IDS course. They discussed at length what should be included in the course content and even what the name of the course should be. Each course was divided into ten or twelve classes and the faculty members who created each course also taught the classes of the course.

The sixth course was still in the process of being created, so I asked to participate in its development. It was to be a course about art. After much discussion, we agreed on a name for the course, IDS 302—*Apollo and Dionysius, Alternative Modes of Perception in the Creative Process*. The course was designed to awaken in students an appreciation for two basic ways in which people perceive and express reality. The course dealt with both the rational, structured and logical perspective represented by Apollo, as well as the innovative, emotional and paradoxical perspective represented by Dionysius. The first half of the course consisted of reading assignments contrasting the rational and emotional sides of the creative experience followed by class discussions. Then, as a demonstration that every creative experience is an example of how these two perspectives intertwine, each student was asked to complete a creative project during the last section of the course. While working on their projects, students met individually with their professors to discuss their progress. In the last weeks of classes, each student presented his or her project to the rest of the class. The projects turned out to be very original and creative and the class and I thoroughly enjoyed the different presentations.

After five years as chair of the nursing department, I decided to retire from administration and become more active in other areas. I became involved with a second IDS course, IDS 201— *Self and Society*. I joined the summer workshop for the course and began teaching it in the fall of 1984. The course was divided into two parts. In the first half students read and discussed how society influences the development of human beings. Students discussed theories of human nature by authors such as Freud, Skinner and Rogers. Then they read and discussed theories about societal influences on people by authors such as Goffman, Linton and Marx. In the second half of the course students studied and discussed readings and films about concrete issues in society such as inequalities, conflict, aggression and mental health.

For the next six years I taught IDS 201 and 302 plus graduate and undergraduate nursing courses. I taught obstetrics to undergraduates in the classroom and the clinical area. My clinical class of ten students worked in Lutheran Hospital in Brooklyn in obstetric nursing. I thoroughly enjoyed teaching students in the labor and delivery room as well as in the prenatal clinic and postpartum area. I also taught IDS classes in summer school and participated in workshops for both classes every summer.

IDS 201 was dominated by two male faculty members who spent their time at the workshops philosophizing with each other instead of preparing the course for the next semester. The women faculty members were frustrated by this behavior. Then another woman faculty member came into the group and a male professor left, giving the women a majority, which they used to vote me in as head of the course. The male faculty members were quite annoyed by this. To add salt to their wounds, in 1988 the faculty from all six IDS courses nominated me to run for the position of Director of the IDS program against the male professor who had formerly been the head of IDS 201. I was elected Director by a vote of 38 to 5. I remained as Director of IDS (later called MDS) for the next ten years.

While I was at Wagner I was elected to a number of college committees including the Graduate Council, Academic Standards Committee, Academic Development Committee and the Faculty Council, the major policy making group at the College. I served as chairperson of the Faculty Affairs subcommittee of the council for seven years, and our major project was the revision of the Faculty Handbook and the Personnel Handbook. In 1987 I was appointed to the College Curriculum Integration and Revision Committee and in 1989 I became a member of the Committee on Academic Structure and Governance of the College

I was hired by Wagner College as an associate professor and was granted tenure in my fifth year there. To be promoted to full professor required a new publication on my part. My friend and neighbor, Ella Handen, was aware that I needed to publish again and took me to a study group at Drew University where we both became part of a project to create a book on the lives of New Jersey women. I researched and wrote biographies of six women that were published in *Past and Present: Lives of New Jersey Women*. These biographies were of Dr Stella Stevens Bradford (1871-1959), Caroline Bamberger Fuld (1864-1944), Dr. Mary Belle Harris (1874-1957), Clara Louise Maass (1876-1901), Dr. Louise Pearce (1885-1959) and Ellen Culver Potter (1871-1958). This publication resulted in my promotion to full professor and to several invitations to speak about these women.

During the 1980's Wagner's financial condition deteriorated steadily and in 1988 the Board of Trustees fired the president, Dr. Sam Frank. The college searched for a new president and selected Dr. Norman Smith, who took over in a time of crisis. During the next 13 years, he managed to turn the college around and make it highly successful. To conserve expenses, Dr. Smith decided to choose faculty members for his top administrators rather than hire outsiders. He offered the position of Vice President for Academic Affairs to Dr. Rogg from the Sociology Department and he asked Mildred Nelson and me to be deans. Mildred was appointed to the position of Dean of Academic Services and Registrar and I was appointed as Associate Dean of Academic Affairs. We both left the Nursing Department and began as college administrators in the fall of 1989.

During the 1980's Mike experienced several changes in his career. He had been with US Lines since 1974 under two supervisors. His first boss was Bart Wilcox, who left the company two years later. Wilcox's boss, Richard Madigan, became Mike's new boss. Madigan was young, bright, capable and a demanding boss. Mike flourished under him as he gave him the freedom to do his job independently. Madigan liked to play racquetball with Mike (he always won and Mike took it good-naturedly). Mike had great respect for Madigan and his boss, Ed Heine, president of the company. They were men of integrity and Mike enjoyed working for them both.

In 1980 Malcolm McLain purchased U.S. Lines. He was originally the founder and president of McLain Trucking Company and then became owner of Sea Land Services Shipping Company. After selling Sea Land, McLain acquired U.S. Lines and immediately began to transfer his own personnel to top administrative positions in the company. Mike hoped that McLain's intention to replace the top U.S. Lines officers would not extend down to his level, but his hopes were thwarted and he lost his position. Previous to Mikes's leaving U.S. Lines, a co-worker of his, Jim Theoharidas, had left to become president of Hellenic Lines, a Greek shipping company in New York City. Mike called his friend who brought him in to meet the top officers of Hellenic Lines. They hired Mike as general manager of financial services.

The financial reporting system at Hellenic Lines was archaic. Almost all modern financial reporting at that time was based on reporting for a period of time, but Hellenic Lines still used the old fashioned shipping company system for reporting based on voyages. Revenues and expenses were associated with each separate voyage of a ship. No financial reporting was possible until the voyage had been completed, which could be several weeks after the financial transitions took place. Mike convinced the company management that good cost control was impossible with such a system. He was encouraged to set up a modern system of financial reporting and control. Mike considered this an exciting challenge and thoroughly enjoyed the opportunity to update the company's system.

It was a time when the shipping industry was enjoying a lull in activity. Revenues were down throughout the industry, resulting in a substantial drop in profits. Because of the reduced level of business for the shipping companies, the cost of shipbuilding had also dropped substantially. The owner of Hellenic Lines decided that this was an ideal time to contract for the building of several new ships, taking advantage of the reduced prices then available. But, unfortunately, he carried this policy too far and subjected the company to extremely high construction obligations. The company was highly leveraged, being heavily indebted to several New York banks. When the company contracted for the new ship building program, the banks became extremely uneasy and decided to call in their debt. The company was unable to meet these obligations and was forced into bankruptcy. The banks seized the company's vessels and sold them at auction, terminating its operations. All the employees were immediately thrown out of work, including Mike. Mike had spent two years developing what he felt was the best financial reporting system in the industry, only to see the company liquidated just as the system was being implemented. The disappointment of seeing his pet system aborted was almost as devastating as losing his job.

When Hellenic Lines went out of business, Mike decided that he no longer wanted to be involved with a business over which he had no control. He was in his early fifties, which was not the best age to be looking for a job. He knew that he would have to retire sometime and he wanted to set his own time for that retirement and not be at the mercy of some large company that would decide it for him. He decided that it would be a good time to go into his own business. Since he had no experience in small business, he decided that operating a franchise business would be the best route to take.

Mike looked at a variety of franchises and very seriously considered Sir Speedy, a printing and copying franchise. However, he finally decided that using his experience and talent in financial management would be a wiser move. So he investigated a number of franchises that offered financial services to small business owners. There were several franchises specializing in this area. He narrowed his choices down to two: General Business Services located in Rockville Maryland and Financial Management Services with headquarters in Jackson Mississippi. He visited both firms, spending a full day at each, and finally decided on General Business Services (GBS). GBS offered their franchisees complete freedom in how they organized and ran their own offices and this especially appealed to him. One of the factors that persuaded Mike to go with GBS was his visit with Tony Humphreys, the regional manager for the New Jersey area. He had his own franchise with GBS and a very lucrative business. Mike was impressed with him and the success of his practice and felt that Tony would be a big help to him in developing his own business.

There was a hefty fee for obtaining a franchise from GBS. We discussed how to pay for this fee and Mike suggested taking out a home equity loan. We had just finished paying off the mortgage on our house and I was opposed to getting another loan on our house. So Mike cashed in a life insurance policy to pay for part of the fee. He assured me that we had enough other financial resources to not only pay off the rest of the fee, but to cover our living expenses while he developed the business. Mike signed the franchise agreement with GBS in January 1984. We went to Maryland to stay with my parents while Mike took the orientation course at GBS headquarters in Rockville.

There were 15 trainees at the orientation and Mike was the only one who stayed with GBS for more than five years. The value of the franchise was especially important during the first years of a new business, so it was understandable that most of the trainees dropped out of GBS once they had established their businesses. Mike, however, felt that tax law interpretations were very complex and that new tools of financial analysis were constantly being developed so that is was very difficult for a single practitioner to remain up to date without the support of a larger organization. To be a first rate financial analyst and tax preparer, in Mike's opinion, required joining an organization that would provide current research in taxes and financial analysis. He was always glad that he stayed with GBS and most of the other trainees who dropped out were not successful in their own businesses after they left.

Mike was well qualified to run his own business in finance. Prior to his experience in the Philippines, he had taught himself advanced accounting as preparation for his position as Treasurer of Union Carbide Philippines. This knowledge gave him the background that he needed to run his own business in finance. In addition to his earned MBA in Finance, he took courses for certification in seven other areas after he acquired his own business. Several of these certifications involved the equivalent of one to two years of graduate study.

Mike looked around the Bound Brook area for a site for his new business. He located an office of about 550 square feet on the corner of Union and Vosseller Avenues in Bound Brook. It was a spacious and clean office in a new building in a busy part of town. There was a nice view from the office and it was across the street from a first rate diner where we ate many meals when we both worked late. Mike was able to arrange a sliding scale of rental payments. He was unable to pay the full rent when he started his business, so the landlord agreed to start off at a much lower rate with the rent escalating a small amount each month for the first year. Mike was able to get nice office furniture at a very reasonable price from Hellenic Lines after they had gone out of business. Our son, Steve, later built a partition to divide one third of the room from the rest of the office so that Mike could have a private office to consult with his clients.

The service that Mike offered was financial analysis and business advice to small business owners to make them become more successful. He also provided accounting services and tax preparation and spent a good deal of time on these services. What differentiated his business, however, was the emphasis on financial analysis and business consulting that he offered. His competition was from accountants, but few of them offered the extensive consultation and financial analysis that he offered.

Mike started out with no clients, so his first job was that of a salesman. He tried three different approaches to selling his services. First he researched new businesses that had been recently registered in the county records. I helped with this research in my spare time. When I brought him a list of new businesses from the county courthouse, he would call each owner and offer his services. Many of these prospects sounded interested in Mike's services and he visited them to explain what he could do for them. However, the vast majority of new businesses that were registered were either half hearted part time ventures or attempts by people who were not capable of operating businesses. Even when these new businesses were sincere attempts by capable people, they were usually short of funds and were generally not profitable clients.

The second approach was the door-to-door system, in which Mike would go to an office park and knock on one door after another to inquire if they had any interest in his services. This was the most time consuming approach and frequently the owner of the business was not available. If the owners were available, however, Mike was in a position to explain his services and prick their interest. Mike spent many full days pursuing this approach and developed a number of long term clients this way, but it consumed a tremendous amount of his time.

The third approach, the one that Mike eventually settled on as his major prospecting tool, was to write a letter catered to one type of business and then mail the letter to about 100 businesses in that specialty. About a week later he would call these businesses and attempt to set up a meeting where he could explain his services in more detail. The idea was to establish enough interest through the letter and phone call that the prospect would be willing to meet with him. It was at the meetings with the prospects that Mike would try to convince them of the value of his services.

Mike gradually developed statistics for this third approach that he used to plan his marketing strategy. He found that out of 100 businesses contacted, he would secure, on average, ten appointments to meet with the owners. Of these ten appointments he could count on securing one client. In my opinion, only someone with Mike's patience and determination could ever have survived this process. Prospecting became a game of statistics. Instead of considering a turn down a rejection, Mike began to think of it as a step toward eventual acceptance. He would say, "Only nine more calls until I get an acceptance." This was characteristic of Mike's optimistic nature. Mike also secured some clients from other accountants. His friend, Bill Woldin, who was gradually retiring, referred some excellent clients to Mike and a fellow GBS franchisee, who was giving up his business, gave him four more clients.

Most new GBS franchisees worked out of their homes and did not hire employees in order to keep their expenses down. Mike had a different approach. He felt that a separate office was important to present a more professional appearance and to avoid the distractions of home activities. He rented an office at the very beginning of his practice. He also decided that his time was needed for prospecting and serving his clients, so he hired a clerical employee as soon as he had a few clients. It took a lot longer to develop his business than he had planned. It was March 15th before he secured his first client and it was over two years before he began to make money.

Mike had assured me when he started his business that we had enough resources to last until the business became profitable and that we would not have to re-mortgage our house. But by the end of the first year while he was still losing money, he told me that it would be necessary to take out a home equity loan. He felt bad that he had to renege on his promise to me, but by that time I was agreeable to whatever he had to do. In the third year Mike's business began to improve and he had enough clients to make a reasonable profit.

Several of Mike's clients became personal friends. One such client was Herbert Patullo. Herbie operated an attractive restaurant in town, Patullo's Tavern, from the early 1950's until he retired in 2000. Mike told me that one of the best marketing opportunities in his business was the fact that there are a large number of mediocre accountants in the world. Herbie currently had such an accountant, and, after getting to know Mike as a fellow Rotarian, he decided to shift his business to Mike. Herbie was concerned about his records remaining confidential and he had heard that Mike was very conscientious about maintaining the confidentiality of his clients' businesses. Mike provided Herbie with accounting service, financial consultation and personal financial planning. Their business relationship blossomed into a strong personal friendship.

In later years Herbie asked Mike to become the treasurer of the Washington Camp Ground Association, a local historic group, and to join the board of trustees of the Swan Historical Foundation. Patullo's Tavern became our favorite place to visit as Herbie provided dance music from local bands on the weekends. We looked forward to dancing every Saturday night and we also hosted family parties in his garden room on Mother's Days and other holidays.

Another of Mike's clients, Bob Fazen, and his wife, Lynn, became close personal friends. Bob, a veteran army officer, decided to set up his own real estate management business when he retired. He acquired as clients several owners of large

commercial buildings in New York City. He was responsible
for leasing the office space, maintaining the buildings and
overseeing any improvements to the properties. One of his
largest clients was a Japanese company that had purchased the
building at 555 Broadway. The company required detailed
financial statements on its operations and Mike's office prepared
these reports for Bob. The design of this reporting system and
the relations with the Japanese owner, including the translation
into Japanese yen, provided an interesting challenge for Mike.
His office communicated with the office in Tokyo and Mike
met with these officers at his office when they came to the
United States.

Several years later, Bob acquired a major new client who insisted
that his own accountants prepare all the reports for his property.
So Bob had to terminate the accounting work that Mike's office
had handled for him. However, Mike continued his service
of tax and financial consultation to Bob. Later Mike saw
samples of the reports that the new accounting firm prepared
and he felt these reports were far inferior to the ones that he
had prepared.

Another interesting client who became a friend was Jim
Beatty, the owner of the Union Avenue Pharmacy in Bound
Brook. Mike acquired him as a client when Jim decided
that he was not receiving good analysis and advice from his
current accountant. Jim asked Mike to take over his account
and Mike provided him not only with monthly accounting
reports, but also a system of financial controls which he felt
were a big help to him in managing the business. Mike later
helped Jim arrange the sale of one of his two stores and,
when Jim retired, he helped him sell his main store in a
manner that minimized the taxes incurred. Mike had frequent
meetings with other GBS franchisees in the area and for a
while he was the regional manager for both the New Jersey
and Eastern Pennsylvania regions. He had the responsibility

of training new franchisees and conducting monthly meetings for each region.

A major factor in the success of Mike's practice was Alice Champion, whom he hired as an accounting clerk in the fall of 1986. She stayed with him throughout the rest of his practice and gradually became his office manager. Any small business is required to submit a variety of reports to government agencies and pay various taxes, mostly associated with payroll. Alice handled all this work for Mike's clients. Only if there were unusual questions or problems would Mike become involved. Alice also handled all of the office routine, ordering supplies, paying bills, reconciling bank statements, thus leaving Mike free to spend his time in meeting clients and analyzing clients' problems.

Throughout the time of his practice, Mike continually tried to increase his knowledge and expand the range of services that he offered to clients. He studied to become a certified financial planner and an enrolled agent to allow him to represent clients to the IRS. He also took several courses to become more expert on tax issues. Small business owners typically plan to sell their businesses and use their sale proceeds to provide for their retirement. However, this sale rarely provides enough money for a comfortable retirement. Mike encouraged his clients, therefore, to fund their own retirement plans. Typically clients would agree with his recommendations, but would fail to act on them. So Mike decided to become certified to sell mutual funds so that he could directly implement the plans that he recommended to his clients. He studied arduously, passed a certification exam and acquired a series of brokerage licenses that allowed him to sell mutual funds and publicly traded partnerships. He also studied to become a licensed life insurance producer, which allowed him to sell annuities. Thus he could not only recommend retirement plans to his clients, but could implement a full range of plans as well.

12

Family Celebrations

While Mike and I were undergoing major career shifts, we continued to enjoy good times and celebrations with our family and friends. During 1979 there were a number of very special events to celebrate. Cathy was at the top of her class at Bound Brook High School. Pete had a successful first year on the Lehigh wrestling team. Steve and Cindy graduated from college and Mike celebrated his 25th reunion from Princeton. There were two major wedding anniversaries in June, our 25th and my parents 50th.

Cathy was in the high school play, *Carousel*. We saw both nights of the production and I cried at both of them, as *Carousel* always affects me that way. Cathy was very good in her part and we so enjoyed watching her act and sing. Cathy had been in every high school play since she was in junior high. She was also in every choral presentation over those years. She excelled in academics and we were very proud of her.

During Peter's freshman year on the wrestling team, Lehigh wrestled many of the major teams including Iowa State, Navy, Penn State, Syracuse and Army. The Army meet at West Point was exciting as Peter wrestled the Army captain, a senior, and defeated him in the last few seconds of the match. Mike's father, sister and brother-in-law came to the meet and were amazed to see Peter defeat the captain from their alma mater's team. We introduced Mike's father to the Army coach after the meet and Dad asked the coach why he didn't recruit Peter for the Army team. The coach replied, "I tried, I tried." The Army coach had visited our house several times and was counting on Peter coming to West Point. He was very disappointed when Peter decided to go Lehigh University instead.

Steve graduated from Tampa University at the end of April. We were so excited at his success in college that we took Cindy and Cathy to Florida for his graduation. We also invited Donna and her two daughters, Heidi and Stephanie, to drive over from their home in Tallahassee to join us for the graduation. Mike put us all up at the Travel Lodge in Tampa. In his senior year, Steve had roomed with his friend, Bryan Fellman, in an off-campus apartment complex. Their room was on the second floor overlooking a pool. They enjoyed jumping off the balcony of their room into the pool, which made me quite nervous. His roommate's parents also arrived for graduation, so we took them all out to a Japanese restaurant the first night that we were there. The chef came over to our table and prepared and cooked the meal right on the table. We savored a delicious meal and enjoyed each other's company.

The following day, we took Steve, Cathy and Cindy to Disney World and loved it just as much as we had the year before. When we returned to Tampa, Donna had arrived with Heidi and Stephanie and was waiting for us at the motel. We all sat in our motel room and caught up on everyone's news. On Saturday morning we attended Steve's graduation and cheered louder than anyone there when he marched across the stage to receive his diploma. After lunch we went to Busch-Gardens Amusement Park and ended the day with an elegant dinner at Tampa's most luxurious eating place, the Columbia Restaurant. There was a three-piece band and we ate and danced until the wee hours of the morning. Steve and Heidi amused us by doing the tango as they had seen it done on a television cartoon of the Flintstones. On Sunday we rented a car, bought some sandwiches and soft drinks and took off for Saint Petersburg Beach State Park. We ate, swam, talked and had a great time. I swam to a sandbar and collected some interesting shells. We flew back to New Jersey on Monday morning, having spent one of the most wonderful family weekends in our lives. How proud we were of Steve!

At the beginning of June, Mike and I drove to Princeton to celebrate his 25th reunion. There was an elegant class dinner on Friday night where we saw old friends and sat with Mike's two college roommates at dinner. On Saturday we took the children with us back to Princeton to march in the "P-rade," in which different classes marched with their families in an assortment of costumes. The costume for Mike's class was Chinese kimonos and as they passed each group of spectators, they would all bow instead of giving the traditional Princeton cheer. After the "P-rade" we drove the children home and returned for the spectacular dinner at Jadwin Gymnasium for all of the alumni. Cindy and her class, the graduating seniors, joined in all the reunion activities. Two days later the graduation ceremony was held in front of Nassau Hall. In a time-honored tradition, the graduation speech was given in Latin and then the diplomas were presented to the seniors. We were filled with pride once more for the accomplishments of a child.

Cindy enjoyed the small classes in her major at Princeton with famous scholars such as Carlos Baker, and she wrote an outstanding senior thesis on Charles Dickens. She made lots of friends at college and thoroughly enjoyed the social life at the club that she joined, Dial Lodge. She also enjoyed being on the women's soccer team. Cindy had demonstrated management skills early in her career at Princeton. She worked for the Refreshment Agency, which provided food services for all the athletic events at the college. In her junior year she was appointed Student Director of the agency. Her first assignment in that position was to manage food services for reunions at the end of her junior year. She was able to save enough money from her food services job to pay for a trip to Europe that summer with Linda Meier, her friend from Bound Brook. They visited Paris, Florence, Venice and Rome and had a marvelous time.

Every weekend in June was a celebration for us. The weekend after reunions was our 25th wedding anniversary. The children surprised us when we came home on Friday night with a most original anniversary gift. They took us upstairs to our bedroom and there was a new double bed with a huge red ribbon and bow tied around it. We were amazed and thrilled. To top it off they took us out to dinner. What a great celebration it was! The children told us how they had shopped together for the bed and each one had tried it out. They discussed whether they should get a hard, medium or soft mattress, and Peter convinced them that we would want a soft mattress. It has been the most comfortable bed we could ever have wished for and we still sleep in it every night.

The following day, on the actual date of our anniversary, the Webers and the Handens gave us a magnificent party to which they invited our many friends. It was a gala event and we enjoyed it immensely. There were many toasts made by the children and old friends including John Sheehan and Jack Handen. Mike's father and sister and my parents were there and one interesting photo showed Mike's relatives towering a foot over my parents who looked like elves next to them. The next weekend our family drove to my parents' home in Kensington, Maryland to celebrate their 50th wedding anniversary. My sister-in-law, Carol, had a big picnic in her back yard for all the relatives on Saturday evening and on Sunday Mother and Father gave a reception at their house for the whole family and some friends. A professional photographer took some great pictures of the entire family and we have treasured our copy ever since.

In July we were invited to the wedding of Tom and Simi Long's daughter in Atlanta, Georgia. The Deipnos decided to drive to the wedding together in John Sheehan's big old car. We left Bound Brook on a Thursday and drove to Kensington, Maryland to spend the first night of the trip at my parents' house. After breakfast we resumed our drive. The second night we stayed in Columbia, South Carolina with Bill and Bonnie Schneider, old friends from Union Carbide. On the third day we arrived in Atlanta and drove to the Longs' home. Lucy was a beautiful bride and we enjoyed the reception after the wedding in the Longs' spacious home. We caught up on the Longs' news at a lovely brunch at their house on Sunday morning and then headed back north. We made one more visit, on the way home, with another couple. Marion and Al Stone had lived next to us in a garden apartment in Plainfield, New Jersey when we were first married. Mike and Al both worked at Union Carbide and took turns driving each other to work. Al hated to get up in the morning, so after Marion pushed him out of bed, he would go into the bathroom and go back to sleep on the bathroom rug. They were close friends and frequently invited us over in the evenings to watch their television set, as we didn't own a set of our own at that time. They continually provided snacks all evening and we marveled at how they stayed so thin when they were always eating. We had not seen the Stones in a number of years and were pleased to see them in their new home in a lovely wooded area of North Carolina. After our visit, we drove to Kensington to spend the last night of our trip with my parents. On Monday morning we headed back to Bound Brook and the following day we left for two weeks at Rockport with Mother and the Webers.

In August Mike and I bicycled to the Jersey shore for a long weekend. We stayed at bed and breakfast lodgings and enjoyed swimming and sightseeing along the coast. We bicycled back to Bound Brook after a four-day mini-vacation just for the two of us. We spent the Labor Day weekend at Rockport with the family and the Deipnos, as was our annual custom, and then returned to work.

In September we attended Mike's 30th reunion from Woodrow Wilson High School in Washington DC. In the fall we bicycled to Princeton with the Handens and spent two nights at the Nassau Inn. We enjoyed touring Princeton and eating in charming restaurants, before bicycling home on Sunday morning. We made several of these trips with the Handens over the years. In November our children came home for Thanksgiving and we had our annual family football game before dinner. The family was invited to the Webers for Christmas dinner and on New Year's Eve Mike and I joined the Webers, as always, for dinner and dancing.

We started 1980 by holding a January Jubilee party at our house. Eighty friends came and it was a spectacular affair. I made and served Swedish meatballs, turkey sandwiches, date-nut bread and shrimp dip. We put out two hams for guests to make sandwiches and provided a variety of snack foods such as nuts, cheese and crackers. We topped off the evening with a big sheet cake and coffee. We had regular social dates each month of the year with different groups of friends. On the first Saturday of each month we met with the Deipnos to discuss a book. On the second Saturday we attended a couples group at our church called the Congregates. This church group was purely social and sponsored a dinner followed by fun and games. Each month a different committee planned and carried out the dinner and entertainment. On the third Saturday we attended a play at McCarter Theater in Princeton with our neighborhood friends Jack and Ella Handen. After the play we went out for a late snack and conversation.

We have always enjoyed giving dinner parties for small groups of our friends. My mother had gradually built up our formal china, silver and crystal patterns to fourteen place settings with Christmas and birthday gifts of each pattern. Our table looked beautiful when it was set for a dinner party of twelve or fourteen friends from Wagner, GBS or Bound Brook. After dinner we usually played parlor games such as charades, Likes and Dislikes, Personality or Marriage Quiz. In charades, teams thought up quotations and gave them to members of the opposing team. Team members had to use gestures, with no speaking, to act out the quotations to the other members of their team. Each team member was timed on how long it took for his or her team to guess the quotation. The team that guessed all the quotations in the shortest time won the game. In Likes and Dislikes, the guests were divided into two teams whose members were instructed to write down on paper five things they liked and five things they disliked. The papers for each team were then shuffled and passed back to their team members. The team members took turns reading the papers handed to them. The members of the other team would confer with each other and decide whose likes and dislikes had just been read. The team that figured out correctly the most writers of the papers won a prize. Personality was played in a similar fashion. Team members were asked to imagine themselves as a type of animal, bird, fish, plant, automobile, cartoon character, athlete, piece of furniture, musical instrument and historical figure. They wrote their choices on pieces of paper, which were shuffled and passed back to team members. The papers were read aloud one at a time and the opposite team had to decide whose paper was being read. The team that figured out correctly the most authors of the papers won the prize. The marriage quiz asked guests to identify facts about their spouses such as the maiden names of grandmothers, names of first grade teacher, names of first sweetheart, shoe sizes etc. The couple who answered correctly the most facts about each other's background won a prize. This was a great game for a Valentine's party.

We loved being with all our different friends, but we also loved just being alone with each other. Friday nights were our special nights and, whenever possible, we went out for a movie and dancing. I was so excited when work was over on Fridays and I could rush home to go out with my Mike. We enjoyed our evenings of movies and dancing together from our early dating times throughout our married life.

During the winter and spring season of 1980 we frequently attended Peter's wrestling matches at Lehigh and he did very well. We also attended Youth Sunday at our church to hear Cathy give a sermon as the representative of the Pilgrim Fellowship youth group. She was very impressive. She was very active in the youth group and would later go on to become a minister. Mike and I celebrated our anniversary in June by biking to the Jersey shore and staying in a little motel on the beach.

The Handens joined our family for the July 4th weekend at Rockport and continued this tradition for the next eleven years. The July 4th holiday in Rockport is vintage Americana. There is a parade with fire trucks, bands, homemade floats and children marching in homemade costumes. Prizes are awarded for the best costumes and floats. Clowns ride in the parade in tiny cars squirting the onlookers with water or throwing candy to the children on the side of the road. After the parade people gather on the town beach and listen to patriotic songs from the bandstand. At dusk a tower of railroad ties with an outhouse on the top is set on fire and everyone watches the gigantic bonfire.

We had a busy fall. In September, Mike was elected to the Bound Brook Board of Education and served on it for the next eleven years. On December 22, Mike's father celebrated his 80th birthday with a big party at his daughter's house in Albany. We celebrated Thanksgiving and Christmas with our family and at the end of the year we gave a formal dinner for seven Wagner couples. After dinner we played Likes and Dislikes and it was a most enjoyable evening.

On January 27, 1981 Mike's mother died. She had been a victim of Alzheimer's disease for eleven years. Her death left much sorrow in the hearts of her close family who had enjoyed her delightful personality and loving care in their lives. In the spring Dad married Helen Honnen, a widow of an old army friend. They were to enjoy twelve years together in their senior years. Dad decided to move down to Helen's house on Sullivan's Island, just north of Charleston, South Carolina. Before he sold his Albany house, he asked his two children, Mike and Shirley, to come to the house and chose those items of their mother's belongings that each one of them would like to have. This plan worked out well as Mike and Shirley took turns choosing the items that they wanted and their interests differed greatly so that there were no conflicts. Mike chose the grandfather's clock that he had helped his grandfather wind each week as a child. Mike and I together chose some china and a number of figurines that his mother bought during her years in Paris. We have treasured these gifts and displayed them in our home over the years.

At the end of March, we gave a dinner party for twelve local friends and played the Personality game after dinner. We were delighted with the clever and humorous responses to the questions. We were surprised to learn that even very serious people can enjoy making fun of themselves in such a game. In May our best friend Beverly Weber turned 50. We joined with a number of her friends to give her a special birthday party. We rented a hall and celebrated the event in style. Several groups of friends put on skits to pay tribute to all that she had done for others. Everyone had a great time and Beverly really enjoyed the occasion.

In June, Cathy graduated from Bound Brook High School and gave the graduation speech. She had been accepted into a number of excellent colleges and chose to enroll at Harvard/ Radcliffe College in the fall. She was the fourth generation in my family to attend Radcliffe. After she arrived at college she found her great grandmother's journal of notes taken as secretary of her Radcliffe class at the turn of the 20th century. Cathy lived in a dormitory in Harvard Yard the first year and made a number of friends there.

In September 1981 we celebrated one of the best decisions we ever made. We purchased the Rockport house from my parents. We gave a party for all the relatives in Rockport to celebrate the occasion. After we bought the Rockport house, we spent a lot of time there in the summers. We spent almost every weekend from May to October there and longer periods when I had vacation time. We would drive up after work on Friday evenings and usually start a game of *Trivial Pursuit* while we waited for other family members and friends to arrive. Steve was the expert at the game and everyone wanted to be on his team. One Friday night we had a good game going when Steve arrived at 2:00 a.m. with his friend Neal. Neal didn't know the answers to the trivia questions, but he seemed to know how to throw the dice. Steve would tell Neal, "We need a nine," and Neal would throw the number he was told. Then Steve would answer the question. In no time Steve and Neal had won the game that the rest of us had been playing for the past couple of hours. Another popular game that we played at Rockport was charades and we were all very competitive about it. The women liked to challenge the men and they usually won much to the disgust of the men.

In the first several summers after we purchased the Rockport house, we made a number of renovations. We installed vinyl tile on the kitchen floor and stained the inside of all the rooms in the house. The house had always been green both inside and out. The relatives referred to it as "the Big Green". Because my aunts and uncles had lived in the house when they were younger, they were concerned that we might change the color of the house when we painted it. I teased my Uncle Frank by telling him that I was going to paint the dining room purple. However, we liked the green color ourselves and stained all the rooms dark green except for the bathrooms. Because of all the guests that we had at Rockport, I told Mike that we needed another bathroom. So in 1983, he and Dick Weber built a bathroom upstairs using a section of one of the big bedrooms.

After we bought the house Mike became worried about using the fireplace, as some of the bricks were loose and the mortar was crumbling. So he and Dick Weber decided to reline the chimney. They tried to find a liner that they could put inside the old chimney, so sparks couldn't go through. They could only find a liner that was six inches in diameter, smaller than the original diameter of the inside of the chimney, but they thought it would work. They dropped the liner sections down the chimney and filled the space between the liner rings and the old chimney with lightweight cement. It took them a week to finish and the chimney seemed solid and safe. However there was one hitch, the flue was no longer wide enough for the smoke to go up the chimney. Dick was so upset over the result that he brought his wood burning stove up from New Jersey so that we could burn wood in a closed space and the smoke was forced up the chimney. This was the only project that didn't come out with the best possible results.

Other projects that Mike and the boys worked on included rebuilding porches, kitchen cabinets and putting vinyl trim on the house. One other project that I really liked was the new picture window that Steve built in the living room. The family spent little time in the big living room because we thought it was too dark a room. Cindy and I decided we should brighten it up with white curtains and lighter colored furniture, but then we had the idea that a big picture window would let in more light and beautify the room. Steve went right to work to accommodate our wishes. He cut a big hole in the front wall of the room, ordered a big plate of glass and built a beautiful big window. He was such an expert carpenter that he seemed to do the whole project without ever taking out a tape measure.

Back in Bound Brook, we started 1982 with another January Jubilee. We invited 120 guests and 100 accepted. On the day of the party there was a severe ice storm, so only 70 guests came to the party. Perhaps that was just as well as 100 people might not have fit comfortably in our house. We had the usual menu and the guests really seemed to enjoy themselves. In early March the Webers treated us to a weekend at Sky Top, a resort in the Pocono Mountains in Pennsylvania. It was a beautiful resort and we enjoyed the scenery, the meals and the square dance on Saturday night.

Peter had a very successful wrestling season that year, winning the regional college tournament and going on to the National College Athletic Association (NCAA) tournament in Ames, Iowa. Mike and I flew out to see him wrestle in the nationals. He was disappointed that he did not make it to the finals, but we were very proud of him. On May 5th I turned 50. I tried not to tell anyone at work, but Cathy sent a big bunch of balloons to my office with a tag saying "Happy 50th". I was really very thrilled to receive them. The Deipnos drove me into New York City and treated me to dinner at the Rainbow Room in Rockefeller Center. It was a wonderful celebration and we dined and danced the evening away.

On July 17, 1982 my mother died of a heart attack while she was swimming at the YMCA. She had suffered a heart attack eight years earlier while in the hospital and the doctors had been able to restart her heart. She was diagnosed as having ventricular fibrillation and her doctor had prescribed medication and a diet to prolong her life. She had religiously adhered to the prescribed regimen and lived a full life up until the moment she died. She donated her body to George Washington University for medical research. Her memorial service was a very moving celebration of her life. The minister asked all her children and their spouses to write down their memories of Ruth, and he prepared a homily that beautifully incorporated their comments. During the service the minister also asked people in the congregation to share their memories of Ruth. My father was touched by the fact that so many of his colleagues attended the service to extend their sympathy. Father continued to live in their house in Kensington and to go to the Smithsonian every day to do his research.

We invited Father to our house for Thanksgiving, along with my brother Steve and his family. We played tag football in the back yard before dinner and charades after a big turkey dinner. It was difficult for Father, as he was grieving over Mother's death. When he returned to Kensington, he announced that he would never leave home again and he kept his word. His world had always been his research and he continued to go to the Smithsonian every day until he was almost ninety. Even after he retired, the Smithsonian provided him with a room in which to do his research.

The following year was an important one for Peter. He won the regional wrestling tournament and went to the NCAA wrestling tournament again. Steve went with Mike and me to Oklahoma University to see Peter wrestle. My brother, Bunkie, and his wife, Ann, also went and told us that they could hear me yelling "Peter" all the way across the stadium. It was an exciting tournament. Peter lost early on for "stalling", something he never did, but the referee had to make the call on one of the two wrestlers, neither of whom was actually stalling. Steve went up to the referee after the match and asked, "Are you blind?" After his loss, Peter wrestled his way up to third place, the highest one could go after a loss. On his way to winning the bronze medal, Peter defeated the top seeded wrestler in his weight class. We were all so proud of him. Bunkie and Ann treated us to dinner at a great restaurant. When we returned to Bound Brook, the big billboard in front of the High School stated, "Pete Schuyler Wins the Bronze."

In the spring we went with the Webers for a weekend at Grossinger's, a resort in the Catskill Mountains and attended a number of weddings of friends. In June our relatives gathered together to celebrate Bat Mitzvah of our niece Becky. Becky did an excellent job in her recitation in the temple ceremony and, afterwards, we all attended a party at her parents' house. At the end of the year we drove to Cambridge to see Cathy participate in a Gilbert and Sullivan musical at Harvard.

At the beginning of 1984, my beloved Grandma Elsie died at the age of 105. She had been such an important influence in my life. We always visited her with our children whenever we came to Rockport. All of her children, grandchildren, great grandchildren and great, great grandchildren were at the funeral service. How grateful we all were for the long and impressive life she had lived and the many lives that she had touched so deeply.

Mike signed a franchise agreement with General Business Services (GBS) early in the year and began his own business in Bound Brook. He joined the local Chamber of Commerce and their dinner dances became enjoyable events in our lives. He later became president of the Chamber and was selected as their "Man of the Year". In May, Peter went to Cedar Rapids, Iowa to try out for the Olympic wrestling team. Mike was too busy with his new business to see Peter wrestle, but I decided that it was a once-in-a-life-time event, not to be missed. I flew out to Cedar Rapids and stayed in a small motel. I couldn't get the key out of the rented car when I arrived at the motel, so I

honked the horn and the motel manager came out to the car
and took the key out of the ignition for me. After I moved into
my room I went to the desk and asked for a pencil sharpener.
The manager gave me a portable sharpener, but I couldn't hold
it and sharpen the pencils at the same time. So I asked the
manager if he would hold the sharpener for me while I sharpened
20 pencils, which he very obligingly did. Peter told his coach
about his mother's naivete and Coach Turner commented, "The
apple didn't fall far from the tree." I cheered Peter on at the
tryouts, where he came in eighth just missing the final team of
six wrestlers in his weight. After the trials Peter took me out to
a unique restaurant in a former boiler house. The steam pipes
in the high ceiling were painted in bright colors and the waiters
and waitresses were dressed in tuxedos and long evening
gowns. The food was fabulous and we had fun discussing
all the wrestlers.

Later in May, Edith Schmidt, the senior nursing professor at
Wagner, retired. We gave a retirement dinner at our house for
her and her Wagner friends. We set up tables for 34 guests in
our family room. People brought different foods and it was a
festive event. Many toasts were proffered and Edith opened
scores of gifts. One lady sitting in the back corner of the room
had a panic attack of claustrophobia and had to be moved to
the center of the room. Otherwise all went well and everyone
seemed to have a good time.

That summer we invited my brothers and their families and
several friends to Rockport. The children also brought their
friends now that the house belonged to our family. For many
years Millie Sheehan, Beverly Weber, Beverly's mother and, at
times, her sister and her friend Jane, visited me in the summer
at Rockport. Mildred Nelson and her niece, Evelyn, were also
annual visitors at Rockport. The Handens came for the July 4th
weekends and the Deipnos came for Labor Day weekends for
many years. We held many picnics on the rocks, went swimming

off the rocks and at the beach, played lots of different games and took our guests to restaurants and shopping on Bearskin Neck in town. We even enticed Dad and Helen Schuyler to come up from Sullivan's Island for a visit and, later, Mike's sister and her family came for a weekend.

Our favorite place to take guests in the evenings was the Studio, a delightful nightclub on Rocky Neck by the ocean in Gloucester, Massachusetts. A piano player named Kay was the entertainer. She played old familiar songs and the audience sang along with her music. Several of the customers with good voices, including our Cathy, liked to sing solos and Kay accommodated them by playing the songs that she knew they liked to sing. One evening Debbie Handen even convinced Cindy, who was normally very reserved, to sing "Rag Mop," much to everyone's delight. Kay also accommodated Mike and me by playing waltzes for us to dance to. At the end of the evening Kay always played "God Bless America" and everyone stood up to sing. In the fall when Mike and I drove to Rockport every Friday night, we would try to arrive at the Studio in time for a few last waltzes. On Saturday evenings we would go out to dinner and the movies and end up at the Studio again.

The following year began with a dinner for Mike's GBS fellow franchisees and another January Jubilee. Some new foods and a game were added to the party. The game took a lot of preparation on our part. We divided the 70 guests into small groups of five. Each group had one thing in common among its members. The guests were given different colored ribbons to pin on their clothes when they arrived. The guests had to find the other members of their group with the same color ribbon. Then they had to talk with their group members until they found out what they all had in common. The first group to discover the thing that they had in common won a prize. Mike and I had grouped them with commonalties such as color of their houses, number of children, year of birth etc. The guests really enjoyed the game and got to know people they hadn't met or known before.

In February 1985, John Sheehan died. He was the most faithful and enthusiastic member of our Deipnosophistical Society. His death was a terrible shock to the group. I had never understood the purpose of a wake until John died. I sat in the funeral parlor both days of the wake looking at John and remembering all the wonderful discussions we had with him over the years. It was our last two days to see him and feel that final closeness with him before he was physically taken from us forever. He and Millie had been married for twelve years and were so happy and in love. Millie continued in our group, but it was never the same without John. His spirit inspired us continually in our discussions.

In March, my cousin, Marrietta Barnes (Mimi) married Joseph Delahant. The wedding was a happy event with delicious food and lots of dancing at the reception afterwards. Mimi's parents, Janet and Frank Barnes, owned one of the other houses in the family complex at Rockport. We grew very close to Mimi and Joe over the years at Rockport. Also in March, Peter tried out for the World Cup Wrestling Team in Colorado Springs and won a position on the United States team. In the middle of March, Peter went to Cuba with the team and won a bronze medal. He wrestled again for the World Cup Championship in Toledo, Ohio at the end of March. In the first match of the tournament, he tore the ligaments between his thumb and his hand. He continued to wrestle during the rest of the tournament with ripped ligaments and ended in fourth place. After the tournament, his doctor told him that he should have an immediate operation so that permanent damage would be prevented. When he recovered from the operation his thumb worked normally.

In May, Mike and I drove to Cambridge to see Cathy graduate from Harvard. She almost didn't receive her diploma. She had been the leader of a large demonstration in Harvard Yard that demanded the divestiture, by the University, of stocks of companies doing business with South Africa. Harvard withheld her diploma from the graduation ceremony, but relented later and gave it to her. This didn't seem to phase Cathy. She was president of Adams House and they had their own ceremony after the official graduation. The students who lived in Adams House made a special diploma for Cathy which everyone in the house signed and it was presented to her by the Master of Adams House. She received a rounding applause from her housemates and always treasured the Adams House diploma more than the official Harvard one.

At the beginning of August Mike and I went to our first GBS convention in San Diego. It was our first visit to that city and we found it charming, with perfect weather. The beaches were beautiful and the historic landmarks were interesting. It was a lovely mini vacation for us. We stayed at the Econo Lodge as the big hotel where the convention was held was too expensive. I spent the rest of the summer at Rockport with Mike joining me on weekends. The "Big Green" was bustling with friends and family all summer long. We continued to go up for weekends in the fall, and didn't close the house until the middle of October. The Deipnos did not come to Rockport for Labor Day weekend after John Sheehan died.

We started 1986 by hosting a dinner for Mike's GBS colleagues and the next week we attended a retirement dinner for Dick Weber. On January 11th, Peter went to a wrestling tournament in Montreal and won the outstanding wrestler award. He also won in his weight class the next two years in the Montreal tournaments. Toward the end of January my father developed cellulitis in his leg and was admitted to the intensive care unit (ICU) of the local hospital for treatment. The doctors discussed amputating his leg, but finally were able to save the leg and cure the infection. He lost some of his flesh in the treatments and had to have plastic surgery on the leg after it healed. He was admitted to a nursing home to recuperate. He refused to enter into any activities of the nursing home, as his only goal was to recover and go home. All of his children visited him while he was ill. I took the train down to see him frequently over the next few months until his leg healed.

In March our family drove to Cape Hatteras to attend the wedding of our niece Heidi. My brother Steve and his family also went and we all stayed in the Econo Lodge near the beach. The two families got together after dinner the first night for a rousing game of charades. The women challenged the men to several matches and won every one. Steve and his wife, Carol, are very competitive at charades and it was a very lively evening. Heidi and Russell's wedding the next day was lovely and the reception was held in a restaurant by the water where we were blessed with a magnificent sunset during dinner. Heidi was the manager of the restaurant and the food and atmosphere were first-rate.

We spent the summer going to and from Rockport and entertaining a number of guests. On Labor Day weekend Cathy and Cindy arrived, along with Peter and his friend Ray Woldin. They all went sailing in Steve's catamaran on Monday, the day that we were to go home. At 6:00 p.m. they had sailed to Loblolly cove, about two miles from the harbor, when the wind died down and they were becalmed. Peter tried to paddle back to the harbor, but he lost the oar. We saw them off the rocks and Peter called to me to get a board and swim it out to him so he could paddle. I did just that but it was to no avail. I climbed on board the boat and told Peter to hail down a lobster fisherman to tow us back with his boat. Peter was embarrassed to do that, but it was getting dark and we had a five-hour trip back to New Jersey to make that evening. So I hailed the fisherman and told him our predicament and asked if he could help us. He thought the incident quite amusing and willingly towed us. We arrive home quite late that night.

We had a couple of other adventures with that catamaran. Another time that Ray was at Rockport, he and Peter took the catamaran out for a sail and it sunk. The Coast Guard came to their rescue, but Ray was in shock. He kept repeating, "The boat just went straight down!" Another incident involved the Webers' grandson, who was out sailing with Steve when the pin holding the mast came loose and the mast fell down. Dick Weber kept telling Steve what a disaster the boat was and that he should get rid of it.

The last catastrophe with the catamaran came when we were towing it behind Steve's truck on our way back to New Jersey. As dusk came upon us, Mike commented, "It's harder to see the boat back there in the dark." Steve looked back and exclaimed, "That's because it's not there!" We were going full speed down Interstate 87 when we lost the catamaran, but we managed to find a place to pull over. A car passed us with people yelling and waving their arms. They pulled over in front of us and told us that they saw the catamaran come loose and careen down the road. Mike and Steve got out of the truck and walked back up the interstate. I sat in the truck expecting to see the catamaran go flying by. After a while I looked back and saw Mike and Steve pulling the boat behind them. Amazing to believe, the catamaran had glided off the highway onto a grassy bank and was unharmed. No accidents had occurred because of it and we were all very relieved. We hitched the boat to the truck again, but the taillights didn't work. Steve rode in the back of the truck the rest of the way home to make sure the boat didn't come loose again. Steve decided to sell the catamaran after that incident and, to the Webers' horror, their son John bought the boat from Steve.

At the end of October we gave a dinner for the members of my Faculty Affairs Committee at Wagner. The seven members of the committee and their wives came for a roast beef dinner, after which we played Likes and Dislikes. In November we drove to Carol and Steve's for another big Thanksgiving dinner and a rousing game of tag football with the relatives. At the end of December, my cousin Mimi delivered her first and only child, Elizabeth, a beautiful ten-pound baby.

We started 1987 with lots of parties, including a buffet for eight GBS franchisees and their wives. On the third weekend in January we visited Dad and Helen on Sullivan's Island. We also visited Father frequently. Cathy was in her first year of graduate school at Union Theological Seminary in New York City. She had majored in religion at Harvard and decided to go into the ministry. She received a score of 800 on her GRE and had no problem being accepted by the seminary. She financed her graduate education with loans and some financial aid from National Association of Congregational Christian Churches Foundation for Theological Studies, as well as a contribution from the Bound Brook Congregational Church. She also worked for Logos Bookstore in New York City during two summers and was paid as a student minister in three different churches that she served during her graduate education. During her second year she also managed a soup kitchen on Broadway down the street from the seminary. She formed deep friendships with the ministers and their wives in two of the churches where she worked as a student. Robert and Katherine Kelly of the Calvary Church in Staten Island were like parents to her and Don and Barbara Mullen became two of her best friends after she worked at their Oakwood Heights Congregational Church in Staten Island. A fellow student at Union Theological Seminary, Ashley Cook, became one of her closest friends. Cathy and Ashley were bridesmaids in each other's wedding.

That spring I spent weekends and vacations helping Mike with his business. We continued with our regular social engagements at church and McCarter Theater and attended the Bar Mitzvah of our nephew, Jody, in June. His recitation in the temple was very well presented and the reception afterward was as splendid as any wedding reception we had ever been to. It was a joyous time for a big family gathering and we all enjoyed the ceremony and reception.

I spent all of July and August in Rockport and we entertained many guests and relatives. All of Beverly Weber's family including her children, her mother, her sister and her sister's children and grandchildren spent a week with us. Our children brought lots of their friends and, of course, the Handen family, Millie Sheehan, Mildred Nelson and her niece came, as usual.

In November we visited Dad and Helen again on Sullivan's Island. The ocean was perfect for swimming and we took long walks on the beautiful beach next to their house. We spent Thanksgiving at Carol and Steve's house in Rockville, Maryland. Carol had started a custom of having all the relatives at her house for Thanksgiving since Father had been ill and didn't want to travel anymore. Our family liked going down to Rockville as we enjoyed the competition of round-robin ping-pong and other games with Steve and Carol's children as well as the big feast that Carol prepared each year. In December, we hosted the Congregates progressive dinner and after Christmas I took the train into New York City and helped Cathy at her soup kitchen. The experience was illuminating.

We started 1988 by giving a party for Dick Weber's 60th birthday. We set up a long table in our family room for 22 guests to honor "King Richard." It was a gala event and Dick thoroughly enjoyed opening the many imaginative and clever gifts that he received. In May, Cindy graduated from MIT with a Master of Science degree in business administration. She had paid for her graduate education by refinancing the mortgage loan on her apartment. At the end of the program, she invited 50 of her classmates to Rockport for a big picnic on the rocks. They had a blast! After she received her graduate degree, Cindy was offered a position at Lotus Corporation. She worked on developing NOTES, the sequel to Lotus 1, 2, 3, and Lotus gave her very generous stock options.

In June Peter tried out for the Olympics again. This time he made the group of six finalists who wrestled off for the place on the Olympic team. He did not win the place on the team, but he came in fifth and we were ever so proud that he got as far as he did. I spent the summer at Rockport, again hosting many visitors. On Mike's birthday in August, Peter gave him a brand new Buick. Mike just could not grasp the fact that Peter had bought him a new car. I think Peter was thanking him for all the years of support that he had given him in his wrestling. Peter bought him custom-made license plates with his initials on them. Mike used the Buick for his business and took special care of that car for the next thirteen years. Mike was so proud of that Buick.

At the end of the year, the Webers treated us to a weekend vacation in New Orleans and we had a marvelous time in one of our favorite cities. We had a comfortable room at the downtown Double Tree Hotel. We ate begniers for breakfast by the river while we listened to a man play a saxophone and watched a colorful parade pass by. We went sightseeing and shopping during the days and in the evenings we dined at charming restaurants and danced the nights away. On Sunday we went to a sumptuous brunch at a very plush restaurant. Jazz musicians paraded throughout the restaurant while we were eating. What a great and generous treat that weekend was for us.

In January 1989 we visited Dad and Helen. They had moved to the USAA Towers, a senior citizen condominium in San Antonio, Texas, as they had felt isolated on Sullivan's Island. Dad wanted to be among friends so that they would continue to have an active social life and not have to deal with the responsibilities of keeping up a private home. They had signed up for an apartment at USAA Towers while it was under construction and, when it was completed, they were one of the first couples to move in. They sold Helen's house on Sullivan's Island just one week before Hurricane Hugo destroyed most of the island. How lucky they were to have sold the house when they did.

Most of the residents at the USAA Towers had backgrounds in government positions or in the military. Dad and Helen enjoyed the social life with other retirees at the Towers. Sumptuous dinners were served to the residents in the elegant dining room and there were private dining rooms if couples wished to entertain a party of guests. Dad and Helen also entertained in their luxurious apartment. They owned a double apartment on the fourteenth floor so that their living space was comparable to Helen's whole house on Sullivan's Island. They were pleased to be able to bring all their treasured belongings when they moved to the Towers.

We had never been to San Antonio, so we had a wonderful time exploring the city. On our first morning there we toured the Towers, drove through Fort Sam Houston and visited an art museum with Dad and Helen. San Antonio was famous for its River Walk recently built along the Medina River. In the afternoon, Mike and I went downtown to explore the River Walk while Dad and Helen took a nap. We came back for cocktails followed by a delicious dinner in the Towers dining room with Dad and Helen. After dinner Mike and I went dancing at the Farmer's Daughter, a country western dance hall. On the second day, we had breakfast and lunch with Dad and Helen and then Dad lent us his Cadillac to go sightseeing. We went back to the River Walk and explored the stores and restaurants along its banks. We toured the Alamo and saw an IMAX movie of the Battle of the Alamo. We returned to the Towers for cocktails and another wonderful dinner with Dad and Helen. After dinner we drove to the Roaring Twenties dance hall for another great evening of dancing. The following day we all went to an outdoor restaurant on the outskirts of town and then to see an old mission. After a prime rib dinner at the Towers, Mike and I went to "Durty Nellie's," a sing-along pub on the River Walk. There were peanut shells all over the floor and a lively crowd was singing familiar songs along with the piano player. We had a great last evening together in San Antonio. On our last day, we had a resplendent champagne brunch at the Towers before flying back to New Jersey. It was a marvelous visit and Dad and Helen seemed very happy in their new environment.

In February we visited Peter at the Naval Academy. He had been the wrestling coach at James Madison University for two years before coming to the Naval Academy, where he stayed for eight years as the assistant wrestling coach. He enjoyed coaching at the Naval Academy, as the wrestlers were first-rate in both sports and academics. The town of Annapolis was charming and we enjoyed visiting Peter there. In June we attended Cathy's graduation from Union Theological Seminary. During the summer she worked in the Logos Bookstore in New York City.

During July we entertained a number of guests at Rockport. Several professors and their families from Wagner visited us including Bill and Deborah Bly, Ammini and Sam Moorthy, Otto and Linda Raths and Walter and Kathy Sweeney. Our children were also there and enjoyed picnics on the rocks and playing games with our friends. Beverly Weber, her mother and Millie Sheehan came up together for a week and Mildred Nelson came for another week. On the last weekend of July we had a big dinner for the Raths, the Sweeneys, Mildred and our children. After dinner we played *Trivial Pursuit* and *Pictionary*. My brothers and their families also visited us in Rockport.

At the beginning of August Mike and I traveled to Colorado Springs for the GBS biennial convention. We had a fantastic vacation in a magnificent setting. We stayed at Motel 6 for $16 a night. We had an immaculate room with a big picture window looking out at Pike's Peak with nothing to obstruct our view of the mountain. Free orange juice and coffee were served in the lobby, so each day I sat on the side of our bed and drank my coffee while I looked at Pike's Peak. What a wonderful way to start each day. After breakfast we walked to the Marriott Hotel where the convention was being held. We attended workshops in the mornings and went sightseeing in the afternoons. One of our favorite spots was the world famous Broadmoor Hotel. We were enchanted by its grandeur in the beautiful setting at the base of the mountains. We walked around the grounds and explored the hotel. We decided to have cocktails in the Penrose Lounge on the top floor and then we went down to the first floor and ate dinner in the Golden Bee restaurant. After dinner we went across the grounds to see the ice show at the Broadmoor World Arena.

One afternoon we drove to the top of Pike's Peak for a fantastic view. We had dinner at McKenna's Pub in Old Colorado City, and then drove to the One-Dollar Movie Theater and saw *Great Balls of Fire,* a delightful biography of Jerry Lee Lewis. On the last evening of the convention, there was a GBS 50's Night held at the Cheyenne Mountain Conference Resort. We had a delicious dinner in a splendid restaurant followed by entertainment and dancing in the lounge. After the convention, we stayed on in Colorado Springs for three more days.

We decided to spend our first free day white water rafting. Sunday morning we drove to Brown's Rafting Company on the Arkansas River and signed up for a trip down the river. We changed into warm clothes and life vests and I wore a pink hat to keep the sun off my face. We got into a rubber raft with three other people and a guide, and took off down the river. Mike fell out of the boat as we went over the first rapids. When he came up the guide pulled him back into the raft. It was an exciting ride, but several miles down, the river widened and the rapids ceased. Our guide steered the raft over to a sandy shoal and some of the young folks got out and climbed up the bank onto a huge rock sticking out over the river. When I saw them, I got out of the raft and followed them. They jumped off the rock into the river, so of course I jumped in right after them. Mike came running up the bank after me and when he saw me jump in he jumped in too. In the river we grabbed each other's hand, lay on our backs and floated down the river together. To me that was pure heaven. Further down the river our guide swam out and pulled us back to shore. Then we all got back into the raft, the river narrowed again, and we rode down the rapids to the finishing place of the trip. A bus was waiting for us and took us back to the starting point where we took warm showers and put on dry clothes.

After that exhilarating experience we drove over to see Royal Gorge. The spectacular view from the top of the gorge is said to be Colorado's top scenic attraction. The narrow gorge is 1,053 feet deep and it is spanned by the world's highest suspension bridge. It was an awesome sight. We ate pizza for dinner at a little snack shop overlooking the gorge and then drove back to our motel. We hung all our wet clothes in our small bathroom where they dried overnight. In the evening we returned to the Cheyenne Mountain Resort and danced until it closed.

The next day we visited the Garden of the Gods rock formations in Colorado Springs, drove to Manitou Springs for lunch in the Tearoom of Marimount Castle, and then visited Cripple Creek, an old gold mining town. We finished the day with country western dancing at the Thunder and Buttons Café. On our last evening we returned to the Broadmoor Hotel for dinner and dancing in the Tavern Restaurant. In the morning we reluctantly left our room at Motel 6 and headed out for lunch at Marimount Castle again on the way to the airport. We said good-by to Colorado Springs and our enchanting vacation there.

When we returned to New Jersey we found out that one of our best friends, Jack Handen, had died while we were away. We had loved Jack and shared so many experiences with him and his wife, Ella. I invited Ella to spend some time with me at Rockport when she was ready. She came for the last week in August. She announced when she arrived that the one thing she had left in her life was an ample amount of money and she made me promise that we would eat all our meals at restaurants and that she would foot the bills. We spent most of the week reminiscing about Ella's and Jack's lives and our times together. It was an illuminating experience for me, and a comforting experience for her. It was a week that I treasured.

Late in the summer our family drove to Raleigh, North Carolina to attend the wedding of Anne Saxby, Mike's sister's youngest child. All of our children went to the wedding and we enjoyed being together as a family as well as being guests at the wedding. We closed the Rockport house for the winter over the Columbus Day weekend. Mike and I had a busy fall at work and enjoyed the Christmas holidays at the end of 1989. On Christmas night we invited 24 of our closest friends for an open house party.

13

Back to the Deipnos

After reading and discussing one hundred books together, the Deipnosophistical Society celebrated by going on a cruise. Following the cruise, the Deipnos continued to read and discuss a book each month together. Beverly Weber remained our archivist through our forty-four years together. She arranged a wide variety of activities for the group and carried on a correspondence with several of the authors that we read, including David McCullough and William Buckley. There were some changes in the group, but the original members, Connie and Mike Schuyler, Beverly and Dick Weber, Simi and Tom Long, and Marion and Bruce McCreary continued to participate in the group. Although the Longs moved to Ohio, they continued to participate in our special events and trips. Four of our early members are now deceased, John and Millie Sheehan and Bruce and Marion McCreary.

There continues to be diversity in the type of books that we read. Some of the favorite books of a number of the members of the group are: *Endurance* by Alfred Lansing, *Washington the Indispensable Man* by James Flexner and *John Adams* by David McCullough. Some authors were also popular. Eight plays of William Shakespeare and six books of David McCullough were chosen for discussion. We also read six books from the

Bible. Three books from each of the following authors were chosen: Mark Twain, Thomas Hardy, David Halberstam and Plato. A few authors were chosen twice, but most authors were chosen only once. Some members of the group had preferences for specific types of books, but most chose a variety of themes to read about.

Mike chose books on historical events such as *Decision in Philadelphia* by Christopher and James Collier and *This Hallowed Ground* by Bruce Catton. He also liked books about people who had deep conflicts in their lives such as: King Arthur in *Idylls of the King* by Alfred Lord Tennyson, Othello in William Shakespeare's play and Job from *The Book of Job* in the *Old Testament*. Mike is always moved when we see a play or movie about King Arthur's wrenching conflict over his favorite knight, Lancelot, and his wife, Guenivere. Othello's frenzied jealously of his wife, Desdemona, and her supposed lover, Cassio, is renown. Shakespeare's description of jealously is very perceptive. When Desdemona is discussing Othello's jealously with Emilia, she says: "Alas the day! I never gave him cause." Emilia replies: "But jealous souls will not be answered so. They are not jealous for the cause, but jealous for they are jealous. 'Tis a monster begot upon itself, born on itself." What Mike found inspiring about Job was his faithfulness to God no matter what happened. He was faithful to God because He was God, not because of benefits God would bestow upon him. Job endured numerous hardships, but he remained loyal to God because of his tremendous faith. Mike also chose biographies of people that he considered noble such as *American Caesar* by William Manchester, a biography of General MacArthur. He relished any biography or writing about Abraham Lincoln.

I continued to like philosophy and chose authors such as Dante, Kant and Ortega. Dante's *Divine Comedy* has been one of my favorite readings since I first read it in the Humanities I course at Harvard. I felt it was too long for Deipnos to read, so I selected only the first book, *The Inferno*. The discussion about it was lively. Immanuel Kant's *Lectures on Ethics* was also well received by the group. I became interested in Ortega because my doctoral advisor at Columbia, Dr. McClintock, had written about Ortega in his own dissertation, *Man and his Circumstances, Ortega as Educator,* and I had read the published copy of it. I managed to get enough copies for all the Deipnos so I used it as my book choice. Our archivist, Beverly Weber, wrote a letter to McClintock telling him how much we enjoyed his scholarly writing and how thrilled we were to learn some more words of Greek origin such as protreptic, heuristic and hypostatize.

As time went on I became more interested in books about civil rights. I chose Mark Mathabane's autobiography, *Kaffir Boy,* about the terrible conditions for blacks in South Africa where he grew up. Martin Luther King's book, *Why We Can't Wait,* was another choice. What a powerful and persuasive writer he was! Through his writings and his speeches he brought about amazing changes for his people in the battle for civil rights. My favorite book about civil rights workers was David Halberstam's book, *The Children*. It is a powerful and wrenching book about young Nashville activists who changed the course of history through their non-violent resistance to the segregation practices in the south in the 1950's and 1960's. In the book, Halberstam follows eight idealists who endured beatings and arrests, risking their lives to improve the lot of blacks. The person I admired the most in the book was John Lewis who never overstepped the goal of achieving change through non-violent resistance. He was able to walk into a surging mob of angry white people without hesitation and was ready to die for the cause. I read John Lewis' autobiography *Walking with the Wind,* and it is the most inspiring biography that I have read. Halberstam is one of my favorite authors and the group has read two other of his books, *The Powers That Be* and *The 50's.* They are both fascinating.

Women's issues also became an avid interest of mine and I chose a number of books about inspiring women for the Deipnos to read, including: Evelyn Keller's A *Feeling for the Organism,* Jill Conway's *Road From Coorain,* Katherine Graham's *Personal History* and Virginia Wolffe's *A Room of One's Own.* A *Feeling for the Organism* is a fascinating biography of Barbara McClintock, who won the Nobel Prize for her research in genetics. *Road From Coorain* is Jill Ker Conway's autobiography of her struggle to grow up in Australia and her move to America where she eventually became the first woman president of Smith College. Her description of the desolate life in Australia is awesome. Katherine Graham's autobiography is a moving account of how she changed into a forceful and successful woman after the tragic death of her husband, Philip Graham.

My interest in history continued and some of my favorite books of history include: Edward Gibbon's *Decline and Fall of the Roman Empire,* Theodore White's *In Search of History* and Daniel Boorstin's *The Discovers.* Boorstin explores how people's mind-sets in different eras and in different parts of the world made them view "reality" in different ways. He shows how people gradually unfolded the truths of the world by removing the beliefs and superstitions that had clouded their vision and understanding. He wrote, "The great discoverers had to battle against the current 'facts' and dogmas of the learned." He presented subjects in the book chronologically, going from discoveries of lands and seas to discoveries in the physical sciences and finally to discoveries about society and its history. I found it interesting that several early major discoveries and inventions were made simultaneously in distant parts of the world.

Beverly often chose classic novels by authors such as Jane Austen, Charles Dickens, Honore Balzac and Gustave Flaubert. She chose two very long novels, *Bleak House* by Dickens and *Pride and Prejudice* by her favorite author, Jane Austen. She chose *Pere Goriot* by Balzac, who was a prolific writer, finishing three or four books a year during his twenty years of writing. Flaubert was nothing like Balzac in his quantity of writing, but his quality was outstanding. He was obsessed with stylistic perfection. He wrote several paragraphs each day and endlessly revised them. He sometimes spent five days working on one page. As a result his writing is awesome and his descriptions are truly beautiful. Beverly chose his most famous book, *Madame Bovary*. Bovary is one of the great figures of fiction, a self-centered impulsive woman who suffered from romantic malaise and yearned for a dramatic affair with an idealized lover above her station in life. I first read *Madame Bovary* at Harvard in Humanities II. As a college professor I assigned this book in many of my classes and had read it more than a dozen times when Beverly chose it for Deipnos. I enjoyed reading it again and again as Flaubert was such a masterful writer.

Beverly also chose books about inspiring individuals such as *Saint Joan* by Bernard Shaw and *Abraham Lincoln* by Carl Sandburg. She too liked history and chose *The Age of Reason*, Volume VII of *The Story of Civilization* by Will and Ariel Durant. This reading was fascinating especially to the history buffs in the group. My Grandma Elsie and her husband were personal friends of the Durants, and their eleven-volume set is our favorite historical collection.

Dick was fascinated by Russian history. His favorite Russian author was Leo Tolstoi and he presented his *Sebastopol Sketches* about soldiers in the trenches of World War I as one of his choices for the Deipnos to read. Dick also chose several of Ralph Waldo Emerson's essays including *Self-Reliance, Compensation, Over-Soul* and *Heroism,* and Sigmund Freud's *Civilization and Its Discontents*. Dick often made copies of articles for the group to read on topics that he felt strongly about and they usually elicited heated discussions.

Bruce enjoyed books about famous explorers and about different cultures. His book choices about explorers included: Samuel Eliot Morrison's *Admiral of the Ocean Sea* about Columbus, Charles Darwin's *Voyage of the Beagle* and Stephen Ambrose's *Undaunted Courage* about Lewis and Clark discoveries. These were all excellent accounts of explorers. His choices of William Prescott's *History of the Conquest of Mexico*, Peter Freuchin's *Book of the Eskimos* and Peter Hessler's *River Town* gave the group an excellent view of three different cultures. When the group discussed *River Town* about life in modern China, we were interviewed and photographed by a reporter from the *Newark Star Ledger* and a nice article about the Deipnos came out in the paper a few days later.

Marion chose six out of the seven books written by David McCullough. She chose his first book, *The Johnston Flood,* in the first decade of the Deipos existence. He was her favorite author and she chose each of his books as soon as it was her turn after it was published. His second book, *The Great Bridge,* about the building of the Brooklyn Bridge by John and Washington Roebling, was a fascinating study of characters. The father, John Roebling, one of the creative geniuses of the nineteenth century, designed the bridge. He was a dynamic man whose life work had been directed toward building this bridge, but he did not live to do it. Before the actual construction of the bridge had begun, John Roebling's foot was caught in the Fulton Ferry slip as a boat entered the slip and ground against his foot. The tip of his boot and toes had been crushed. His toes had to be amputated but he developed lockjaw from tetanus and died three weeks after the accident. His son, Washington Roebling, a modest man, became the chief engineer at the age of 32 and accomplished the tremendous feat of building the Brooklyn Bridge.

The third McCullough book Marion chose was *The Path Between the Seas*, a magnificent account of the building of the

Panama Canal and the amazing work of Dr. Gorgas and his colleagues in ridding Panama of yellow fever. The fourth book of his that was chosen, *Mornings on Horseback,* is a biography of Theodore Roosevelt and the fifth and longest book, *Truman,* is an excellent biography of the 33rd president. McCullough's latest book, *John Adams,* was chosen by Bruce in honor of Marion, who was no longer with us when it was published.

Marion was interested in human struggles. A fascinating book that she chose was *Adrift* by Steven Callahan. It is the story of a man whose schooner sank in the Atlantic Ocean and he found himself adrift on a five-foot raft with three pounds of food and eight pints of water. He was alone in his raft for seventy-six days before he found land. Nine ships passed him without seeing his flares. His ingenuity in obtaining food and water, plus his determination to survive, finally pulled him through the ordeal.

Another gripping book that Marion chose was Betty Mahmoody's *Not Without My Daughter.* It was a true story of an American woman who married an Iranian doctor and went to Iran with him to visit his family. Once they were in Iran, her husband would not let her and their four-year-old daughter return to the United States. They were treated like prisoners and guarded so that they could not escape. The book is an engrossing story of Betty Mahmoody's harrowing experience in trying to escape with her daughter from Iran and her final return to her own country. Whenever it was Marion's turn to choose a book she would read a number of books before making her selection. Thus she always presented us with a captivating book to read.

John chose books about momentous events in history. Two of his favorite books were *The Great Hunger* by Cecil Woodham-Smith and *The Great War and Modern Memory* by Paul Fussell. *The Great Hunger* is an account of the potato famine in Ireland in the 1840's that caused the death of one million peasants from starvation. It is a horrifying story written by a master writer and the Deipnos were enthralled by it. *The Great War and Modern Memory* was a book of great scope and depth about World War I. It won two national book awards and was given outstanding reviews. Lionel Trilling wrote, "It was an original and brilliant piece of cultural history and one of the most deeply moving books I have read in a long time."

John was discerning in his choice of books and we all admired his choices. Another of his favorite books was *Washington, the Indispensable Man* by James Flexner. This book gave a magnificent picture of Washington and his influence at the birth of our country. John also chose a book on the history of the Jewish people, *The Indestructible Jews* by Max Dimont. It was a dramatic and inspiring story. John's turn for presenting a book kept turning up on Labor Day weekend when the Deipnos met at our Rockport house. This happened for five years in a row, so we knew we would have a good book and a good discussion for those weekends.

Millie chose a number of biographies of both men and women. Her books were about interesting and famous people such as Abigail Adams, Disraeli, Queen Victoria, Gandhi and Dr. Squibb, the founder of the company where she worked for most of her life. She also chose books about people who were victims of the culture in which they lived. She chose Oliver Goldsmith's *The Vicar of Wakefield*, the classic nineteenth century novel about a young man who was held captive by his parents who continually threatened to disinherit him if he did not obey their demands. She also chose *The Scarlet Letter* by Nathaniel Hawthorne. It is the story of Hestor Primm, a woman in a strict puritan society who was mortified by being forced to wear a scarlet letter "A" on her dress because she had committed adultery. Henrik Ibsen's play, *The Doll House,* an example of a woman frustrated by a strict hide-bound society, was also a choice of Millie's.

In August 1974, Lysle and Artie Heney were invited as guests to a Deipno meeting. They were members of our church and we thought that they might enjoy a literary discussion. The book being discussed was *Lectures on Ethics* by Imanuel Kant. I led the discussion and the Heneys seemed to enjoy the evening. From then on they came each month and became the sixth couple in the group. Lysle and Artie met as students at the University of Minnesota. They both received Bachelors of Science in chemistry and Lysle went on to earn a Ph.D. in chemistry. Lysle is an avid reader and interested in a variety of subjects besides chemistry. Artie and Lysle are devoted to each other and he especially appreciates her cooking.

Lysle chose a number of books of the Bible as his book selections including *Ecclesiastes, Daniel* and *Jeremiah.* He led the discussions of these books perceptively. One of his favorite books that he chose was Mary Baker Eddy's *Science and Health with Key to the Scriptures.* Lysle's mother was a Christian Scientist and he was deeply influenced by her faith. Others of his favorite books were Thomas Paine's *Rights of Man,* Oscar Wilde's *The Picture of Dorian Gray* and Daniel Boorstin's *The Discoverers.* One very interesting book that Lysle chose for the Deipnos to read was *Not Quite a Miracle* by Jon Franklin and Alan Doelp. It is a fascinating description of the cutting edge of microsurgery of the brain.

Artie chose classic short novels such as J.D. Salinger's *Catcher in the Rye,* Edith Warton's *Ethan Fromm,* Jack London's *White Fang* and Stephen Crane's *The Red Badge of Courage.* Crane's book was one of her favorites that the group read. Other books chosen by the group that were among her favorites included: Thoreau's *Walden,* Sinclair Lewis' *Main Street,* Helen Keller's *The Story of My Life,* James Clavell's *Shogun,* Jonathan Swift's *Gulliver's Travels* and Paine's *The Rights of Man.*

Walden, an early choice of Beverly, was a book that we all enjoyed because of the fascinating details about nature that

Thoreau noted in his writing. *Shogun* was long and intriguing. It was hard to believe that medieval Japan was so much more advanced than England in hygiene and living conditions at that time. Helen Keller's life was inspiring to say the least. She had been at Radcliffe College at the same time as my Grandmother Jane and those who knew her were amazed at her brilliance and accomplishments.

Carol DeHaan came to a Deipno meeting for the first time in 1974. She was a volunteer worker in the Hiillcrest School library where Beverly was the librarian. Carol attended college while her children were in Hillcrest School. She majored in English and Beverly thought that she might be interested in participating in literary discussions, so she told her about our group. Carol seemed interested in becoming a part of the group. She came to our meetings sporadically during the 1970's, but in early 1980 she became a regular member of the Deipnos for the next ten years.

Carol liked Shakespeare and chose two of his plays soon after she joined the group. She chose *King Lear* and *Anthony and Cleopatra* and did an excellent job of leading the discussions of the plays. We sympathized with poor King Lear who was old and felt unloved by his children. He was truly a tragic figure and died of grief after all three of his daughters died in tragic ways. Carol also chose Charles Dickens' *Great Expectations* and a book by Winnie Mandela, *Part of My Soul Went with Them*. Carol left the group at the end of 1989. She moved to Newark and became active in the community there. In April 2002 she invited the Deipnos to dinner at her apartment in Newark and at that meeting she rejoined the group and became a regular member again.

In 1982 the Deipnos accepted three new people into the group. Marion McCreary brought Brian and Sue Edwards to our meeting in February. Brian was an English professor from Australia who had come to the United States on a sabbatical.

He and his wife met Marion, who was a real estate agent, and she showed them a house to rent. They were a delightful couple and became regulars at our meetings during the year that they were here. Brian chose Gabriel Marquez' novel, *One Hundred Years of Solitude*, the story of the Buendia family. The Deipnos thoroughly enjoyed his choice. At the end of his sabbatical, Brian and Sue returned to Australia, but Brian wrote to the Deipnos regularly for years afterward.

In October of 1982, the McCrearys' brought another friend, Si Mack, a retired minister in his eighties. He joined our group as a regular member and chose two memorable books for the group to read and discuss. He first chose Owen Wister's *The Virginian,* a story that we remembered from our childhood. Our favorite remark from the book was the riposte by the Virginian, "Smile when you call me that!" Another book that he chose was M. Scott Peck's *The Road Less Traveled.* Peck, a practicing psychologist, integrated traditional psychology and spiritual insights to show people how to achieve serenity while embracing reality. Si came to the Deipno meetings regularly until he died in 1986. We all enjoyed his friendly optimistic personality while he was with us.

In 1988 the Webers brought Shelia and John Fuhrmann to a Deipno meeting. They were interested in joining the group and the group welcomed them. Shelia chose two very interesting books, Mark Twain's *Puddinhead Wilson* and John Irving's *Cider House Rules.* John chose Tom Wolff's *Bonfire of the Vanities,* which was very long, but enjoyable reading. The Fuhrmanns remained in the group less than three years, but we thoroughly enjoyed them while they were with us. John was a great raconteur of jokes and stories and laughed at his own jokes with more gusto than anyone else.

In 1990 Gerry and Connie D'Alessandro joined the Deipnos. Gerry was a professor at Wagner College and he and I developed the masters program in International Business together. We taught together in the Interdisciplinary Program and he also served on the Faculty Affairs committee with me for several years. In 1990 he told me that he and his wife would like to join our book club. After the Deipnos met Gerry and his wife, Connie, they were pleased to invite them to become members of our group. They stayed with the group for the next ten years. When they first joined the Deipnos they lived in Union, New Jersey, but later they sold that house and moved into their summer home in Belmar on the Jersey shore. It was an hour's ride from Bound Brook, but members of the group often drove down early to walk along the boardwalk before the meeting. Sometimes in the fall I would go for a swim in the ocean before the meeting.

The D'Alessandros were a delightful couple. Gerry was an avid reader and truly loved teaching the liberal arts courses in the Interdisciplinary Program at Wagner, even though he was a professor in the Business Department. Connie had been an elementary school teacher during her career, but after her retirement she also did a great deal of reading. She was a very outgoing gregarious person and took great personal interest in the members of our group. Both Gerry and Connie liked reading the books and the discussions in the Deipno group. Connie was an excellent cook and served us gourmet meals in both her Union and Belmar houses.

After they joined the Deipnos, Gerry chose classic books about human struggles including: John Steinbeck's *Grapes of Wrath*, Erick Remarque's *All Quiet on the Western Front*, Gay Talese's *Unto the Sons*, Ernest Hemmingway's *A Farewell to Arms* and Tobias Wolff's *This Boy's Life*. Connie chose well known novels such as F. Scott Fitzgerald's *Tender is the Night*, Amy Tan's *Joy Luck Club* and Carson McCullers' *The Heart is a Lonely Hunter*. This last book was McCullers' first novel, which she wrote at the age of twenty-three. The group had not read it before and

SCHUYLER

was really impressed with the quality of her writing. She was able to capture the ambience of a small southern town and describe its inhabitants with amazing discernment and clarity. We thought this book was a masterpiece for such a young author and Connie did an excellent job of leading the discussion about the book and its author. The D'Alessandros left the group in 1999, because the long ride up to Bound Brook was becoming difficult as their nighttime vision deteriorated. We sorely missed them after they left the group. Gerry died a few years later, but we continue to visit Connie at her house in Belmar. She is a good friend and we enjoy our visits together.

In 2001 when Mildred Nelson and I retired from Wagner College, she asked me if she could join the Deipnos. Of course I was delighted and she has become a regular member. She has chosen three books so far: Russell Martin's *Beethoven's Hair,* Barbara Ehrenreich's *Nickel and Dimed* and Michael Beschloss' *The Conquerors.* She has coped well with leading discussions and seems to enjoy the group. I am thrilled to be able to see her regularly now that we are retired.

In July 2002 another couple joined the Deipnos, Jim and Joan McCoy. They came as visitors to the group at my request. I had chosen the book, *A Beautiful Mind,* the biography of Nobel Prize winner John Nash by Sylvia Nasar, and I needed someone to explain Nash's game theory to me and to the Deipnos. Jim McCoy was a good friend of mine at Wagner College where he had been chairman of the Math Department before he retired. I asked him to come to our meeting to explain Nash's theory. He was a perfect choice for this challenge, as he had written his doctoral dissertation on part of John von Neumann's game theory, a forerunner to Nash's theory. Jim brought a diagram for each Deipno and brilliantly explained Nash's theory to the group. He brought his wife, Joan, with him and the Deipnos liked them so much that we asked them to join the group and gave them a copy of the next assigned book. We had been trying to find a new couple to join the group after our loss of the D'Alessandros. The McCoys were just the right couple for the group, and we were thrilled when they accepted our invitation.

Jim McCoy had been head of the central computer system at Wagner College, as well as chairman of the Math Department. He had helped me innumerable times in my efforts to enter sections of the Wagner catalogue on the central computer system. His personality was cheerful and kind and he almost always had a smile on his face. Jim and Joan McCoy attended the University of Oregon together where she earned a M.S. in Biology and he received a M.S. and Ph.D. in Mathematics. After raising five children, Joan made a decision to go into a new career. She attended Wagner College, where tuition for her was free, and earned a bachelor's degree in nursing. She was a brilliant student and has really enjoyed her work in oncology nursing.

Jim and Joan are perfect for membership in the Deipnos. They are interested in reading and discussing intellectually stimulating books, and their easygoing personalities enable them to withstand some of the strong debates in the group. They entertain all of us royally when it is their turn to be hosts and they both have chosen stimulating classics for the group to read when they were discussion leaders. The group is delighted to have them as members.

During its existence the group has enjoyed a number of special events together such as trips to interesting places and holiday gatherings at Rockport, where we spent Labor Day weekends together for a number of years. At Rockport we all chipped in to pay for the food and to help with preparing and cleaning up after the meals. The Deipnos often brought their children with them over Labor Day weekend and the children played some rip-roaring tag football together. Most of the families drove up to Rockport on Friday night and we had snacks and drinks for them when they arrived. On Saturday the Deipnos and their families went swimming, walked to town for lunch, shopped on Bearskin Neck or just sat on the porch and chatted while watching the tag-football game. We usually had a big picnic on the rocks on Saturday evening and watched spectacular sunsets. Then we returned to our house for round-robin ping-pong and other games. On Sunday mornings John and Millie always went to church. Often the older children and some of the adults organized games such as volleyball. Before the Deipno meeting on Sunday evening we would all gather at the big dining room table for a feast of roast ham, turkey and all the fixings. After dinner the smaller children went to bed and the older ones played games in the dining room while the Deipnos discussed the book in the living room. Whoever was the designated host for the meeting provided refreshments.

On Labor Day weekend of 1982 we had the biggest crowd ever staying at the Rockport house. There were twenty-four of us sleeping and eating in the house. The group included grandchildren as well as children of the Deipnos. The McCreary's three daughters came—Jan, Gay and Amy—along with Jan's fiance and Gay's husband and four children. We put all of Gay's family in the downstairs bedroom with the children on sleeping bags while Stan, Jan's fiance, slept on a cot in the shed. We managed to find beds for everyone else. We had gigantic picnics on the rocks both Saturday and Sunday to accommodate so many guests and the McCreary grandchildren loved climbing all over the rocks. John presented his book, *The Indestructible Jews* to the Deipnos on Sunday night and led a spirited discussion. The next year was our last Deipno meeting at Rockport. I led the discussion on my book, *In Search of History* by Theodore White, one of my favorite authors, and the activities over the weekend were similar to previous years.

In 1984 John Sheehan developed cancer of the liver. He was in the hospital and could not come to Rockport. He died in

February 1985 and left a great void in our group. The Deipnos never seemed interested in returning to Rockport as a group, knowing that John would not be with us. His spirit continually kindled our memories in the following years and we missed him dearly.

The Deipnos went on a number of trips to historic places. The books that we chose to discuss on these trips usually had some connection to the place that we visited. In April 1977 we spent a weekend in Gettysburg, Pennsylvania. Mike chose *This Hallowed Ground,* Bruce Catton's book on the Civil War, for the group to read and discuss. Visiting the museum and the battlefield in Gettsyburg gave us a more intimate view of Catton's book. The Longs joined us at our motel there and participated in the group's activities, as they always did on our special trips. The McCrearys brought their youngest daughter, Amy, and we brought our youngest, Cathy. They were friends and enjoyed doing things together on Deipno trips.

In December 1978 the Deipnos drove to Kensington, Maryland and stayed at my parents house while we visited Washington DC. My parents were in Brazil and gave us permission to use their house. They had five bedrooms and one couple slept in the basement. We had a wonderful time together and did a good deal of sightseeing in Washington. Amy and Cathy were the only children with us and they enjoyed visiting museums and monuments with us. Beverly chose Robert Remini's *Revolutionary Age of Andrew Jackson* and did a fine job of leading the discussion. I was the hostess as it was easy for me to prepare food in my parents' house. We also found some great restaurants in the city.

In May 1980 the Deipnos drove to Williamsburg, Virginia for a long weekend. The restoration at Williamsburg is a fascinating place for seeing history in action. Mike led the discussion on Fawn Brody's *Thomas Jefferson.* It was a new biography of

Jefferson, exposing the relationship with his slave, Sally Hemings, as well as with the painter, Maria Cosway. The group found the book interesting and enjoyed discussing the emotional side of Jefferson. We ate at some charming historical inns and enjoyed each other's company.

The next summer we visited Philadelphia. It was Mike's book again and he chose *The Federalist Papers* that were written by Alexander Hamilton, John Jay and James Madison. Mike did an excellent job of leading the discussion. Philadelphia is proud of its colonial heritage and has preserved its historical buildings well. It was interesting to visit the places where our forefathers had written the seminal documents of our country. On Sunday we found a fascinating tour of old colonial homes that had been restored by young couples in the city. We also found some outstanding restaurants for meals and continued our discussion all weekend.

In May 1982 we chose a place closer to home, but no less charming, than the more famous places that we had visited. Mike and I found an elegant Victorian inn just north of New Hope, Pennsylvania. The Golden Pheasant had six large bedrooms with beautiful Victorian furniture and fireplaces. The owner let us rent the whole house for the weekend so that we had the inn's charming living room all to ourselves for our discussion. Our favorite spot for relaxing was the large hanging swing on the front porch under lovely wisteria. We bicycled down the towpath to New Hope during the days and shopped at the quaint shops there. We ate dinners together in picturesque restaurants and chatted together on the porch of "our" house. We discussed Mike's book choice, *The Bretheren* by Woodward Armstrong about the justices on the Supreme Court and brought in refreshments to serve in the living room of our delightful inn.

John noticed how much Mike enjoyed the hanging swing on the porch of the Golden Pheasant, so he gave Mike an identical swing for his birthday in August. We took it to Rockport and hung it on a beam at one end of the big front porch there. It has been there ever since and everyone who comes to Rockport enjoys swinging on it. We have innumerable pictures of family and friends sitting on that swing. The trip to New Hope was our last special trip for some time. After John Sheehan died the group did not participate in any special trips for a long time. We continued to meet each month and Millie came regularly, but it was never quite the same without John.

In the summer of 1991 we went on a vacation with the Webers, the McCreary's, the Longs and Millie to Annapolis, Maryland. Our son Peter was the assistant coach at the United States Naval Academy and he found us a house to rent right on the Severn River, with a picturesque view from its deck. It was a nice place for a reunion with the Longs whom we had not seen for a long time. Peter took us on a tour of the Naval Academy and we shopped in Annapolis, a quaint town on the river. Beverly made an appointment with Eva Braan, the Dean of St. Johns' College, to discuss their curriculum, which is based on the series, *The Great Books of the Western World.* When we arrived at the college, Dean Braan welcomed us and took us into one of the seminar rooms. We sat around a long table and compared the Deipno readings with the required readings of St. Johns' students. We had read most of the books in their curriculum. In a thank you letter to Dean Braan, Beverly referred to our visit to St. John's as the "highlight" of our weekend in Annapolis. The weather was ideal, the view from our house on the river was beautiful and our meals at enchanting restaurants were delicious. It was a wonderful vacation and reunion with the Longs.

In 1995 we lost another longtime member of our group. Marion McCreary died, leaving another tremendous void in the Deipnos. Marion and Bruce had joined the group at its inception. Marion was one of our most loyal and dedicated members. Her book choices were always popular and she led discussions in an enthusiastic fashion. She was enthralled with the books that she chose and she and Bruce often visited the sites mentioned in her books. They visited Johnstown Pennsylvania to see the site of the great flood and Brooklyn to walk over the great bridge. She adored Bruce and he would do anything to make her happy. She loved the members of the Deipnos and was known for her thoughtfulness of others.

After Marion and Bruce celebrated their 50th anniversary at a gala dinner party given by their children, Marion was taken to the hospital with severe pains in her abdomen. She had immediate surgery and the doctors removed 90% of her stomach, which had become gangrenous from lack of blood supply to the area. She had stoically suffered pain for quite some time without telling anyone. After the surgery, Marion had to receive nourishment through tubes. I recommended a doctor from New York University Medical Center who specialized in conditions like Marion's. He recommended a system of nourishment that could pump predigested liquid food into Marion. She could wear the pump like a backpack so that nourishment would be continually pumped into her system. Marion survived with this system for another year and was able to enjoy several special family events during that time. She died in August 1995 and, like John Sheehan, she is deeply missed by all of us who loved and admired her. She wrote a weekly newspaper column for the local paper for many years and was well known in the Bound Brook—Middlesex community.

At the turn of the century the Deipnos took two more special trips. In January 1999 we planned a trip to Key West, Florida on the Martin Luther King weekend. The Heneys did not want to go and Millie felt that she was not physically up to the trip. Beverly, Dick, Bruce, Mike and I arranged to meet Tom and Simi at the Dewey House in Key West on Friday evening. We planned to fly out of Newark on Friday morning. We rented a limousine to drive us to the airport and we almost didn't get there in time due to a severe ice storm. When we arrived at the airport, all flights had been cancelled because of the storm. We stood in one of the long lines to inquire about our flight. Dick was very agitated and went off to get a cup of coffee. When he returned with no coffee he announced with great disgust that coffee cost $1.50 and he would never pay such an outrageous price. Five minutes later he announced that he was going to take the train back home and that he would never fly again. He kept his word. When we were finally able to talk with a ticket agent we were told that no planes would leave before Saturday afternoon and we would have to get in another line to change our tickets. As we waited patiently in the line a woman ahead of us lost her composure and started screaming at the ticket agent. As we stood there watching her, a customer service agent came up to us and quietly told us to follow her, which we did. She took us to another ticket desk and exchanged all our tickets for the first flight out on Saturday afternoon. We thanked her and then took a taxi back home.

On Saturday Dick drove us all back to the airport, but declined to join us as we flew off to Miami arriving at 8:00 p.m. There were no connecting flights to Key West so we lined up to rent a car, which we finally got at 10:00 p.m. Mike drove us down the keys and we arrived at Dewey House in Key West after midnight. The Longs were waiting up for us and showed us to our room. The hotel was very accommodating and did not charge us for Friday night. We all met for the complementary breakfast in the morning. We only had a day and a half in Key West but we enjoyed every minute of it. The Dewey House had belonged to the famous educator John Dewey and had been renovated into an elegant small hotel. It was right on the beach and provided a large breakfast on the porch adjacent to the beach each morning.

After breakfast on Sunday we decided to split up to visit the different sights that interested us. Mike and I drove to Bahia

Honda State Park, which we had visited on our vacation to Key West the year before. The ocean at Bahia Honda was a beautiful turquoise color and very clean, perfect for swimming. The ocean at Key West was not appealing for swimming as it was dirty and gray and very few people swam in it. After an hour of swimming and a nice lunch at the State Park dining room, we returned to Key West for dinner with the Deipnos. Tom Long had discovered a roof top restaurant and made reservations for us. After dinner we returned to Dewey House and held the discussion in our spacious room. Tom had chosen the book, *Slouching Toward Gomorrah* by Robert Bork, about the decline of civilized conduct and personal integrity in our country today. The discussion was vigorous, and we all enjoyed being together again.

On Monday we enjoyed a relaxed breakfast and then said good-by to the Longs. The rest of us flew to Miami and, as we walked through the airport toward our flight to Newark, Beverly suddenly came running back to us yelling, "You won't believe this!" All flights to Newark had been cancelled because of high winds in Newark Airport. We again waited in line for further directions and heard ticket agents repeating that they could not provide accommodations for stranded passengers, as they were not responsible for weather conditions. Luckily a customer service agent came to our rescue a second time. He took us aside and told us that the airline would give us free lodging and meals in a Miami motel. Tuesday morning we flew back to Newark and were relieved to be home again. But we all agreed that we had a wonderful time together despite the mishaps.

Our first trip of the new century was a visit to Cape May, New Jersey in May 2002. We chose this location so that Dick could come without flying on a plane. Millie was having problems with her heart and wanted to stay close to her doctor, so she did not come with us. Mike and I had visited Cape May in November of 2001 for a brief getaway and we found a perfect inn for the

Deipnos. The Peter Shield Inn was similar to the Golden Pheasant Inn in New Hope. It was an elegant old white mansion right on the beach. The bedrooms were large with fireplaces and wonderful views of the beach and ocean. There was a charming sitting room on the second floor looking out over the ocean. It had enough comfortable chairs for all ten of us to sit on during our discussion and the inn served wine and cheese there from 5:00 to 7:00 p.m. every evening.

On the first night Beverly found a superb restaurant for dinner in a picturesque Victorian house. On Friday morning we enjoyed the inn's complementary breakfast while discussing current events with the Longs. In the evening we decided to go to the Lobster House for dinner, and then Mildred led the discussion on her book, *Beethoven's Hair,* in our upstairs sitting room. We talked until after midnight and truly enjoyed each other's company. We decided to eat our last dinner in Cape May at the Peter Shield Inn, which was also a five-star restaurant. We had a big round table next to the front window and enjoyed the piano music as we ate our delicious meals. On Sunday morning we all headed home after a delightful vacation together.

In August Millie Sheehan died. She looked forward to being with John again and seemed to accept death with serenity. She had moved into a nice apartment in a senior citizen residence for the last few years of her life. Her memorial service was held in the auditorium of the complex so that her friends could easily attend the service. Mike spoke at the service and described Millie as "a lady—a woman of high moral and ethical principles, of impeccable manners who was always concerned about the welfare of those around her." Mike continued, "Millie was cheerful and vivacious and her bright spirit enlivened every gathering where she was present." Millie was a loyal participant in the Deipno meetings. She and John never missed a meeting of the group and Millie continued that record after John's death.

Mike commented, "Millie was one of our dearest friends and took special interest in every one of our children and grandchildren." She frequently visited our home in Rockport and continually contributed things that were needed there. She made curtains for several rooms and needlepoint pictures for the walls, and gave us gifts for "no specific reason, just thought you might like it." She was a part of our lives for thirty years and she is sorely missed.

The Deipnosophistical Society has been a vital part of our lives. We love all the members we have known and the books that we have read and discussed together. John Sheehan summed up our feelings in the following poem, which he wrote:

The Fifth Gift

What can the earth be made of
Asked the learned men of yore.
Air and fire, water, earth
The elements are four.
Ah, but we are wiser now.
We know the earth is more.
Something else the world did ask:
What has the man who's blessed?
Why, fame and health, power and wealth,
These four gifts are the best.
But just as elements no more
Are found to number only four,
So do we find that we who're blessed,
Of more than four gifts are possessed.
We Deipnos have the gift of health,
Perhaps some power, fame and wealth.
But a fifth and far more precious gift
Lifts us above the common run.
We have the gift, which kindles flame
To fuse our souls and make us one.

This gracious gift—a cement that binds,
Stronger than kith or kin,
So that without rancor, heat or anger
We can resolve the problems
Of poetry, politics and art,
Religion, philosophy or heart.
With fervent gratitude and humble pride,
With all vain pretense aside—
We Deipnos are a happy band,
A blessed company—an elite,
The sifted few who reside
On the sunny side of the street.

14

From Academia to Administration

In July 1988 Wagner College hired a new president, Dr. Norman Smith. Prior to his arrival, the college was deeply concerned over its continued viability. The previous president had driven the college into serious debt so that "financial exigency" had been declared. After Smith assumed the presidency his vision and determination turned the situation completely around. He stabilized financial conditions, upgraded the facilities, beautified the campus and raised the academic caliber of the college. As a result of these improvements, Wagner became a more desirable college for outstanding students and we were able to increase enrollment without sacrificing the new higher academic standards. Under President Smith's leadership Wagner earned a reputation as one of the finest small liberal arts colleges in the country.

When Smith took over he instituted a number of restrictions because of the college's budgetary constraints. He announced that there would be no automatic replacements of administrators, faculty or staff. Budgets for new library books and equipment were drastically reduced. Part-time faculty were cut back and full-time faculty were asked not to teach overloads or tutorials unless they did so voluntarily. No salary increases were allowed for administrators, faculty or staff and the student work budget was cut back dramatically. The president replaced vacancies in top administrative posts with faculty members, which reduced the number of full-time faculty. With losses of faculty to administrative positions, leave of absences, retirements, and resignations, the number of full-time faculty dropped from 81 to 68 in Dr Smith's first year at the college. During the fall of 1988 several measures were considered to alleviate the budget deficit. The president worked to convert the college's short-term debt into long-term debt and several large grant proposals were written. There was talk of using some of Wagner's facilities for a health care center and of closing Wagner's study abroad program in Austria, which was no longer profitable to the college.

The president was concerned about the development of Wagner's faculty while the college's budget was so constrained. In November we became aware of the New York University Faculty Resource Network, which provided opportunities to small liberal arts colleges to develop their faculty at New York University (NYU) under a large federal grant. NYU was entertaining applications for membership in the network and we applied and were accepted. Membership entitled us to place up to fifteen of our full-time faculty with NYU each semester as university associates. In this capacity, our faculty could audit NYU courses, use their libraries and work on research projects with NYU professors free of charge. We were also eligible to have several of our faculty members become network scholars in residence at NYU during their sabbaticals. The program would pay Wagner $10,000 to replace each of these faculty members while he or she was at NYU. Soon after we joined the network NYU accepted fifteen Wagner faculty members as university associates and three as network scholars. This was a real honor for Wagner College, as most colleges in the network were only awarded one scholar in residence position. I became the liaison officer from Wagner and attended meetings with the deans and vice presidents of the other colleges in the network. These meetings gave us the opportunity to work on common faculty development and curricula concerns, and allowed me to give presentations on some of Wagner's new programs. The liaison officers visited several of the colleges represented in the network. I was very impressed with visits to Morehouse and Spellman colleges in Atlanta and Dillon and Xavier colleges in New Orleans.

At the beginning of 1989 President Smith began a rigorous effort to upgrade Wagner College. He appointed eleven faculty members to an academic restructuring committee to investigate a number of well-known liberal arts colleges and use their findings to develop a better academic structure and government at Wagner. He hoped an improved structure would reduce the duplication of faculty effort and allow more time for scholarly development of faculty. He suggested that committee members who were not personal friends should go in teams of two to visit at least two colleges. I was appointed to the committee and went with Bob Volyn, an economics professor, to visit Muhlenberg College and Drew University. We talked to the vice president of each college and brought back some interesting findings. Bob and I also found that we had wrestling sons in common. The restructuring committee met weekly and during spring vacation to discuss the merits of models from different colleges. The committee presented three models to the Wagner faculty at a preliminary workshop held at the president's house one Saturday. After a full day of deliberations, one of the two models was eliminated and it was decided that the other two models should be officially brought before the entire faculty at a special faculty meeting in May. Copies of the two models were distributed to all faculty for study, and at the May meeting the model with14 departments was approved by faculty vote. The president was not satisfied and he continued to pare down the number of departments. Five years later the faculty voted to eliminate departments and condense the academic structure to five Faculties presided over by faculty chairs. The old academic departments were integrated into the five Faculties, which were entitled Humanities, Performing and Visual Arts, Professional Programs, Sciences and Social Sciences.

I continued as the director of the interdisciplinary studies program (IDS). The president was interested in all aspects of the Wagner curriculum and soon after he arrived, he called me into his office to discuss the IDS program. I told him the history of the program and some of the problems since its inception in 1976, and he expressed a desire to upgrade the program. He called a meeting of several professors who had been key figures in developing and teaching IDS courses over the past 13 years. These professors had been paid for their work originally by a large outside grant. However the funds from the grant had dried up and, with a deficit college budget, the president was unwilling to pay faculty to revise the IDS program. The faculty in his office stated that they would not work on a revision unless they were paid. I piped up and said that I could get a group of IDS faculty to work with me on the revision without pay. Everyone looked at me in disbelief, but the president said that he was willing to let me try. I asked three outstanding professors who taught in IDS to work with me without pay to revise IDS. They all agreed immediately. I also enlisted the help of other professors as consultants and began some background work in preparation for a summer workshop.

First I went to Columbia University to see my doctoral advisor, Dr. McClintock. I asked him to be a consultant to our IDS revision committee and he agreed. I visited several colleges over the next month to inquire about their interdisciplinary programs. I attended conferences at Iona College and Drew University on their core programs and interviewed the directors of similar programs at Upsala College and Fairleigh Dickenson University. The last of these was revising its own program and agreed to give a workshop at Wagner for our committee.

The revision committee at Wagner was made up of four professors from different disciplines: Otto Raths from physics, Ammini Moorthy from Biology, Bill Bly from literature and myself with a background in literature, philosophy and science. We worked from 9:30 a.m. to 4:30 p.m., Monday through Friday, for six weeks. Dr. McClintock spent a number of days with us as a consultant and other Wagner professors gave us input at different times. These consultants came from a variety of disciplines including economics, theatre, religion, philosophy, history and nursing. I reported our progress to President Smith, and he approved the revised IDS program, which was renamed Multidisciplinary Studies (MDS) so as not to confuse it with the old IDS program. The faculty approved the MDS program at the December meeting of the whole faculty.

On the last day of our workshop I took the committee members out to lunch in my brand new red Hyundai. Mike and I invited the members of the committee and their families to our house in Rockport to celebrate all our work. We had picnics on the rocks and delicious meals at the house followed by round-robin ping-pong and other games such as *Trivial Pursuit* and charades. The children enjoyed shopping for souvenirs on Bearskin Neck, swimming off the rocks or at the beach and playing lots of games. We all had a great time together.

During the summer of 1989 four new professors joined the MDS program. Marilyn Kiss, a Spanish professor, became my most enthusiastic MDS faculty member and a loyal friend. She would become the course leader of two MDS courses over the next 14 semesters. She and I always taught sections of the same courses, and shared our ideas for content and teaching strategies. We discussed our progress almost daily. Cindy Carlson, a brilliant professor of English literature, gave the MDS faculty many insights for interpreting literature during our summer workshops. The other two new faculty members, Pat Lutz, a professor of chemistry, and Juliet Niehaus, a sociologist, both became course leaders for MDS and later chairpersons of their respective departments. Drs. Kiss, Lutz, Raths and Moorthy and I taught in MDS throughout its existence. Course leaders during MDS existence included: Professors Bly, Moorthy, Henkel, Niehaus, Lutz, Stearns, Dean and Kiss. Drs. Dean and Kiss were course leaders for the longest time and both were a tremendous help to me in developing the course syllabi and handout books each semester.

In September President Smith appointed me Associate Dean of Academic Affairs. He appointed Mildred Nelson as Registrar and Dean of Academic Services. We moved from the building that housed the nursing department to the registrar's office in Cunard Hall. Our new home was the former Cunard mansion of the shipping magnate who owned Cunard Lines. It had deteriorated over the years, but it still had hints of its former splendor. There were sparkling chandeliers hanging from some of the ceilings, ornate marble fireplaces in two rooms and ivory statues in the corners of the hall. I was fortunate to have one of the marble fireplaces and a big bay window in my office. We were in the center of the campus and every one who walked by my big window waved to me. It was a grand place to work. Mildred and I would stay in Cunard Hall until we retired. There was a group of very friendly and efficient women working in the registrar's office next to me and they became wonderful friends. The business office was across the hall and also had friendly personnel, who were a great help to Mildred and me.

One of my first tasks as Associate Dean was to write an annual report for the college, which I would continue to write for the next twelve years until I retired. The annual reports were 25-35 pages long and covered academic activities plus changes and accomplishments in curricula, faculty, students and administrators. Both undergraduate and graduate curricula were discussed in reference to requirements for general education, electives and majors. All changes in courses and programs were reported. Each department was discussed separately and activities of faculty in each department were listed. Academic services such as the library, academic advisement and career planning were described. A profile of the faculty was given including their ages and salary ranges, hiring, retiring, and firing, as well as promotions and merit prizes awarded to them.

In the annual reports, I described the activities of the faculty organizations—Academic Policy Committee, Committee of Chairs, Faculty Personnel Committee and the Faculty Hearing and Appeals Committee. A review of the meetings of the Committee of the Whole, nicknamed COW, was included and finally the activities of the top academic administrators were reported. Researching all this information took a good deal of time, especially obtaining reports from department chairs with an updated list of activities of their faculties. It was an interesting job putting all the information together and typing the reports, but at times it was frustrating. The end result, however, proved helpful for writing annual reports for the Middle States Association of Colleges and Universities and the New York State Department of Education. The Middle States team that came to survey the college in the last year that I was working there, commented on the value of my annual reports of the previous ten years, stating that the reports gave them a comprehensive view of the college.

In November 1989, soon after I became Associate Dean, I was sent to a conference of deans of Lutheran colleges held in Guernovaca, Mexico. Mike joined me on this visit, as did the spouses of several of the other deans attending the conference. The purpose of the meeting was to have the deans observe the program for US students who visited Mexican families for a semester to practice their Spanish and learn about a foreign culture. The deans and their spouses stayed in a monastery in Guernovaca and enjoyed eating and discussing the program together. The Lutheran Council that sponsored the trip assigned each of the deans a Mexican family to visit. Mike and I visited a family living in a one-room shack next to the railroad tracks. The home was immaculate and owner most gracious. There were several pictures displayed of the son who worked in America and sent home funds to support the family. They were very proud of him. We also visited a larger family in a barrio on the outskirts of the city. We were impressed with the program and I gave a presentation about our trip at the Wagner Faculty Forum when I returned.

In the spring semester of 1990 the new MDS program was initiated. There were sixteen sections of each course in the new program and all students were required to take the four courses in the first four semesters at Wagner College. Over the years over forty faculty members would teach in the program. The unifying theme of MDS was the individual and his or her relationship with society. Aspects of this theme were to be presented in four courses, each representing one of the four basic disciplines of the liberal arts—the humanities, the natural sciences, the social sciences and the arts.

The course that I taught throughout the existence of MDS was MDS 101 *Perspectives on Human Nature*. In this course students were assigned readings of Plato, the Bible, Kant, Freud, Marx and Sartre. They then used the theories of these writers to analyze young people in literature and cinema who were confronted by difficult life situations. Students were asked to read autobiographies of Jill Conway and Tobias Wolff, and novels by Doris Lessing, Toni Morrison and Gustave Flaubert. They were also required to see films about individuals having to make hard choices. The assigned films were *Medea, Cinema Paradiso, My Left Foot, Chariots of Fire* and *Europa Europa*. When the course was taught, assignments on films were alternated with reading assignments to give students more time to read each book. The classroom discussions were lively and the students seemed to enjoy the assignments.

In MDS 102 *Science and Technological Progress* students
discussed problems as well as benefits that have resulted from
modern scientific and technological discoveries. The readings
and films assigned helped students view the cultural changes
that evolved as a result of these discoveries. Assignments
included books and films on scientific discoveries, the history
of science and biographies of famous scientists. The course
concluded with a best seller, *And the Water Turned to Blood,*
about Dr. JoAnn Burkholder's recent discovery of pfiesteria
piscicida, a deadly aquatic organism that was killing thousands
of fish and even attacking humans in the estuaries of North
Carolina. Dr. Burkholder endured tremendous pressure from
politicians and other scientists concerning her discovery of the
organism that was killing so many fish in Pamlico Sound. These
organisms were nourished by waste from large hog farms. The
waste was washed down the river into Pamlico Sound where it
stagnated in the closed bay that was not cleansed by the ocean.
Later this organism was also found in the Chesapeake Bay. The
owners of the hog farms, supported by the politicians, felt that
knowledge of her discovery could result in onerous legal
restrictions and they tried to discredit her research. Other
scientists, who were jealous of her, also tried to deny or cover
up her findings. This assignment helped students understand
the politics and prejudices that can interfere with scientific
progress. We invited Dr. Burkholder to speak at Wagner and
she was well received by MDS students and members of the
community at large.

MDS 201 *Challenges of Society: A Global Perspective*
considered the emergence of modern society and analyzed
how individuals have shaped economic, political and social
thought and how they have been affected by it. Each society
included in the course was examined, starting with an
historical overview, followed by an analysis of a specific
crisis in the society and concluding with a discussion of
modern worldwide parallels of the crisis. Students explored

societal crises such as freedom of speech, plagues, poverty, and civil rights. The societies considered were classical Athens, medieval Europe, South Africa and the United States. Readings and films assigned related to these issues in the different societies. Each semester that the course was taught we invited men and women with AIDS to speak to all the sections of the class about how they coped with the disease. Students seemed very interested and asked them lots of questions, which they answered freely.

In MDS 202 *The Arts: A Cultural Response* students examined how individuals had reacted to events in different cultures through artistic expression in music, theatre, painting and creative writing. Rather than try to give an historical overview of art, this course considered the functions of art within different cultures at different times and showed that art responded to the needs of society. In classical Greece art served as an act of religious worship. During the neoclassical period of the European tradition art acted as a servant of society and followed certain rules. In many societies art acted as protest, either against previously established aesthetic rules in the Romantic period in Europe and the Jazz Age in the USA, or against modern atrocities committed by society such as war. Reading and film assignments gave examples of artistic expression in response to events in different cultures and circumstances.

Prior to the introduction of the MDS program, a series of eighteen meetings were held with MDS faculty to prepare them to teach the courses. A workshop was given in January 1990 for final preparation of faculty who would be teaching the first course in the new program. In May and June two workshops were held to prepare faculty to teach two more new MDS courses for the first time in the fall. The last of the new MDS courses was first taught in the spring semester of 1991. Workshops were stimulating experiences for the faculty, allowing them to contribute knowledge from their disciplines and learn from their fellow faculty members in other disciplines. Several faculty in the MDS program took advantage of the NYU Faculty Resource Network to enhance their knowledge about certain areas of MDS. Professors Carlson, Kiss, Moorthy, Niehaus and Rappaport became university associates at NYU during the 1989-1990 academic year, and other professors took advantage of NYU writing seminars in the summer.

Teaching strategies as well as course content were discussed in the MDS workshops at Wagner. Faculty shared their experiences in teaching and learned new strategies from each other. They decided that seminar style classes were most effective in helping students explore ideas together. Students were held accountable for doing their assignments and class participation was included in determining their final grades. I always had my students sit in a circle for discussion. I learned all their names on the first day of class so that I could call on the more reticent ones for discussion. When they saw that others listened to them respectfully, they learned to share ideas and discuss them with each other. The MDS professors found that seminars generated intellectual excitement in students as they shared their minds and feelings.

There was a lot of work involved in directing the MDS program. Each semester books had to be ordered for courses, along with desk copies for the course professors. I printed syllabi for each course and distributed them to the professors. There were a number of articles and excerpts from books that I had bound together in handout books for students in each course. I had to obtain permission from the copyright holder for each article before including it in the handout books. Course leaders helped me prepare the handout books. At the end of each semester I held a workshop to review student evaluations of each course and refine the course as needed. Changes were incorporated into the course for the next time that it would be taught and syllabi and handout books were revised to reflect the changes.

It was also my job to evaluate part-time teachers in all the MDS courses once a year.

In the summer of 1990 Mike and I invited several MDS faculty up to Rockport again. We enjoyed sitting out on the rocks talking and watching our sons diving for lobsters. Steve was an experienced diver, but Peter was a novice. One afternoon they went down together as partners and after a while Steve and his cousin Andy came up with about a dozen lobsters. I asked them why Peter wasn't with them. They looked sheepish and said he had gone off on his own. One of our guests said that he thought he heard Peter say that his oxygen tank was defective. I started to panic. Someone ran up to the house to call the harbor patrol. Steve and Andy just threw their bag of lobsters on the seaweed and dove back into the water. I got so excited that I dove into the water fully clothed in a summer dress. As I swam out toward where Peter was supposed to be, he popped out of the water holding up a lobster looking very pleased. He asked me what was wrong and I told him how worried we all were. He was totally embarrassed and refused to look at anyone when he got out of the water.

I came out of the water in my wet dress onto the rocks. Cindy was standing there with three friends staring at me. She introduced me to one of them saying, "Mom, this is Denis." Cindy had been reluctant to bring Denis to meet me as she was trying to win his heart and she didn't want me to do some crazy thing to embarrass her and ruin her chances with him. I had just blown it for her and, to make it worse, I blurted, "DENIS? Oh I promised not to embarrass Cindy in front of you!" Later Cindy told me how embarrassed she was that I had revealed to Denis that she was pursuing him. However, Denis thought the whole incident was hilarious and he married Cindy anyway. He said he always liked her mother because she was so down-to-earth. Otto Raths never tired of telling this story to anyone who would listen.

In the spring of 1991 the last of the four new courses in the
MDS program was to be introduced. In January we had a
workshop to prepare the faculty to teach the course. After the
workshop, Mike and I held a celebration at our home for all the
MDS faculty and their spouses or friends. Forty guests came
and we had a great time playing quiz games about MDS content
and gorging on lots of homemade food and drinks. After the
last new course had been taught, we invited a large group of
MDS faculty and their families to Rockport. They enjoyed eating
lobster, walking and swimming at the beach and sitting on the
rocks. We played games and ate big meals in the dining room
and on the rocks. The Barchittas and the Raths both brought
their 13 year-old sons, who enjoyed tossing the football in the
yard. They also tossed pillows in their room and after a vigorous
pillow fight one of the old Rockport pillows burst its seams and
there were feathers everywhere in the room. Luckily it was a
small room so the feathers were soon gathered up. The next
week Otto came to my office at Wagner with a large bundle. It
was a big pillow to replace the one that gave out. Mike liked
that new pillow and has used it ever since on our bed at Rockport.

Soon after President Smith came to Wagner he took me aside
and told me his view of the academic honors ceremony at the
college. He was very disappointed with it and wished to put
more emphasis on academic achievement. He spoke of the effort
that went into sports banquets to reward the top athletes and
said that he would like to do something comparable to recognize
top scholars at the college. He asked me to take on the challenge
of setting up a banquet with substantial awards for academic
scholarship. I accepted his challenge.

The first academic awards banquet was given in May 1990.
The college rented the same catering hall that the athletic
banquets used and over 400 students and parents attended that
first dinner. The president had specific directions that he wanted
carried out for the dinner. He told me to remove awards for

leadership and extra curricula activities that had previously been given at the honors award ceremony. He made a rule that all awards must be for academic achievement and include at least a one hundred dollar stipend. All students on the dean's list were to receive a certificate in a leather binder and all special awards were to be put on wooden plaques with checks taped to the back of them. Special prizes were awarded by departments, alumni or honors groups. Previously many awards had been small amounts of money or books. In order to meet the president's stipulation that all awards must be $100.00 or over, I had to contact departments or honors groups and ask them to increase the amount of their awards. Most of the alumni awards were endowed with enough funds that the amount of the awards could be increased, but some needed more money in the endowment to be able to give an annual amount of $100.00. It took a lot of time and tack to contact all the award donors and obtain enough funding for all the special awards. The president of the board of trustees, Dr. Donald Spiro, agreed to donate $500 annually for an award to the outstanding senior and I ordered a specially engraved trophy to be presented with his check. The senior with the highest overall grade average was selected to receive this award each year.

Early in the spring semester I contacted the computer center to obtain the names of all the students on the dean's list. The president's secretary, Judy Lunde, typed the students' names on preprinted certificates. I spent many a late evening stuffing leather folders with hundreds of dean's list certificates and putting them in envelopes with the students' names on the outside. Department chairs sent me the names of students they had chosen to receive special awards. I gave these names to Judy Lunde and she typed them, along with the name of the awards, on specially prepared parchment. After Judy prepared these awards she sent them to me. Each award had to be covered with a plastic sheet and hammered onto a wooden plaque. There were 125 awards so I asked a group of seven friends on the faculty to help me with this task. I took them to dinner in the dining room first and then we all hammered away and Marilyn Kiss took pictures of the "hammering gang" each year. Each year I gave Judy a book for herself or her grandchildren in appreciation for all her help. I could never have accomplished all the preparations without such wonderful friends.

The first dinner was a bit harrowing. The catering hall was constructing a new parking lot. On the day of the dinner it rained all day and the parking lot became a sea of mud. In desperation I called the vice president of development, a kind and friendly man, Dr. David Long. He arranged with the restaurant owner to secure alternative parking and the dinner was a success, even though 400 people barely fit into the restaurant. After that experience, the president announced that all future academic honors dinners would be held in the Wagner College dining room looking out over the New York skyline and the Verrazano Bridge.

The academic awards banquet became so popular that in a few years the number of guests had increased to 700. The dining room could not accommodate that many people so we decided to have two dinners, one for underclass students and one for graduating seniors. Even then we had 400 or more at each dinner. A few years later we decided to also give a dinner to honor graduate students for academic achievement. Thus, in addition to all my other duties, I was in charge of three large festive academic awards banquets every spring.

However, it was rewarding to see how helpful so many people were to me in preparing for those dinners. The dining room staff truly made the dinners into banquets. The controller worked with me to get the funds for awards. The department heads found enough money for their awards and chose the recipients of them. The president's secretary, Judy Lunde, typed the names on hundreds of certificates and awards and always claimed it was an easy task. My hammering crew gave freely of their time and always worked with enthusiasm. The maintenance crew set up the stage and humored me when I got nervous just before the dinner began. And, finally, Mildred Nelson helped me lay out the awards on tables on the stage before the dinner began. We had a good system. I put numbers on the backs of the awards that corresponded with the numbers on the descriptions of the awards being read by the provost as each student came forward to receive his or her award from the president. The president liked my system because he could just pick up the awards in order as the provost read the names in the same order. I continued to arrange these academic banquets for twelve years until I retired. Mike came to all the banquets to give me moral support and I was so grateful for his comforting optimism and love.

I frequently worked late at night and on weekends to prepare for the academic awards dinners. Mike came into Wagner with me whenever I had to work on weekends or holidays. While I worked on the dinners he studied for various certification examinations. To become a certified financial planner he had to study for six exams that would give him credit for six courses. He also studied for examinations to obtain licenses to sell life insurance, mutual funds and partnerships. Another important examination that he studied for would certify him to represent clients before the IRS. He passed all the examinations on the first try. Studying for all these exams took a lot of time and he needed to be away from his office to concentrate on his studies. Mike studied at my secretary's desk in the room that had been the living room in the old Cunard mansion. There was a beautiful fireplace next to him and a magnificent chandelier over head. I worked in my office next door with another marble fireplace and high ceiling. We would get together for snacks and lunch at a small mahogany table and discuss what we were doing. It was like playing house and we loved being together. If we went in on Sunday morning we would go over to the student dining room and have Sunday brunch. On Saturday and Sunday evenings we would find a movie to see on our way home and then go dancing until midnight.

One other big job that the president assigned me was the annual completion of the Wagner College Bulletin, the catalogue that was distributed to schools and students. The 230-page undergraduate bulletin contained data about all aspects of the college and there was a similar bulletin for the graduate programs that I also prepared. The two bulletins were published in alternate years. Developing these bulletins required continual interaction with department heads and other administrators to obtain the information needed. Luckily I was a member of the Committee of Chairs so that I could keep track of all the courses that were dropped, added or revised. I arranged a meeting with all department heads to proofread the bulletin before it went to the final printing.

I typed the entire bulletin on the college's central computer system. Jim McCoy, the director, helped me out whenever I was stymied by the computer. Sometimes I was frantic when I thought that I had lost a section of the bulletin, but he always recovered it for me. The final version of the bulletin had to go to the printer before August 1st, so I did the final proofreading at Rockport each July. Harry, the printer, and I sent a number of Federal Express packages to each other in the summer. I also chose and inserted all the pictures in the bulletin and obtained the approval for the cover from the president. I produced a bulletin every year until I retired. Mike also accompanied me to Wagner while I was working on the bulletin on weekends.

I was on a number of committees during my last years at Wagner. I continued on the Committee of Chairs, the Graduate Council, and the Orientation, Retention, and Commencement committees. I was also active on a number of faculty committees that I enjoyed immensely such as the Women's Caucus and the Faculty Forum. Both of these committees, as well as MDS workshops, encouraged faculty to share knowledge, exchange views on pedagogy and course content and focus on intellectual and academic issues. The Women's Caucus encouraged women to serve as guest speakers in a number of areas including women in science and women in the workplace. I led a discussion on Henry James's *Portrait of a Lady* at a Women's Caucus meeting, where writings by and about women were often discussed. The Caucus developed activities for Women's Month each year and helped create a gender studies minor for the college.

The Faculty Forum offered faculty the opportunity to speak to their colleagues on their research and interests. The forum often worked in conjunction with the Women's Caucus. One spring eleven faculty women gave presentations at the Faculty Forum on women's issues. I was one of them and presented a paper on Mary Belle Harris, a reformer of women's prisons.

Marilyn Kiss and I attended a number of seminars related to MDS topics that were given by the humanities department at Princeton University. After lunch we enjoyed exploring the campus and the town of Princeton. Our favorite place to visit was the college bookstore.

In the 1990-1991 academic year Wagner was preparing for an accreditation visit from the Middle States Commission on Higher Education. Every faculty member was assigned to one of eight committees involved in writing the report for the accreditation. I was on the Faculty, Organization and Administration Committee with two of my closest friends, Julie Barchitta and Marilyn Kiss. Julie was the chair of our committee. As with all accreditation visits a great deal of time was spent at weekly meetings writing a comprehensive description of each area of the college activities for the upcoming visit.

That same year the college was searching for a new vice president of academic affairs. Dr. Mordechai Rozanski was chosen and began his tenure at the college on January 1, 1991. Dr. Rozanski was short, jolly and full of energy. His goal was to develop a comprehensive plan for the college's academic structure and programs. He was able to enlist enthusiastic support from the faculty. He promptly organized the Committee on Academic Change (CAC) as a strategic planning committee to review the curriculum and recommend changes. He recommended focusing on the liberal arts core, distribution requirements and majors, as well as issues of coherence and compatibility among the various elements involved. The CAC met for the first time in March with the goal of resolving key issues before publication of the next bulletin. CAC would fulfill the recommendation of the Middle States commission for continual involvement of the faculty in the ongoing academic planning of the college. The members chosen to be on the committee included most of the leaders at the college, many of them faculty who taught in MDS. It was a joy to me to be a part of such a vital committee.

In his first month at the college Dr. Rozanski appointed me as Director of Graduate Studies. He took a group of faculty to the American Association of Colleges (AAC) conference in Washington DC. Drs. Kiss, Kaelber and Raths and I were chosen to go because of our involvement in the core curriculum. We brought back a number of ideas that could be used by the CAC. During his first year Dr. Rozanski made progress with CAC and also worked to improve other aspects of the college such as establishing a system of Dean's Merit Scholarships to entice better students to come to Wagner.

In the fall of 1992 Dr. Rozanski decided to combine and improve the Academic Advisement and Career Planning Offices. He appointed me as the new director of the combined office in addition to all my other jobs. I had the east wing of the New another picture for his or her ID photo. I used paper with two columns of squares down the middle. My secretary typed the names of everyone in the college next to the boxes. Mildred and Marilyn came to my aid and during the summer we pasted 1800 pictures into the boxes on the sheets of paper. I then took these pages to the printer and he copied them and bound them in a cover to distribute to all 1800 people. There were two sections to the book: the undergraduate students and the administrators, faculty and staff. The books were beautiful and I might have had to do another one for graduate students, but a quirk developed that brought an end to any further picture directories. Some male students called some female students in the book and soon the book was nicknamed the "Stalker Book." The president was disappointed that we couldn't keep on publishing the book, but he felt it would not be good public relations to continue with it even if only a few students complained that they were being bothered. I was not disappointed.

In 1996 a search committee was formed to look for a new provost. President Smith wanted a well-known individual for the position who could make Wagner College recognized nationally. In the spring of 1997 Dr. Richard Guarasci was hired. Gary Sullivan went back to managing the theatre department and became his former happy self. Dr. Guarasci was nationally known for his innovative college program and he had published a book describing it. Guaraci visited Wagner several times during the spring and early summer to prepare for his new role at the college. He spoke to the faculty at a COW meeting about his plans for reviewing and improving the curriculum. He formed an ad hoc curriculum review committee with representatives from every department and worked with them during the summer to develop a new curriculum. MDS as a program ceased to exist, but MDS courses were to continue and be used in the new curriculum.

Administration Building renovated to house the new Center for Academic Advisement and Career Development. I advertised for heads of each part of the new center. While I was in the midst of this endeavor, Dr. Rozanski went to Italy to interview students for our MBA program. He called me about one of the resumes for the position as head of academic advisement. He told me that he was impressed with one candidate who had a doctorate. I told him that I had doubts about the personality of the candidate as an advisor to students even though he had a Ph.D. Dr.Rozanski told me to go ahead and hire him anyway, so I did. The first thing he did as head of Academic Advisement was to insult the secretary and make her cry. I called him in the next day and fired him. Everyone was surprised at the firmness and speed of my decision, as I was usually reluctant to assert myself so strongly. Soon after this we interviewed a capable young woman, Christine Hagedorn, for the position and she turned out to be a great success.

We also found an excellent person to be in charge of Career Development, Professor Tony Carter. He was a faculty member from the Business Department and did an excellent job of running Career Development in addition to his faculty workload. He revamped Career Development and developed an innovative mentor program. Dr. Walter Rohrs, Coordinator of Internships, also became part of Career Development. Christine Hagedorn took on the job of International Student Advisor and we hired two more people to be part of the academic advisement team. Being Director of the center gave me another big task. At the end of each semester I met with Mildred Nelson and Christine Hagedorn to go over all the undergraduate transcripts to determine which students should be put on probation or dismissed. Letters were sent to all students involved. I performed the same task for all the graduate students at the end of each term and sent warning letters to those whose grade averages fell below B-. I had the unpleasant job of notifying graduate students when they were dismissed for poor grades.

In October of 1992 my secretary was offered a higher paying position in the personnel department and I had to hire someone else. What a blessing that turned out to be! I found Ann Dillon, who was the best secretary and friend I could ever have wished for. She stayed with me until I retired and I loved her! In January 1993, Dr. Rozanski surprised everyone by accepting the presidency of Guelph College in Canada. What a blow that was. Mildred Nelson was appointed Acting Vice President of Academic Affairs while a search committee looked for a replacement for Dr. Rozanski. Other search committees were looking for a new Vice President of Development and Deans of Admission and Students. Dr. Linda Basch was shortly hired as Vice President of Academic Affairs and Provost. She took over her new position on August 1, 1993. The other three positions were filled within the year. The new Dean of Students, Diedre Shaffer, attached herself to Mildred and me and looked to us as mentors. We shared a lot of laughs, and sometimes sorrows, with her over the next eight years.

At the beginning of the fall 1993 semester Dr. Basch arranged to meet with each chairperson to discuss his or her program and with each faculty member to get acquainted. One of the first things she did was to take a group of key faculty to the AAC conference in Washington DC. Dr. Basch's tenure at Wagner was brief. She had a number of good ideas but rarely did she succeed in fulfilling them. For instance, she was especially interested in the issue of diversity in the curriculum. She called together an ad hoc committee, made up of several faculty and administrators to write a proposal for an AAC grant to help the college address this issue. Unfortunately Wagner did not obtain the grant. Dr. Basch also sought to develop courses about the United Nations where students would be involved at the United Nations for practical experience. She was unsuccessful in this attempt also. In some areas her endeavors were successful. She participated in workshops with the Women's Caucus to develop a new minor in gender studies

and she developed a Faculty Mentor's Program in which faculty could submit plans for student enrichment experiences in New York City. Mildred Nelson and I were on her committee to approve the faculty plans and assign appropriate finances from an American Lutheran grant to carry them out. Dr. Basch established a council of student representatives to meet with her monthly to discuss student interests and problems. She held a provost meeting with Mildred and me every Friday afternoon. In the spring of 1994, President Smith promoted Mildred Nelson to vice provost and me to associate provost at the same time.

Dr. Basch worked well with students and faculty, but the president was not satisfied with her ability in budgeting, funding proposals and planning. During the summer Dr. Basch left the college and Professor Sullivan was appointed Interim Provost. Gary Sullivan had been a very successful manager of the theatre department for a number of years. President Smith felt that with his management experience Gary could handle the provost position for a while until a national search for a permanent provost could be conducted. Gary gamely took over the provost position, but it was quite a strain on him, especially writing reports for the Middle States commission and the New York State Department of Education. Mildred helped him with these reports and we both supported him as much as we could.

Early in 1995 while we were in an administrative heads meeting, President Smith announced that he had a project that he was excited about. He wanted to produce a directory of everyone in the college with a picture next to each name. He looked right at me and said, "I think that the only person who could do this is Connie Schuyler." I gulped and he continued, "Do you think you could produce such a book?" Of course I said, "yes." This job in addition to all my other tasks was truly a challenge. I decided to use the ID pictures from the Security Office. I sent a letter to everyone on campus telling them what I was trying to accomplish and offered everyone the opportunity to substitute

Administration Building renovated to house the new Center for Academic Advisement and Career Development. I advertised for heads of each part of the new center. While I was in the midst of this endeavor, Dr. Rozanski went to Italy to interview students for our MBA program. He called me about one of the resumes for the position as head of academic advisement. He told me that he was impressed with one candidate who had a doctorate. I told him that I had doubts about the personality of the candidate as an advisor to students even though he had a Ph.D. Dr.Rozanski told me to go ahead and hire him anyway, so I did. The first thing he did as head of Academic Advisement was to insult the secretary and make her cry. I called him in the next day and fired him. Everyone was surprised at the firmness and speed of my decision, as I was usually reluctant to assert myself so strongly. Soon after this we interviewed a capable young woman, Christine Hagedorn, for the position and she turned out to be a great success.

We also found an excellent person to be in charge of Career Development, Professor Tony Carter. He was a faculty member from the Business Department and did an excellent job of running Career Development in addition to his faculty workload. He revamped Career Development and developed an innovative mentor program. Dr. Walter Rohrs, Coordinator of Internships, also became part of Career Development. Christine Hagedorn took on the job of International Student Advisor and we hired two more people to be part of the academic advisement team. Being Director of the center gave me another big task. At the end of each semester I met with Mildred Nelson and Christine Hagedorn to go over all the undergraduate transcripts to determine which students should be put on probation or dismissed. Letters were sent to all students involved. I performed the same task for all the graduate students at the end of each term and sent warning letters to those whose grade averages fell below B-. I had the unpleasant job of notifying graduate students when they were dismissed for poor grades.

In October of 1992 my secretary was offered a higher paying position in the personnel department and I had to hire someone else. What a blessing that turned out to be! I found Ann Dillon, who was the best secretary and friend I could ever have wished for. She stayed with me until I retired and I loved her! In January 1993, Dr. Rozanski surprised everyone by accepting the presidency of Guelph College in Canada. What a blow that was. Mildred Nelson was appointed Acting Vice President of Academic Affairs while a search committee looked for a replacement for Dr. Rozanski. Other search committees were looking for a new Vice President of Development and Deans of Admission and Students. Dr. Linda Basch was shortly hired as Vice President of Academic Affairs and Provost. She took over her new position on August 1, 1993. The other three positions were filled within the year. The new Dean of Students, Diedre Shaffer, attached herself to Mildred and me and looked to us as mentors. We shared a lot of laughs, and sometimes sorrows, with her over the next eight years.

At the beginning of the fall 1993 semester Dr. Basch arranged to meet with each chairperson to discuss his or her program and with each faculty member to get acquainted. One of the first things she did was to take a group of key faculty to the AAC conference in Washington DC. Dr. Basch's tenure at Wagner was brief. She had a number of good ideas but rarely did she succeed in fulfilling them. For instance, she was especially interested in the issue of diversity in the curriculum. She called together an ad hoc committee, made up of several faculty and administrators to write a proposal for an AAC grant to help the college address this issue. Unfortunately Wagner did not obtain the grant. Dr. Basch also sought to develop courses about the United Nations where students would be involved at the United Nations for practical experience. She was unsuccessful in this attempt also. In some areas her endeavors were successful. She participated in workshops with the Women's Caucus to develop a new minor in gender studies and she developed a Faculty Mentor's Program in which faculty could submit plans for student enrichment experiences in New York City. Mildred Nelson and I were on her committee to approve the faculty plans and assign appropriate finances from an American Lutheran grant to carry them out. Dr. Basch established a council of student representatives to meet with her monthly to discuss student interests and problems. She held a provost meeting with Mildred and me every Friday afternoon. In the spring of 1994, President Smith promoted Mildred Nelson to vice provost and me to associate provost at the same time.

Dr. Basch worked well with students and faculty, but the president was not satisfied with her ability in budgeting, funding proposals and planning. During the summer Dr. Basch left the college and Professor Sullivan was appointed Interim Provost. Gary Sullivan had been a very successful manager of the theatre department for a number of years. President Smith felt that with his management experience Gary could handle the provost position for a while until a national search for a permanent provost could be conducted. Gary gamely took over the provost position, but it was quite a strain on him, especially writing reports for the Middle States commission and the New York State Department of Education. Mildred helped him with these reports and we both supported him as much as we could.

Early in 1995 while we were in an administrative heads meeting, President Smith announced that he had a project that he was excited about. He wanted to produce a directory of everyone in the college with a picture next to each name. He looked right at me and said, "I think that the only person who could do this is Connie Schuyler." I gulped and he continued, "Do you think you could produce such a book?" Of course I said, "yes." This job in addition to all my other tasks was truly a challenge. I decided to use the ID pictures from the Security Office. I sent a letter to everyone on campus telling them what I was trying to accomplish and offered everyone the opportunity to substitute another picture for his or her ID photo. I used paper with two columns of squares down the middle. My secretary typed the names of everyone in the college next to the boxes. Mildred and Marilyn came to my aid and during the summer we pasted 1800 pictures into the boxes on the sheets of paper. I then took these pages to the printer and he copied them and bound them in a cover to distribute to all 1800 people. There were two sections to the book: the undergraduate students and the administrators, faculty and staff. The books were beautiful and I might have had to do another one for graduate students, but a quirk developed that brought an end to any further picture directories. Some male students called some female students in the book and soon the book was nicknamed the "Stalker Book." The president was disappointed that we couldn't keep on publishing the book, but he felt it would not be good public relations to continue with it even if only a few students complained that they were being bothered. I was not disappointed.

In 1996 a search committee was formed to look for a new provost. President Smith wanted a well-known individual for the position who could make Wagner College recognized nationally. In the spring of 1997 Dr. Richard Guarasci was hired. Gary Sullivan went back to managing the theatre department and became his former happy self. Dr. Guarasci was nationally known for his innovative college program and he had published a book describing it. Guaraci visited Wagner several times during the spring and early summer to prepare for his new role at the college. He spoke to the faculty at a COW meeting about his plans for reviewing and improving the curriculum. He formed an ad hoc curriculum review committee with representatives from every department and worked with them during the summer to develop a new curriculum. MDS as a program ceased to exist, but MDS courses were to continue and be used in the new curriculum.